BISTRO | LAURENT | TOURONDEL

NEW AMERICAN BISTRO COOKING

LAURENT TOURONDEL AND MICHELE SCICOLONE

JOHN WILEY & SONS, INC.

WILEY

For my family, Mum, Dad and Adelynn, many thanks and much love

This book is printed on acid-free paper. ∞

Copyright © 2008 by Laurent Tourondel. All rights reserved

Published by John Wiley & Sons, Inc., Hoboken, New Jersey
Published simultaneously in Canada

No part of this publication may be reproduced, stored in a retrieval system, or transmitted in any form or by any means, electronic, mechanical, photocopying, recording, scanning, or otherwise, except as permitted under Section 107 or 108 of the 1976 United States Copyright Act, without either the prior written permission of the Publisher, or authorization through payment of the appropriate per-copy fee to the Copyright Clearance Center, Inc., 222 Rosewood Drive, Danvers, MA 01923, (978) 750-8400, fax (978) 750-4470, or on the web at www. copyright.com. Requests to the Publisher for permission should be addressed to the Permissions Department, John Wiley & Sons, Inc., 111 River Street, Hoboken, NJ 07030, (201) 748-6011, fax (201) 748-6008, or online at http://www.wiley. com/go/permissions.

Limit of Liability/Disclaimer of Warranty: While the publisher and author have used their best efforts in preparing this book, they make no representations or warranties with respect to the accuracy or completeness of the contents of this book and specifically disclaim any implied warranties of merchantability or fitness for a particular purpose. No warranty may be created or extended by sales representatives or written sales materials. The advice and strategies contained herein may not be suitable for your situation. You should consult with a professional where appropriate. Neither the publisher nor author shall be liable for any loss of profit or any other commercial damages, including but not limited to special, incidental, consequential, or other damages.

For general information on our other products and services or for technical support, please contact our Customer Care Department within the United States at (800) 762-2974, outside the United States at (317) 572-3993 or fax (317) 572-4002.

Wiley also publishes its books in a variety of electronic formats. Some content that appears in print may not be available in electronic books. For more information about Wiley products, visit our web site at www.wiley.com.

Design by Vertigo Design NYC

LIBRARY OF CONGRESS CATALOGING-IN-PUBLICATION DATA:
Tourondel, Laurent.
   Bistro Laurent Tourondel : new American bistro cooking / Laurent Tourondel and Michele Scicolone.
      p. cm.
   Includes index.
   ISBN: 978-0-471-75883-9 (cloth)
   1. Cookery, American. I. Scicolone, Michele. II. Title.
   TX715.T7185 2007
   641.5'973—dc22

2006032501

Printed in China

10 9 8 7 6 5 4 3 2 1

ACKNOWLEDGMENTS

I would like to express my heartfelt gratitude to the following people, all of whom made invaluable contributions to this book:

My editor, Pam Chirls, who turned the manuscript into a beautiful book;

My co-writer, Michele Scicolone, for putting my thoughts into words;

Ellen Silverman, for the beautiful photographs;

My agent, Judith Weber, for her belief in this book and good advice;

Michele Gentile, for carefully testing the recipes;

Charlotte March, for being not only the smartest and prettiest assistant a chef could ask for but also one hell of an eater;

Fred Dexheimer and Jennifer Lordan, for the thoughtful wine pairings;

Marc Sarrazin of De Bragga & Spitler, for helping me learn more than I ever thought possible about meat and providing outstanding products;

Louis Rozzo, for always delivering the freshest and highest-quality seafood;

Francis Staub, for providing me with his exceptional cookware;

Jennifer Baum of Bullfrog and Baum, for her work as my publicist;

My sous chefs, Emile Bousquet, Amy Eubanks, Marc Forgione, David Malbequi, Liran Mezan, Mathieu Palombino, and Steve Wambach;

And my partners, Jimmy Haber and Keith Treybal, for their vision and support.

CONTENTS

FOREWORD

Laurent Tourondel is an inspired chef. A man who enjoys the respect of his clientele at his wonderful restaurants, he is admired and lauded by the critics, but most importantly he is truly respected by his peers. I have known Laurent personally for many years, and I have long admired his culinary talents, but above and beyond that I have always found him to be immensely likeable and warm.

Like me, Laurent grew up in France and first learned how to cook at home alongside his grandmother and mother. He continued his education at culinary school and then under some of the best talents in Europe, including Jacques Maxim and Pierre and Claude Troisgros. These experiences clearly shaped him. First, learning how to cook in the home with the best possible local ingredients teaches respect for the products, and further, there can be no substitute for the kind of culinary education Laurent received under his mentors. He learned to love food by eating it and enjoying it at home and then solidified his mastery of the classic techniques by working with the great chefs under whom he flourished.

I met Laurent when he worked under Claude Troisgros at the highly successful restaurant CT. It quickly won 3 stars from the *New York Times,* which is a major accomplishment. Since then Laurent traveled and worked outside of New York, drawing inspiration from all the places he has visited and worked. Over the years, he continued to amass accolades and attention across the industry, but luckily he decided to come back to New York City and make it his home.

In 1999 Laurent opened Cello on the Upper East Side of New York, and it was an instant success. Laurent's creativity was evident in the cuisine and his distinct sensibility emerged. He maintained the high standards he had learned over the years of classical training in France and elsewhere, but then he went a step beyond and was not afraid to integrate his own unique ideas. At Cello, he also proved his capability as an excellent pastry chef.

As a chef, I understand how satisfying cooking at home for one's family and friends can be. It is totally different from cooking in a restaurant, and it always makes me happy to be able to slow down and get back to good food and simple techniques. It is something that I relish and I know that Laurent does, too. With this book Laurent has created something that you can really use and cook from in your home, whether it is dishes from BLT or something he remembers from his childhood.

I know that I am looking forward to enjoying Laurent's inspirations while I am taking time to cook in my home—and I am confident that eager home cooks from all over will find so much enjoyment from it as well.

Eric Ripert
Executive Chef and Co-Owner
Le Bernardin

INTRODUCTION

Whenever someone mentions the word "bistro," it makes me think about the restaurant that my grandfather would take me to when I was a boy in France. It was called L'Hostellerie du Théatre and it was located next door to my grandfather's music school. He was a musician and a *chef d'orchestre*—what we call here a conductor.

I felt like a king when I went there with him because no matter how crowded the place was, there was always a table for my grandfather, usually his favorite quiet one in the back. I can still remember the waiter calling out, *"Monsieur Michon à la table cinq!,"* and everyone looked up as we walked by. We would eat wonderful warm and homey French food, like *steak frites,* a full-flavored beef steak with crisp, salty fries; *coq au vin,* a rooster braised with red wine and mushrooms; meltingly tender braised veal tongue with *sauce charcutière,* made with onions, white wine, chopped cornichons, and mustard; and *blanquette de veau,* veal chunks stewed in a delicate creamy sauce. For dessert there was a delicious fruit tart with a crisp, buttery crust filled with peaches, apples, figs, or whatever fruit was in season, or my favorite—fresh strawberry ice cream, molded in a stainless-steel bowl called a *coupe.*

I have heard that the word "bistro" became popular after 1815, when the Russian army seized Paris. In the bars and cafés, soldiers would demand quick service and shout a Russian word that sounded like *bistro.* Not everybody agrees with this explanation, however, since "bistro" does not appear to have entered into the French language before 1884. Other possibilities are often cited. One is *bistraud,* a word in the Poitou dialect, meaning "a lesser servant." The other is *bistouille* or *bistrouille,* a drink made from brandy and coffee, the kind of beverage you might order in a café or bistro. Whatever its source, *bistrot,* spelled with a final, silent "t" in France, came to mean a small informal restaurant, and the proprietor was called the *bistrotière.*

Though it may have started out as a place to grab a quick meal, to me a bistro suggests an informal, comfortable restaurant where the food is generous, straightforward, and full of flavor. The cooking seems familiar, like the meals I enjoyed at home or at the bistro with my grandfather, and the recipes do not change, though the chef will make every effort to personalize his cooking by adding a fresh herb or vegetable in season. Everyone, or at least almost everyone, can find something he or she likes to eat at a bistro.

When I first came to America, I sought out restaurants that had the same kind of spirit as the bistros in France. I found what I was looking for in good steakhouses. The casual, friendly atmosphere was the same, and the food, even though prepared differently, was always appealing, uncomplicated, and comforting. I also discovered that steakhouses allowed me to order my food exactly as I wanted it, specifying the cut, the doneness, the sauce, and the side dishes. This kind of restaurant does not exist in France where, instead, the chef composes a plate of food, but I quickly learned to prefer it.

A few years ago I got together with my business partners, Jimmy Haber and Keith Treybal, and we decided to open a new restaurant in New York City. Having worked in restaurants around the world, I told them that in my mind, the perfect restaurant would be a cross between the cozy bistro I remembered from my childhood and the friendly and warm steakhouse restaurants I discovered in America. An elegant, contemporary design would encourage guests to feel at ease and relaxed. I wanted the atmosphere to be welcoming for a single person having a meal at the bar, a couple out for a romantic evening, or a group of people gathered for a subdued business luncheon or a lively family dinner.

We agreed on the concept for the new restaurant, but I needed to find a name for it that would embody all of my ideas. I wanted to call it something that would be not only catchy and distinctive, but also reflect my regard for American cooking as well as my French roots. I wanted to make it clear that it had elements of both a bistro and a steakhouse, done my way.

"BLT Steak" seemed to say all that. I suggested it to my partners and the first thing they said was that they thought I meant a bacon, lettuce, and tomato sandwich. That was fine by me, because I love a good BLT! But when I explained that in this case BLT stands for Bistro Laurent Tourondel, they agreed that it was the ideal name.

We found a great location and immediately set to work. The menu would be based on robust fare like top-quality beef steaks in classic cuts such as rib-eye and porterhouse, and I sought out the city's finest purveyors. In addition to meats, fish, and chicken cooked to order, I wanted to give diners the choice of their preferred sauces and side dishes. Seasonal vegetables would be a big part of our menu, such as fat asparagus and tender, buttery peas in the springtime, and ripe heirloom tomatoes layered with crisp, sweet onions for summer meals. Wild mushrooms would take center stage in the fall, either baked with a tasty stuffing, sautéed with garlic and herbs, or simmered in a sauce, and there would be luscious creamed spinach and fried onion rings for winter meals. Generous portions with side dishes served separately would enable everyone at the table to taste and share, the way you would enjoy meals at home. To welcome the guests, every meal would begin with a gigantic hot popover topped with a crown of toasty Gruyère cheese.

I was trained as a pastry chef in the classic French tradition, and I don't think any meal is complete without dessert. You may be surprised that so many of the desserts in my restaurants, and in this book, are all-American favorites like fresh fruit pies and cobblers, towering layer cakes, and sundaes, but these are the kinds of desserts that I can't get enough of in my travels around this country. I'll never forget the first time I walked into an American diner and spotted a row of sky-high layer cakes on a counter and a refrigerator case full of luscious fruit pies. I felt the sense of joy that a child does in a candy shop and I couldn't wait to try them all. A slice of rich, spicy carrot cake layered with cream cheese frosting in a puddle of hot butterscotch sauce, or a warm fruit pie made with tart-sweet apples in winter and plump, juicy blueberries in the summer, topped with a scoop of homemade ice cream, or pineapple upside-down cake with piña colada sauce still give me that joyful feeling that I love to share, so I added these items and others like them to our menu.

To complete the meal, I worked with our wine director, Fred Dexheimer, to come up with an extensive list of food-friendly wines. Our approach was to offer wines from around the world that our clients would be comfortable with, primarily from small producers. We looked for wines at every price

point made from interesting grape varietals that are typical of their growing region, or *terroir*. To make selecting wines less complicated, we organized our wine list both by grape varieties, for example, Chardonnay, Pinot Noir, and Cabernet Sauvignon, and by aromatic and stylistic characteristics, such as fresh-crisp, spicy-exotic, and earthy-soulful. I find that most guests really enjoy this way of choosing, both for convenience and adventure.

Not only did the menu and wine list at BLT Steak have to be just right, but I also wanted the restaurant to be beautiful, not one of those super-masculine, rough-and-tumble places with cigar smoke in the air, decorated with dark wood paneling and stiff leather chairs, or—worst of all—with stuffy waiters in white coats. I explained what I wanted to the talented designer, Michael Bagley, and he came up with a perfect look. The rich color scheme is cream, chocolate, and butterscotch, while the tabletops, floors, and trim are done in warm wood tones. Soft suede banquettes and sepia photos of old New York complete the decor. The design is contemporary, warm, and luxurious all at the same time. We gave the waitstaff brown bib aprons and put up a big blackboard menu so that I could change it every day and let guests know at a glance what was freshest in the market.

BLT Steak became a popular dining destination and the model for my other restaurants that have followed. My partners and I have since opened branches of BLT Steak in Washington, DC, Los Angeles, Puerto Rico, Dallas, Scottsdale, and Miami.

I love the atmosphere at BLT Steak, but many New Yorkers first met me when I was the chef at Cello, an elegant restaurant that specialized in seafood. After it closed, I have often been asked if I would consider opening that type of classic restaurant with formal food presentation and service again. Though I like cooking fish and appreciate the elegant style of restaurants like Cello, I also enjoy a good fish shack, the kind you might find on the coast of Maine or the east end of Long Island, where I can eat a delicious lobster roll or a clam bake right on the beach. I began to think of ways that I could combine elements of these two styles in one restaurant.

I was lucky to find the perfect Manhattan location for BLT Fish, where I could have both an informal fish shack on the ground floor and a modern, sophisticated restaurant above. It's like having two different restaurants in one location.

The romantic upstairs dining room is light and airy and there is a retractable glass roof. The soft color scheme is inspired by the delicate shades on the inside of a seashell. The open kitchen is a feature I really like. It reminds me of being at a party at someone's home, where guests congregate in the kitchen. People love to feel like a part of the action and watch the cooks preparing their meals.

The menu specializes in grilled or roasted fish, available filleted or whole. Only the freshest varieties from around the world make it to the BLT Fish kitchens, including Belgian Dover sole, Nova Scotia lobster, and New Zealand pink snapper. They are good simply cooked, but like the meat dishes we serve at BLT steak, you can enhance the seafood with your choice of sauce, such as Curry-Lemongrass (page 200) or Soy-Caper Brown Butter (page 140), and side dishes such as Silver Dollar potatoes (page 224), Sea Salt-Crusted Sunchokes (page 232), or Honey/Cumin-Glazed Carrots (page 215). Upstairs at BLT Fish is cool and elegant, but always relaxed and lively, the way I like my restaurants to be. When guests are seated, we welcome them with hot Chive-Cheddar Biscuits (page 119) served with sweet butter, coarse sea salt, and good maple syrup. Meals end with a big glass jar of homemade cotton candy placed on every table so everyone can help themselves. Many of my customers say that the candy reminds them of childhood visits to the circus, or summers spent at the shore.

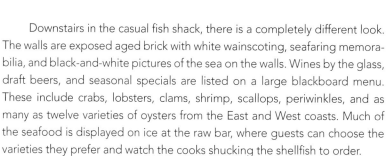

Downstairs in the casual fish shack, there is a completely different look. The walls are exposed aged brick with white wainscoting, seafaring memorabilia, and black-and-white pictures of the sea on the walls. Wines by the glass, draft beers, and seasonal specials are listed on a large blackboard menu. These include crabs, lobsters, clams, shrimp, scallops, periwinkles, and as many as twelve varieties of oysters from the East and West coasts. Much of the seafood is displayed on ice at the raw bar, where guests can choose the varieties they prefer and watch the cooks shucking the shellfish to order.

Baked clams and creamy chowder are popular starters and there are great sandwiches, like the BLT Grilled Tuna with avocado, tomatoes, bacon, and tapenade (page 112); the crunchy Spicy Soft-Shell Crab Sandwich (page 115); and our famous Lobster Roll (page 110)—soft, rich brioche rolls full of chunky lobster meat in tarragon-flavored mayonnaise.

For my next restaurant, which I called BLT Prime, I wanted to focus on dry-aged beef. Dry aging means that large cuts of meat are placed in a temperature- and humidity-controlled cooler for a period of time so that they can develop a deeper, nuttier flavor and become more tender. I wanted to control the dry-aging process so that I could determine for myself when the beef had reached its optimum state and was ready to be enjoyed. To do this, I installed a glass-enclosed refrigerated aging room. The room is located close to the front entrance at BLT Prime so that everyone would know at a glance that it is a restaurant that is serious about beef.

Japanese Kobe, American Wagyu (Kobe), and Prime beef in a variety of different cuts are the stars at BLT Prime, but there are also lamb T-bones, racks, and shanks as well as veal porterhouse and hanger steaks, and chops. There is a good selection of seafood favorites as well, like swordfish, Bluefin tuna steaks, and jumbo shrimp. To complement the main courses, the line-up of seasonal side dishes includes blue cheese tater tots, barbecued onions, and creamy corn succotash. For dessert, there are classics like warm raspberry bread pudding, strawberry sundaes, and chocolate tart with pistachio ice cream.

We reproduced BLT Steak's warm color palette, and a huge skylight brings the city sky into the comfortable, sophisticated room. Fortunately, the space allowed us to have an open kitchen like we have at BLT Fish so guests can see what normally goes on behind the scenes. It adds to the restaurant's informality and lively atmosphere and creates a casual vibe.

Our next restaurant was BLT Market in the Ritz-Carlton Hotel, across from Central Park in New York City. Even though it is in a glamorous hotel, I think of it as a neighborhood restaurant, or at least the kind of restaurant I wish I had in my neighborhood. It reminds me of Parisian bistros where elegant diners meet for a quick meal that ends up stretching for hours, fueled by laughter, good conversation, and great food. The menu is based

on seasonal produce and local ingredients, and I am working with several farmers in the New York area who raise special varieties of produce that you won't easily find anywhere else.

The restaurant has a casually elegant look, with soaring windows on all sides that flood the room with natural light. There is a big outdoor terrace facing Central Park, where diners can enjoy cocktails and dine in fine weather, and watch the horse-drawn carriages driving by. And we also have a small gourmet specialty shop, like a French *épicerie*.

The latest version of the BLT concept is BLT Burger. Burger has a more casual look than the other BLT restaurants and the menu focuses on a variety of burger choices as well as hearty salads and a fun kid's menu. For side dishes, there are classic accompaniments like Rosemary-Parmesan French Fries (page 230) and Fried Onion Rings (page 212), and to drink there are milkshakes in unique flavors such as Mocha Mudslide, Rocky Road Oreo, and Pecan Pie, as well as all of the standards. Adult diners might prefer to choose one of our forty varieties of beer, including forty on tap, or one of the spiked milkshakes like the "Grandma's Treat" that features bourbon, caramel and vanilla ice cream. Of course, there are burger-friendly wines available and an extensive cocktail list featuring both frozen drinks and smoothies.

HOW TO USE THIS BOOK

I am often asked about my style of cooking and how I come up with my recipes. Usually, the dishes that we serve start out with ideas that I perfect in the restaurant kitchens. These ideas are based on the things I learned at home from my mother and grandmothers, from my training as a chef, from my experiences cooking and eating all over the world, and ultimately from my personal tastes. I think it is much more fun to cook what I like to eat, and what you will find in this book is a collection of some of my favorites.

As I developed these recipes, I thought a lot about the way that I cook at home. I do not often make dishes in my home kitchen that are a lot of trouble since I don't have the time, the equipment, or anyone to clean up after me! In these pages, you will find that many of the recipes take very little effort and are made with ingredients that you can find in your local supermarket or farmers' market.

I suggest that you start out by trying just one or two new recipes from this book at a time. Try a new salad or main course and add it to a menu of dishes that you already feel comfortable with, especially if you are entertaining guests. Among the dishes that a new cook might want to try are the Marinated Mushrooms/Tomatoes/Cilantro (page 20), the Peel and Eat Shrimp (page 31), the Chopped Vegetable Salad/Creamy Oregano

Dressing (page 50), the Carrot-Cilantro Salad/Ginger-Orange Dressing (page 48), the Macaroni/Tomatoes/Spicy Sausage (page 77), Braised Swordfish/Tomatoes, Olives, and Capers (page 128), and the Baked Black Sea Bass/Tomato/Eggplant/Honey/Sherry Vinegar (page 138). Corn, Bean, and Sausage Chili (page 105) and the BLT Grilled Tuna Sandwich (page 112) would also be good choices for a novice cook, as well as any of the grilled steaks, American Kobe Burger/au Poivre Sauce (page 148), Tapenade-Stuffed Leg of Lamb (page 167), and Roasted Rosemary-Lemon Chicken (page 183). Barbecue Sauce (page 195) and Maître d'Hôtel Butter (page 201) are also easy to do, as well as the Grilled Corn/Herb Butter (page 217), Oregano-Breaded Tomatoes (page 220), and Creamed Spinach (page 210). For dessert, the Dried Apricot Bread Pudding (page 249) or the Chocolate-Espresso Cookies (page 241) are simple and satisfying to make.

More experienced cooks will also discover many new and exciting recipes to try, such as, Beef Carpaccio/Portobello Mushrooms/Mozzarella (page 34), Duck Liver Mousse/Port Gelée (page 41), Camembert Beignets/Smoked Duck Salad (page 70), Octopus Salad/Lemon-Bergamot Dressing (page 72), Anise Duck Tortellini (page 81), Crispy Red Snapper "Chinese Style" (page 131), Chestnut/Apple/Celery Soup (page 100), Cream of Corn/Corn Fritters (page 98), Steak and Foie Gras Sandwich (page 111), 5-Spice Caramelized Long Island Duck (page 190), or Fried Stuffed Jalapeños (page 214). The more challenging desserts include Passion Fruit Crêpes Soufflé (page 250), Cinnamon-Pecan Sticky Loaf/Crème Anglaise (page 269), and "Barbie" Raspberry Layer Cake (page 267).

Read each recipe through before you begin to be sure that you have the utensils you need and understand the steps you will be taking. If any of the ingredients are unfamiliar, take a look at the Glossary (page 12), where I have explained many of the unusual items. There is also a list of places where you can purchase ingredients that might not be available in a typical supermarket (see Sources, page 274). Another advantage of reading the recipe through before you begin is that you will feel more confident if you know exactly what is needed and the steps you will be taking. There is nothing more frustrating than finding that you are missing an ingredient when you are in the middle of cooking. Often, by reading the recipe through you will find that some of the preparation can be done ahead of time, such as chopping and measuring.

Always allow yourself plenty of time. You don't want to feel rushed or pressured when trying out a new recipe.

Look for recipes appropriate to the present season so that you will have access to the best ingredients. Out of season produce will never give you the flavors that you want to get from your cooking.

I have included a lot of suggestions for which dishes to serve together, but you should feel free to mix and match them according to your taste.

The same is true for pairing up your menu with an appropriate wine. I have made suggestions for ideal wines and beers to serve with many of the recipes in this book, but you can regard these suggestions as inspirations so that if you cannot find the exact wine that I mentioned, you can ask for something similar.

I find that I keep just a few favorite beer and wine varieties at home for myself and visitors. Sparkling wine is a must. Whether an inexpensive cava from Spain or grand vintage Champagne for special occasions, few things are better than sharing a glass of bubbly with friends.

I always keep a crisp, refreshing white wine in my refrigerator at home, such as a Sauvignon Blanc or dry-style Riesling. Whites are often overlooked in home use, but I think they are perfect for stimulating the appetite, especially during the summer. Both of these wines go with a wide variety of foods.

A lot of my friends prefer red wines and I find Pinot Noir to be very versatile. It has really surged in popularity in recent years and many people are surprised to find that it goes great with both meat and fish.

A sweet wine at the end of the meal is optional but always fun. For a simple yet indulgent dessert, I like to have a glass of chilled late-harvest Riesling with some fresh-cut ripe fruits.

My goal with this book is to bring you a taste of the food we prepare in our restaurants every day. When you are in your kitchen, I hope you will have fun and take pleasure in cooking as much as I do, whether it is a delicious sandwich just for you, a weeknight meal for your family, or a party for a group of friends.

It is my pleasure to share my way of cooking with you. Whether you are a regular at BLT or have yet to visit us, I hope you will enjoy this book and be inspired to join me in the kitchen.

INGREDIENTS

When I was a boy, I learned to shop for food with my grandmother. We would go to the market and she would show me what to look for: the fish that glistened as if it was just caught, the well-cut meat with the best color, the vegetables and fruits that were ripe and in season. She patronized certain vendors, yet there were others she avoided because she did not like their wares, or the way they were kept. She was very picky and she knew how to make every ingredient count!

Though we may no longer go to the market daily with a basket in hand, you can still be picky. Shop at farmers' markets when you can. They are often the best sources for fresh local produce, eggs, meat, and even fish. Often, you will find unusual varieties that are naturally raised or even organic. Because they are not mass produced, laden with preservatives, or shipped over long distances, the flavor of these foods will be more likely to remain intact and they will be more nutritious for you and your family.

Seek out artisan bakers and cheesemakers in your area who make specialty products. Good cheese and fine bread can make even a simple meal seem special. Don't overlook ethnic markets either, especially for fresh spices, exotic produce, and condiments. Ethnic grocers often have a bigger and more interesting selection than supermarkets. Because these items sell quickly, they are often fresher and more flavorful.

At BLT restaurants, we use two types of beef. The first is Certified Angus brand. Angus cattle are named for the region in Scotland where they originated hundreds of years ago. Only certain types of grain-fed Angus qualify for this brand because the company's standards for selecting cattle are extremely high, far exceeding the USDA's requirements for Prime beef. Only a small percentage of beef earns the Certified Angus designation.

The other beef that we use comes from the Wagyu variety of cattle, a special breed first raised in Japan. It is sometimes called American Kobe, named for the Japanese city. Because of the type of food they eat and the way the animals are raised, Wagyu meat has a higher fat content, so it is especially tender and flavorful.

Both Certified Angus and American Kobe beef are my top choices because they have a lot of marbling, which is really just another name for the flecks of fat in the beef. Marbling is the main contributor of juiciness, flavor, and tenderness—the attributes we all look for in beef.

At BLT Prime, we have a special temperature-controlled room for aging our beef. The meat is left uncovered so that the air can circulate around it and the temperature is constantly regulated so that it stays above freezing, but below 36°F for between ten and twenty-eight days. This treatment is called dry aging and it is one of the reasons our steaks taste so special. During the aging process, enzymes in the meat break down the fibers so it becomes more tender. The meat loses a lot of its moisture and shrinks by about 10 or 15 percent as the flavor becomes richer and more intense. It requires a real expert to choose the right cut for aging and judge when the meat is just right. Until about twenty years ago, most beef was aged this way.

Today, most of the beef sold in retail stores has been wet aged. This means that the cuts of meat are packed in vacuum-sealed plastic bags for shipping and storage. It doesn't lose any of its moisture and it can be sold in as few as seven days, so the process is cheaper. The meat ages, but it never develops the nutty, rich quality and concentrated flavor of dry-aged beef.

HOW TO BUY AND COOK A GREAT STEAK

FIND A GOOD BUTCHER The right butcher can make all the difference. Find one with real knowledge of retail cuts of meat, aging, and yes, even cooking. He or she can guide you on the right cut of meat to buy for whatever you are making and save you from a lot of disappointment.

WHAT DO YOU PREFER? Some people like their steaks so tender that they can be cut with a fork, while others like meat that is a little chewy. Some pre-

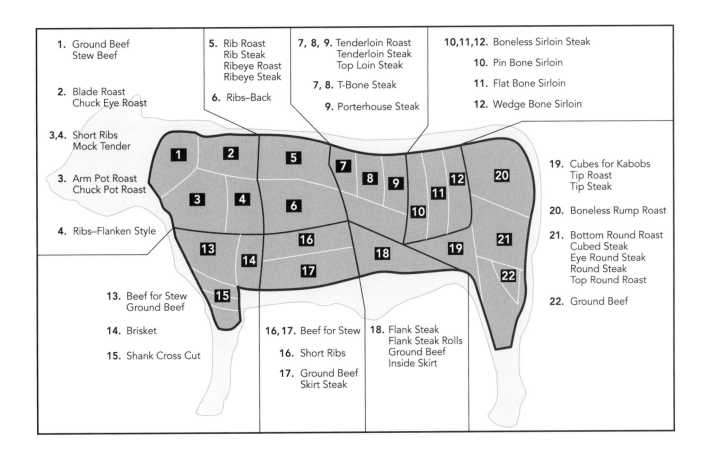

1. Ground Beef
   Stew Beef

2. Blade Roast
   Chuck Eye Roast

3,4. Short Ribs
   Mock Tender

3. Arm Pot Roast
   Chuck Pot Roast

4. Ribs–Flanken Style

13. Beef for Stew
   Ground Beef

14. Brisket

15. Shank Cross Cut

5. Rib Roast
   Rib Steak
   Ribeye Roast
   Ribeye Steak

6. Ribs–Back

16,17. Beef for Stew

16. Short Ribs

17. Ground Beef
   Skirt Steak

7, 8, 9. Tenderloin Roast
   Tenderloin Steak
   Top Loin Steak

7, 8. T-Bone Steak

9. Porterhouse Steak

18. Flank Steak
   Flank Steak Rolls
   Ground Beef
   Inside Skirt

10,11,12. Boneless Sirloin Steak

10. Pin Bone Sirloin

11. Flat Bone Sirloin

12. Wedge Bone Sirloin

19. Cubes for Kabobs
   Tip Roast
   Tip Steak

20. Boneless Rump Roast

21. Bottom Round Roast
   Cubed Steak
   Eye Round Steak
   Round Steak
   Top Round Roast

22. Ground Beef

fer a mild flavor, while others want their meat full of beefy richness. There are cuts of steak to satisfy every taste, but it is important to know what you want.

SOME POPULAR STEAKS

Steaks from the rib, loin, and tenderloin are the most tender because they are cuts from the parts of the animal that are exercised the least. These are the meats that I feature at BLT restaurants. I cook our steaks and chops first on a very hot wood-fired grill to give the meat a good crust, color, and a slightly smoky flavor. Then the steaks are transferred to a broiler to ensure that they will cook to perfection. Follow the cooking method instructions below for each cut for the best results.

PORTERHOUSE STEAK In the early nineteenth century, a porter house was a coach stop where travelers could dine on steak and ale. Around 1814, a porter house–keeper in New York City began to serve a cut of beef that included part of both the flavorful top loin and the buttery soft tenderloin. Now known as porterhouse steaks, these should be cut from two to three inches thick and are best when broiled.

T-BONE STEAK With its T-shaped bone, this is one of the easiest steaks to recognize. It comes from the center of the short loin. It is similar to the porterhouse but with a smaller section of tenderloin and a smaller tail. T-bones should be cut from one to three inches thick and are best when broiled.

RIB-EYE This cut comes from the rib and is preferred for its excellent flavor and tenderness. A rib-eye steak should be about 1¼ to 1¾ inches thick and is best when grilled.

DELMONICO STEAK The Delmonico steak originated in 1843 as the house cut at the famous Delmonico's Restaurant in New York City. The meaning of the Delmonico steak has changed over the years and from place to place. It is some-

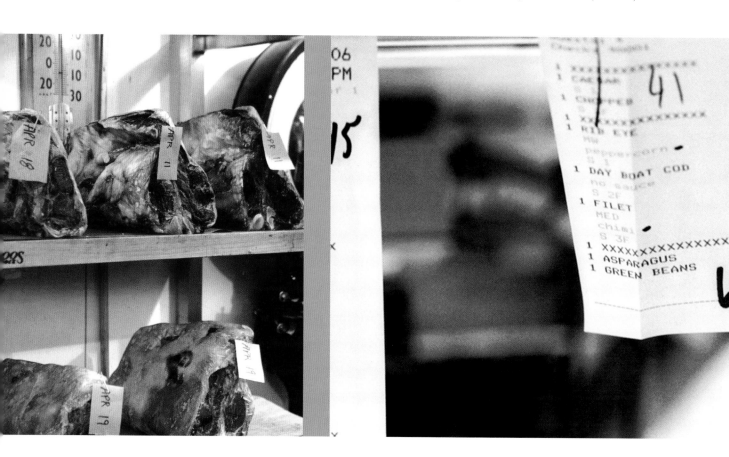

times called a Spencer steak. A typical Delmonico is cut from the short loin, next to the rib end. It should be about 1½ to two inches thick and is best grilled.

FILET MIGNON OR TENDERLOIN Filet strips come from the short loin and are cut before any other steaks. A filet can be cut into individual portions for steaks or it can be roasted whole. A filet steak should be about two inches thick. Wrapped in pastry, a whole filet mignon becomes Beef Wellington. The center portion of the filet, enough for two, is known as the Châteaubriand. Filet mignon and Châteaubriand are best when pan roasted.

NEW YORK STRIP STEAK OR SHELL STEAK After the tenderloin strip has been removed from the short loin, the remaining meat can be cut into shell steaks. Shell steaks are called by a variety of names, such as strip, New York strip, and Kansas City strip. This steak should be about 1½ to two inches thick and is best grilled.

BLT DOUBLE-CUT STRIP STEAK Our customers loved the New York strip steaks described above so much, we decided to come up with this larger,

juicier version to serve two. The steaks are about three inches thick and are cooked and served on the bone. I don't know of another restaurant that serves this type of steak.

I like to cook it either on a barbecue grill or with a combination of pan searing and roasting. See the Chef's Tip for Grilled BLT Double-Cut Strip Steak (page 160) for an explanation of the combination method.

SIRLOIN STEAK There are several different steaks that come from the sirloin or hip. In general, they are rather large, thin, and only moderately tender and flavorful. They taste best grilled.

FLAT-IRON STEAK There are varying accounts of how the flat-iron steak got its name, but most sources indicate that it comes from the triangular shape of the cut, like an old-fashioned flat iron. These steaks come from the top shoulder of the chuck. It is a very tender cut that is best for grilling.

HANGER STEAK A hanger steak is a strip of meat that hangs between the last rib and the loin. It has a grainy texture and is somewhat chewy, but the flavor is first-rate. It is sometimes called a butcher steak, because at one time it was rarely sold in the market and the butcher just took this flavorful cut home for his own enjoyment. These steaks are best when grilled.

FLANK STEAK A thin, flat steak with a distinct grain that runs the length of the meat, flank steaks come from the belly area, and are chewy with beefy flavor. Always carve flank steak thinly and cut it against the grain to minimize the chewy texture. They are best when grilled.

SKIRT STEAK Best known as the steak for fajitas, skirt steaks come from the diaphragm or short plate. This cut is long, narrow, and flat, with a chewy texture and good flavor. Carve it like flank steak, diagonally across the grain into thin slices. They are best when grilled.

UNDERSTAND MEAT GRADES

The United States Department of Agriculture (USDA) inspects meats for wholesomeness, but grading for quality is voluntary and paid for by individual packers.

Steaks graded Prime are of the highest quality. Most Prime meat goes to restaurants or better meat markets. It is well worth seeking out a source for Prime meat in your area.

Choice and Select grades are the most widely available. Choice meat can vary greatly, so it pays to know what to look for. Select grade meat has the least amount of marbling and tends to be dry, tough, and lacking in flavor. It is the most common grade found in retail stores.

SHOP CAREFULLY

Look over the steaks in the meat case and be selective. What you want is a thick, even cut. It won't cook evenly if the meat is thick in one part and thin in another.

Except for certain cuts like hanger or flank steaks, the meat should be at least one inch thick, and preferably two. When buying more than one, choose steaks that are of the same size so that they will cook in about the same amount of time.

FAT IS YOUR FRIEND

At least as far as a steak is concerned! An even distribution of fat flecks throughout the meat will ensure good flavor, tenderness, and juiciness.

Don't trim off excess fat before cooking a steak. Fat around the edge helps to keep the meat moist and adds flavor. You can always trim it away when you eat the steak.

STORAGE

Store meat in the coldest part of the refrigerator (at the back of one of the center shelves) or in the meat compartment (usually at the bottom). The temperature of the refrigerator should be between 35°F and 40°F. Use the meat within one to three days of purchase.

COOK IT JUST RIGHT

Broil it, grill it, or sauté it—done right, any of these methods will yield a good steak. The most important thing is to not overcook it. For best flavor, texture, and juiciness, cook a steak to rare or medium-rare. Here are some tips for cooking steak:

BROILING Cooking meat or other foods on a pan under direct heat is known as broiling. This method is especially good for steaks and other thin pieces of food because they acquire a crisp, brown crust. Most home ovens come equipped with broilers. Some can be set to low or high heat, while others have only one setting; I find the best method of regulating the cooking in a home broiler is to adjust the placement of the pan. The farther the pan, and the steak, is from the heat, the more slowly it will cook. For a thick steak, start cooking the meat close to the heat so that its surface is about two inches away and leave it there until it is nicely browned on both sides. Then adjust the distance of the pan farther from the heat to finish the cooking. Thinner steaks can be cooked three inches from the heat and will probably be done by the time they have browned on both sides.

GRILLING Whether done on an indoor grill, a grill pan, or an outdoor bar-becue, grilling is similar to broiling, except that the food is placed over, not under, the heat source and grilled foods acquire the characteristic striped markings from contact with the ridges of the grilling surface. The advantage of an outdoor grill is that you can use aromatic charcoal or wood chips to add a distinctive smoky flavor to foods. The same principles apply to grilling as to broiling, except that if you are cooking on a grill pan or grill where the distance from the heat is not adjustable, you can move the food to a cooler part of the grill to finish cooking.

PAN ROASTING When cooking thick steaks such as filet mignon, or a châ-teaubriand for two, the method I prefer is pan roasting. I cook the meat in a small amount of oil or butter in a skillet, then transfer the skillet to a 375°F oven. This way, the meat gets a good brown crust on the stove top, and cooks evenly through in the oven.

MEAT AND POULTRY COOKING TEMPERATURE CHART

No matter which cooking method you use, it is best to judge the cooking of meat and poultry with an instant-read thermometer. Using this type of thermometer takes away all the guesswork. Test the temperature by inserting the tip of the thermometer into the thickest part of the meat away from the bone. Leave the thermometer in until the dial stops moving, but remove it if you continue the cooking.

Handle the meat carefully with tongs. Don't pierce it with a fork as it cooks. This will allow the juices to escape.

Always let cooked meat and poultry rest for a few minutes after cooking. Cover it loosely with a foil tent to keep it warm. Resting allows the juices to settle into the meat and the temperature to even out. You will even notice a slight increase in the temperature after the meat has rested. Thicker, larger cuts of meat need a longer resting time than smaller cuts.

MEAT	FAHRENHEIT	CELSIUS
Beef		
Rare	120°–125°	45°–50°
Medium-Rare	130°–135°	55°–60°
Medium	140°–145°	60°–65°
Medium-Well	150°–155°	65°–70°
Well	160°	+70°+
Lamb and Veal		
Rare	135°	60°
Medium-Rare	140°–150°	60°–65°
Medium	160°	70°
Well	165°+	75°+
Pork	160°–170°	65°–70°
Chicken and Turkey	165°–175°	75°–80°

FISH AND SHELLFISH

Freshness is the key to buying good seafood. Shop at a market with a good turnover and knowledgeable, well-trained staff. Keep in mind that all fish and shellfish should smell of the sea without any off odors. In fact, if the market does not smell right, shop somewhere else.

WHOLE FISH A whole fish is easier to judge than fillets or steaks. Take a look at the eyes. They should be rounded and full, not sunken. You may have heard that cloudiness in the eyes is an indicator that the fish is not fresh, but this is not the case. The eyes of many varieties of fish become filmy when they are caught.

The scales on the fish should be intact and look bright. If scales are missing, it can mean that the fish is old or it has been mishandled.

Ask the salesperson to show you the gills. The color should be bright red with no signs of browning. If you can get close enough to the gills, smell them. They should smell fresh and clean, not fishy.

If possible, touch the fish. It should feel firm and spring back when pressed.

FISH STEAKS AND FILLETS Avoid purchasing prewrapped fish since the packaging will make it more difficult to judge the quality.

Steaks and fillets should have a pearly, moist look to them without any traces of drying or browning.

Fish fillets should appear solid without flaking or separation. Steaks should be cut into even slices so that they cook evenly. To prevent over-cooking, buy steaks that are at least one inch thick.

SHELLFISH Lobsters, crabs, clams, and mussels should always be alive when purchased.

To choose a lobster, ask the fishmonger to lift it from the tank. The tail should flap and the legs should move. Fresh crabs also should move their legs when touched.

Clams and mussels should close their shells tightly when touched. Discard any that have broken shells or that do not open up when cooked.

In this country, scallops are usually sold shelled. They should look plump and creamy white to pale pink in color, and moist with no cracks or separations in the flesh. Sometimes scallops are soaked in a preservative to keep them fresh. Avoid them and look for so-called "dry" scallops.

Whole shrimp are more flavorful than those sold without their heads, but they can be hard to find. Since there are many varieties of shrimp from different waters, color is not always an indicator of flavor. All shrimp should be free of black spots—a sign that they are not fresh.

STORING SEAFOOD It is a good idea to carry a cooler bag and ice packs to the store when you go to buy seafood because it must be kept very cold. Use it as soon as possible after you buy it.

Store fish wrapped, in the refrigerator on a top of a bowl of ice until you are ready to use it, changing the ice as it melts.

Clams and other mollusks in their shells should be removed from the plastic bag and placed in a shallow pan loosely covered with damp news-paper. Lobsters should also be taken out of the plastic bags, but do not remove the bands that keep their claws closed.

Both clams and lobsters should be stored in the refrigerator in a pan covered with a damp cloth. Crabs should be stored in a paper bag that is punctured for ventilation.

GLOSSARY

BREAD For sandwiches and croutons, I use rustic French or Italian-style ciabatta bread with a crunchy crust, chewy interior, and good flavor.

BREAD CRUMBS Unless stated otherwise, I like to use panko, which are Japanese-style bread crumbs. They have a coarser texture and stay crisp longer than regular crumbs, especially in fried foods.

CHOCOLATE At BLT restaurants, I use Valrhona, an incredible French chocolate with exceptional quality. It is made from top-quality cocoa from a variety of blended cocoa beans, including some that are quite rare. It is widely used in professional kitchens around the world and readily available. We use several varieties in the kitchen, including extra bittersweet and white chocolate. I am particularly fond of their milk chocolate.

CHILES I use a variety of different types of chiles at BLT. Most of the heat is in the seeds, so scrape them out if you want to tone down the heat. I usually leave them in. Make sure you wear disposable plastic gloves when handling fresh chiles and be especially careful not to touch your eyes.

CREMA DI CARCIOFI Literally, "cream of artichokes" in Italian, this is a puree of artichoke hearts and seasonings. You can find it in many Italian groceries.

HERBS I always use fresh herbs in my recipes. Dried herbs really don't have the same flavor so I don't recommend substituting the dried for the fresh.

Most varieties of fresh herbs are widely available, and if you are lucky enough to have a garden or even a sunny window box, you can grow some of them yourself.

MIRIN A low alcohol, sweet wine made from rice, it is typically used in Japanese cooking.

OLIVE OIL I use extra-virgin olive oil exclusively from France, Spain, and Italy. It has a good flavor that is excellent for most purposes, including sautéing. For vinaigrettes, I like Le Moulin Dores, a French oil that is very flavorful.

OTHER OILS For frying and those occasions when we don't want the dish to have the full flavor of extra-virgin olive oil, I use peanut oil for deep frying because it does not burn as easily and adds a good flavor, canola oil for dishes where I prefer a neutral flavor, and grapeseed oil for certain mild vinaigrettes. Nut oils are delicious in salad dressings, but they must always be very fresh.

SALT For most cooking purposes, I use fine sea salt. Sea salt comes from evaporated seawater. The flavor varies slightly depending on where the salt was harvested and the minerals that remain in it. The salt crystals can be fine or coarse. Fine is best for an all-purpose salt, while coarse crystals are good for a finishing salt, brining, or when you want to grind salt to your own specifications.

Kosher salt is pure sodium chloride without any remaining minerals, so the flavor is always uniform. Kosher salt has been used for ages in the process of certifying foods as kosher.

Pink salt is not a general-purpose salt like sea salt and kosher salt. It is actually a combination of potassium nitrate or saltpeter, salt, and food coloring that chefs use to keep pâtés fresh and impart a rosy color.

Do not confuse this type of pink salt with table salts that are naturally pink, such as the kind from the Himalayas.

BLACK PEPPER Like other spices, the flavor of black pepper fades quickly once it is ground. Freshly ground not only is more flavorful, but you can also control the coarseness of the grind.

GREEN PEPPERCORNS These are the unripe berries of the *piper nigrum* vine, from which both black and white pepper are produced. Green peppercorns are most commonly sold pickled in brine or vinegar, or freeze-dried. Thai cooks sometimes use fresh green peppercorns.

SRIRACHA A fiery red hot sauce used throughout Southeast Asia that is made from ground chiles, garlic, vinegar, sugar, and salt.

CHAPTER ONE

2500 g

W hite asparagus is the same species as green asparagus. The only difference is that they are grown under a mound of soil to prevent them from getting sunlight and turning green. They are thicker and more tender than green asparagus and their flavor is milder. Typically, they are available in the early spring, but since they are grown all over the world, you can usually find them year-round. | SERVES 6

GRILLED WHITE ASPARAGUS | EGG | PROSCIUTTO | BLACK TRUFFLE VINAIGRETTE

Dressing

6 tablespoons black truffle oil

2 tablespoons sherry vinegar

2 teaspoons black truffle puree (see Sources, page 274)

Fine sea salt and freshly ground black pepper to taste

12 very large white asparagus spears (green asparagus can be substituted), peeled and trimmed

24 thin slices (about 8 ounces) prosciutto, preferably San Daniele

6 tablespoons Maître d'Hôtel Butter (page 201)

About 1 tablespoon white vinegar

6 large eggs

CHEF'S TIP: *Be sure to grill the asparagus quickly over high heat so that they do not become soft and the butter does not burn.*

WINE SUGGESTION: SAUVIGNON BLANC, WESTERLY, 2003, SANTA YNEZ VALLEY, CALIFORNIA. *A crisp and refreshing Sauvignon Blanc with aromas of grapefruit, lime zest, and herbs.*

MAKE THE DRESSING In a medium bowl, whisk together the truffle oil, vinegar, and truffle puree. Season with salt and pepper.

COOK THE ASPARAGUS Bring a large pot of salted water to a boil. Add the asparagus and cook until tender yet still crisp, 2 to 3 minutes. Cool the asparagus in a bowl of ice water. Drain and pat dry.

PREPARE THE ROLLS On a flat surface, arrange 2 slices of prosciutto with their long sides overlapping slightly. Spread the prosciutto with a thin coating of the Maître d'Hotel butter. Place 1 or 2 asparagus spears at the short end of the prosciutto and roll it up. Repeat with the remaining asparagus and prosciutto.

POACH THE EGGS Fill a wide, shallow pot two-thirds full of water and add 1 tablespoon or so of white vinegar. Bring the water to a simmer, not a boil, over medium heat.

Fill a large bowl halfway with ice water.

Carefully crack an egg onto a small plate or saucer. When the water simmers, tip the plate to slide the egg into the water. Repeat with the remaining eggs. When the eggs are firm and white, approximately 3 minutes, remove them with a slotted spoon. Transfer the eggs to the ice water to cool and stop the cooking.

GRILL THE ASPARAGUS Preheat a barbecue or stovetop grill to high heat. Brush the grill lightly with oil. Place the asparagus rolls on the grill. Cook, turning occasionally, until the prosciutto is browned and crisp on all sides, about 2 minutes. Transfer the asparagus to serving plates.

TO SERVE Drizzle the dressing over the asparagus. Remove the eggs with a slotted spoon and allow the water to drain off. Place a poached egg on each bundle. Serve immediately.

When I was growing up in France, all my mother had to do when she wanted to cook leeks was lean out the window and ask our next-door neighbor for some fresh picked from his garden. I remember that their mild onion flavor was sweet and delicate because they were fresh. | Fourme d'Ambert, a creamy cow's milk blue cheese from the Auvergne region of France, goes well with the leeks, but another blue such as Italian Gorgonzola can be substituted. | SERVES 6

LEEKS VINAIGRETTE | FOURME D'AMBERT

Leeks

6 large leeks

Fine sea salt and freshly ground black pepper to taste

½ cup walnut oil

¼ cup sherry vinegar

3 tablespoons chopped fresh chives

6 ounces Fourme d'Ambert, Gorgonzola, or other creamy blue cheese

1 recipe Caramelized Walnuts (see page 273), sliced

PREPARE THE LEEKS Remove the outer layer of the leeks and trim off the root ends and the darker green portions at the top. Wash thoroughly. Tie the leeks together, 3 in a bunch, with kitchen twine so that they will hold their shape when cooked.

BOIL THE WATER Bring a large pot of salted water to a boil. Add the leeks. Simmer the leeks until tender when pierced with a knife, about 15 minutes. Drain and shock by plunging them into a bowl of ice water. Drain well and squeeze the leeks gently in a paper towel to eliminate excess water. Remove the strings. Cut the leeks crosswise into ¾-inch slices.

TO ASSEMBLE Arrange the leek slices with one cut side down on serving plates. Season them with salt and pepper and drizzle with the oil and vinegar. Sprinkle with the chives.

TO SERVE Place a little of the cheese on each piece of leek. Scatter the sliced walnuts over all. Serve immediately.

WINE SUGGESTION: SEMILLON/SAUVIGNON BLANC, BUTY WINERY, 2003, COLUMBIA VALLEY, WASHINGTON. *A crisp, nutty white Bordeaux-style blend with aromas of citrus, figs, and peaches.*

M ushrooms, ripe tomatoes, and fragrant cilantro make a delicious appetizer for a summer barbecue, or served as a side dish salad with a grilled steak. Toasting and crushing coriander seeds brings out their flavor and aroma before adding them to the dressing. | These mushrooms can be made ahead to the point where they are cooled and refrigerated for up to 3 days. Drain them slightly and season them with the lemon juice, remaining oil, and cilantro just before serving. | SERVES 6

MARINATED MUSHROOMS | TOMATOES | CILANTRO

5 tablespoons extra-virgin olive oil

2 tablespoons minced shallots

1 teaspoon minced garlic

3 sprigs fresh thyme

1 tablespoon toasted and crushed coriander seeds (see page 272)

1 bay leaf

½ teaspoon ground black pepper

1 heaping tablespoon tomato paste

1 pound small white button mushrooms, washed and trimmed

Fine sea salt to taste

2 cups dry white wine

1 tablespoon freshly squeezed lemon juice

2 tablespoons chopped fresh cilantro

MAKE THE BASE In a large skillet, heat 3 tablespoons of the oil over medium-low heat. Add the shallots and garlic and cook until soft but not browned, about 4 minutes. Reduce the heat if they begin to color. Add the thyme, coriander, bay leaf, and pepper. Cook for 1 minute. Stir in the tomato paste and cook 2 minutes more.

COOK THE MUSHROOMS Stir in the mushrooms and cook for 5 minutes, stirring occasionally. Season with salt. Add the wine and bring to a simmer. Cover and cook until soft, about 10 minutes more. Cool the mushrooms in the cooking liquid.

TO SERVE Spoon the mushrooms and some of the cooking liquid into a bowl, drizzle with the lemon juice and the remaining 2 tablespoons oil. Sprinkle with the chopped cilantro.

WINE SUGGESTION: SAUVIGNON BLANC, WESTERLY, 2003, SANTA YNEZ VALLEY, CALIFORNIA. *A crisp and refreshing Sauvignon Blanc with aromas of grapefruit, lime zest, and herbs.*

Aioli is a heady garlic mayonnaise traditional in France as a sauce for poached fish and vegetables. These tomatoes are sauced with aioli that I Americanized with a Cajun spice blend and Tabasco sauce. The sauce is also delicious spread on chicken sandwiches or as a dressing for boiled shrimp, potato salad, or hard-cooked eggs. | Follow this salad with Tapenade-Stuffed Leg of Lamb (page 169) and Pan-Seared Hen of the Woods Mushrooms (page 225). | SERVES 6

BABY VINE-RIPENED TOMATOES | BACON | SPICY AIOLI

Salad

24 baby vine-ripened tomatoes (red and yellow if available), about 1½ pounds

1¼ cups Tomato Vinaigrette (page 60)

2 tablespoons chopped fresh cilantro leaves

Spicy Aioli

3 egg yolks, at room temperature

2 tablespoons Dijon mustard

1 tablespoon Cajun spice mix, such as McCormick Cajun Spice Blend

2 teaspoons Madras curry powder

1 garlic clove

1 cup extra-virgin olive oil

½ cup soybean oil or canola oil

1 tablespoon freshly squeezed lemon juice

3 dashes Tabasco sauce

12 slices (about 1 pound) thinly sliced bacon, cooked (see page 43)

1 cup trimmed baby arugula leaves

MARINATE THE TOMATOES Cut the tomatoes in half. Place them in a bowl with the Tomato Vinaigrette and the cilantro. Marinate at least 30 minutes.

MAKE THE AIOLI Place the egg yolks in a food processor with the mustard, Cajun spice mix, curry, and garlic. With the machine running, slowly add the oils. Add the lemon juice and Tabasco. If the sauce does not look smooth and emulsified, pour it into a jar with 3 tablespoons of warm water. Cover and shake the jar until the sauce is smooth.

ASSEMBLE THE SALAD Drain the tomatoes. Arrange the tomatoes on 6 plates. Top each salad with 2 slices of bacon. Drizzle the aioli around the plates. Garnish with the arugula.

WINE SUGGESTION: PINOT NOIR, NAVARRO VINEYARDS, 2003, ANDERSON VALLEY, CALIFORNIA. *A crisp, fresh Pinot Noir with aromas of cranberries, cherries, violets, and slight notes of spice.*

Artichokes are members of the thistle family and are related to sunflowers. To recognize a good artichoke, look for those that are plump and crisp—they should make a kind of squeaking noise if you gently squeeze them. | Creamy goat cheese and tangy tapenade are a delicious flavor contrast to the sweet flavor of artichokes. | SERVES 6

POACHED ARTICHOKE | GOAT CHEESE | TAPENADE

6 large artichokes

3 lemons, cut into twelve ½-inch-thick slices

1 onion, sliced

3 tablespoons fine sea salt

3 sprigs fresh thyme

1 bay leaf

Goat Cheese Cream

8 ounces fresh goat cheese

1 cup heavy cream

3 tablespoons mayonnaise

1 teaspoon freshly squeezed lemon juice

1 pinch cayenne

Freshly ground black pepper to taste

Tapenade

1 cup pitted Kalamata olives

1 anchovy fillet

2 teaspoons freshly squeezed lemon juice

½ garlic clove

½ cup extra-virgin olive oil

PREPARE THE ARTICHOKES With a large knife, cut off the top ¾ inch of each artichoke. Cut off the stems even with the base. Trim off the spiny tips of the artichoke leaves with scissors. Place a lemon slice on the top and bottom of each artichoke. Tie the lemon slices in place securely with kitchen twine. Repeat with the remaining lemons and artichokes.

COOK THE ARTICHOKES In a pot large enough to hold all of the artichokes upright, bring about 2 or 3 inches of water to a boil. Add the onion and season the water with 3 tablespoons of salt and the herbs. Stand the artichokes in the liquid. Bring to a simmer and cook for 30 minutes, or until the artichoke bottoms can easily be pierced with a paring knife. Remove the artichokes and turn them upside down to drain and cool completely. Cover and chill.

FINISH THE ARTICHOKES Remove the strings and lemon slices. Spread the leaves open slightly, gently pull out the center leaves, and carefully scoop out the fuzzy chokes with a small spoon.

MAKE THE GOAT CHEESE CREAM Crumble the goat cheese into a food processor. Add the cream. Pulse until blended. Add the mayonnaise, lemon juice, cayenne, and salt and pepper; blend until smooth.

MAKE THE TAPENADE Place the olives, anchovy, lemon juice, and garlic in a food processor. Process the mixture, adding the oil slowly. Blend until smooth.

TO SERVE Spoon the goat cheese cream into the center of each artichoke and top with a tablespoon of tapenade. Serve immediately.

WINE SUGGESTION: SAUVIGNON BLANC, HONIG VINEYARD, 2004, NAPA VALLEY, CALIFORNIA. *A crisp, mouthwatering Sauvignon Blanc with aromas of grapefruits and fresh-cut grass, and a tangy acidity.*

Buffalo chicken wings, named for the city where they originated, are fried, dunked in hot sauce, and served with celery sticks and blue cheese dip. At the BLT Fish Shack, we make this version with rock shrimp. Rock shrimp are tender and sweet, but other varieties of small shrimp can be substituted. Just be sure that they are very fresh when you purchase them, with a firm texture and no dark spots. | SERVES 6

FISH SHACK "BUFFALO-STYLE" ROCK SHRIMP

Sauce

1 cup Frank's Red Hot Sauce

⅓ cup clarified unsalted butter (see page 271)

2 teaspoons Worcestershire sauce

Batter

1½ cups cornstarch

1 cup all-purpose flour

1¼ teaspoons fine sea salt

1¼ cups club soda or seltzer

Vegetable oil for frying

1½ pounds rock shrimp, shelled and deveined

4 cups shredded iceberg lettuce

4 to 5 tender celery stalks, cut into twenty-four 3 x ½-inch sticks

Blue Cheese Sauce (page 197)

MAKE THE SAUCE In a large saucepan, whisk together all of the ingredients. Heat gently. Keep warm.

MAKE THE BATTER In a large bowl, stir together the cornstarch, ½ cup of the flour, and the salt. Add the club soda and whisk just until smooth. Do not overbeat or the batter will be tough.

HEAT THE OIL Fill a deep fryer or large deep pot about one-third full of oil. Heat until the temperature reaches 350° F on a deep-frying thermometer.

FRY THE SHRIMP Dredge the shrimp in the remaining ½ cup flour and shake off the excess.

Add a handful of shrimp to the batter and stir until coated. Remove the shrimp 1 at a time, allowing the excess batter to drip back into the bowl.

Slip the shrimp into the hot oil, making sure that they do not touch each other and stick together. Fry until golden brown, about 3 to 4 minutes. Remove with a slotted spoon. Drain on paper towels. Repeat with the remaining shrimp.

TO SERVE Add the fried shrimp to the warm hot sauce and stir gently to coat completely.

Place ⅔ cup of the lettuce on each plate. Mound the shrimp on top and serve immediately with the celery sticks and blue cheese sauce.

BEER SUGGESTION: SIERRA NEVADA PALE ALE, CHICO, CALIFORNIA. *A crisp, hoppy beer with notes of citrus and pine.*

Some specialty markets carry zucchini or other squash blossoms out of season, but if you grow them, you will have an abundance of flowers all summer long. The ones with the narrow stems will not produce a vegetable, but the blossoms are great stuffed and fried. | On summer days, I like to serve the tomato compote cold on chilled plates and place the freshly fried zucchini blossoms in the center. The contrast between the hot and cold is especially nice. | Serve this with the Grilled BLT Double-Cut Strip Steak (page 159) and the Creamed Spinach (page 210). | SERVES 6

STUFFED ZUCCHINI BLOSSOMS | TOMATO COMPOTE

Tomato Compote

20 plum tomatoes

¼ cup extra-virgin olive oil

Fine sea salt and freshly ground black pepper to taste

Filling

¼ cup panko bread crumbs

1 shallot, finely diced

1 sprig fresh thyme

1 teaspoon extra-virgin olive oil

10 anchovy filets, drained

4 ounces artichoke spread (*crema di carciofi*; see Sources, page 274)

6 ounces fresh mozzarella, diced

5 ounces mascarpone, about ¾ cup

¼ cup freshly grated Parmigiano-Reggiano cheese

1 egg

12 large zucchini blossoms

MAKE THE COMPOTE Bring a pot of water to boiling. Add the tomatoes a few at a time and cook for 30 seconds. Remove the tomatoes with a slotted spoon and transfer them to a bowl of ice water.

Cut the tomatoes in half crosswise and remove the stem ends. Squeeze out the tomato juice and seeds.

Heat the olive oil in a large, heavy-bottomed pan over medium-high heat. When almost smoking, carefully add the tomatoes. Cook, stirring frequently, until the tomatoes are cooked to a thick sauce, about 20 minutes.

Puree the tomatoes in a blender or food processor until almost smooth. Season the sauce with salt and pepper. Keep warm.

MAKE THE FILLING Place the ¼ cup panko crumbs in a food processor or blender. Grind the crumbs until very fine.

In a small skillet, cook the shallot with the thyme and olive oil until translucent. Add the anchovy filets and cook, stirring, until the anchovies dissolve and form a paste. Scrape the mixture into a bowl and remove the thyme stems.

Pass the artichoke spread through a fine strainer or food mill to remove any larger pieces.

Add the artichoke spread, mozzarella, mascarpone, Parmigiano-Reggiano cheese, egg, ground panko, and salt and pepper to the bowl. Stir until well blended. Transfer the mixture to a piping bag or heavy duty plastic bag with

Coating

1 cup all-purpose flour

3 eggs

2 cups panko bread crumbs

Canola oil or vegetable oil for frying

one corner cut off. Use a rubber spatula, holding the bag, top folded down two or three inches, in one hand, and the spatula in the other hand. Twist the top to close the bag.

STUFF THE ZUCCHINI BLOSSOMS Wipe the zucchini blossoms clean with a damp cloth. Gently open a flower and pinch out the stamen. Holding the zucchini flower open with 1 hand and the pastry bag in the other, fill the flower three-quarters full. Fold the ends of the flower petals over to seal it shut. Repeat with the remaining flowers and filling. Set aside.

COAT THE BLOSSOMS Spread the flour in a wide, shallow dish and the panko in another. In a shallow bowl, beat together the eggs. Gently dredge the flowers in the flour, then in the eggs, and then in the panko. Stand the blossoms upright, with the stem at the top, on a plate. Refrigerate 1 hour.

COOK THE BLOSSOMS Heat about 3 inches of oil to 375°F in a heavy pot with a frying thermometer or in a deep fryer according to the manufacturer's directions.

Add the blossoms a few at time so that they do not touch. Cook the flowers for 3 to 4 minutes, or until golden brown. Remove the flowers with a slotted spoon and drain on paper towels. Sprinkle with salt. Cook the remaining flowers in the same way.

TO SERVE Spoon some of the warm tomato compote on a plate and top with 2 zucchini blossoms per serving.

Use a top-quality sushi-grade tuna, such as Bluefin, for this dish, one of the most popular appetizers at BLT. I layer the diced raw tuna with creamy avocadoes and dress the salad with an Asian-inspired dressing. The dressing is also good on tuna carpaccio or other raw fish. | Crispy fried shallots add a nice texture contrast. At the restaurant, I serve this with homemade potato chips, but grilled ciabatta bread is good with it, too. | SERVES 6

BLUEFIN TUNA TARTARE | AVOCADO | SOY-CITRUS DRESSING

Crispy Shallots

Peanut oil for frying

3 tablespoons finely chopped shallots

2 tablespoons Wondra flour

Fine sea salt

Dressing

1½ teaspoons wasabi powder

3 tablespoons reduced-sodium (lite) soy sauce

2 tablespoons white mirin

1 tablespoon mustard oil

1 tablespoon rice wine vinegar

1 teaspoon honey

Freshly ground black pepper to taste

18 ounces fresh Bluefin tuna, trimmed and cut into ⅛-inch dice

6 tablespoons extra-virgin olive oil

2 ripe Hass avocados, peeled and diced

Toasted sliced ciabatta bread

FRY THE SHALLOTS Pour the oil into a small saucepan to a depth of about 1 inch. Heat the oil until a small piece of shallot sizzles rapidly when added to the pan. Toss the shallots with the flour. Carefully add the shallots to the oil and fry until golden brown, 30 to 60 seconds. Remove the shallots with a fine mesh strainer and drain on paper towels. Season with a pinch of salt.

MAKE THE DRESSING In a medium bowl, stir together the wasabi powder and 1 tablespoon water to make a smooth paste. Whisk in the soy sauce, mirin, mustard oil, vinegar, and honey. Add black pepper. Set aside.

MAKE THE TARTARE Toss the tuna with the olive oil, and salt and pepper. Season the avocadoes with salt and pepper.

TO SERVE To mold the tuna into a disk, place a 3-inch tartlet ring or an empty tuna can with the top and bottom lids cut out on a chilled plate. Fill the ring with a layer of avocado and top with the diced tuna and fried shallots. Lift off the ring. Drizzle the dressing around the tuna.

SERVE with the ciabatta or homemade potato chips.

CHEF'S TIP: *When molding this salad, wrap a potato half about the same diameter as the mold in plastic wrap. Spoon the tuna and avocado into the mold and use the covered flat side of the potato as a tamper to press the tuna and avocado neatly, evenly, and quickly into the mold.*

WINE SUGGESTION: RIESLING, "EROICA," DR. LOOSEN/CHATEAU STE. MICHELLE, 2003, COLUMBIA VALLEY, WASHINGTON. *A dry-style Riesling with aromas of white peach, melon, and spices.*

Tiny, silvery-gold sardines swim in large schools and reproduce quickly, so they are always plentiful. Marseilles in southern France is famous for its abundant catch, and locals like to enhance their reputation by fabricating tall tales about how a sardine so huge that it blocked the entire harbor once swam into port! | My father's favorite way to eat grilled sardines is on a slice of buttered, grilled bread with a dash of vinegar and a sprinkle of sea salt. | SERVES 6

GRILLED SARDINE CROSTINI | RED ONION | TOMATOES

Tomato Salad

2-inch piece of fresh ginger, peeled

½ cup extra-virgin olive oil

2 tablespoons sherry vinegar

Fine sea salt and freshly ground black pepper to taste

2 cups cherry tomatoes (red, yellow, and orange, if possible)

2 tablespoons julienned Thai basil

2 tablespoons chopped red onion

18 fresh sardine fillets

2 cups Tomato Vinaigrette (page 60)

6 slices country bread, ½ inch thick, toasted or grilled

6 thin slices bacon, cooked until crisp (see page 43)

18 small leaves fresh Thai basil

MAKE THE GINGER JUICE Grate the ginger on the large holes of a grater. Wrap the grated ginger in the corner of a lint-free cloth. Squeeze the ginger over a cup to extract the juice. You should have 2 tablespoons of juice.

MARINATE THE TOMATOES In a medium bowl, whisk together the oil, vinegar, ginger juice, and salt and pepper until blended. Add the cherry tomatoes, basil, and onion. Taste for seasoning. Let stand at room temperature for 30 minutes.

GRILL THE SARDINES Pat the sardines dry with paper towels. Brush the cut sides with olive oil and season with salt and pepper. Preheat a grill pan over medium-high heat until a drop of water sizzles when flicked onto the pan. Grill the sardine fillets skin-sides down for 1 minute. Turn them and grill 1 minute more. Remove the sardines to a plate.

SERVE THE CROSTINI Divide the Tomato Vinaigrette among 6 plates. Place a slice of toast on top of each. Divide the tomatoes over the toast. Top each with 3 sardine fillets, 1 slice of bacon, and 3 basil leaves. Serve immediately.

WINE SUGGESTION: ROSÉ, SOLA ROSA, 2004, CALIFORNIA. *A crisp and clean Rosé wine with aromas of fresh-picked strawberries, wildflowers, and spice.*

Remove with a slotted spoon. Drain on paper towels. Repeat with the remaining shrimp.

Though some sources credit the maître d' of the Casino Club on Narragansett Pier for inventing this recipe in 1917, there are many others that indicate it was popular at least ten years earlier. After cooking the clams, strain and freeze the broth. Use it for seafood soups. | SERVES 6

CLAMS CASINO

2 cups dry white wine

1½ cups sliced shallots

½ cup chopped fresh parsley

2 tablespoons chopped garlic

3 sprigs fresh thyme

48 littleneck clams, scrubbed with a brush

Filling

1 cup (2 sticks) unsalted butter, softened

1 cup panko bread crumbs

3 tablespoons minced fresh parsley

2 tablespoons finely diced Serrano or prosciutto ham

2 tablespoons chopped fresh chives

2 teaspoons minced shallots

2 teaspoons minced garlic

Fine sea salt and freshly ground black pepper to taste

MAKE THE BROTH Place the wine, shallots, parsley, garlic, and thyme in a large saucepan. Bring the liquid to a boil.

COOK THE CLAMS Add the clams to the broth. Cover and cook, shaking the pan occasionally, 5 to 7 minutes, or until you begin to hear the clams popping open. Remove the opened clams to a bowl. Cook any unopened clams a little longer. Discard any that refuse to open.

Let the clams and the cooking liquid cool slightly.

PREPARE THE FILLING In a large bowl, stir together the butter, panko crumbs, parsley, ham, chives, shallots, garlic, and salt and pepper. Mix well.

STUFF THE CLAMS Remove the clams from their shells. Place half the shells in a large baking pan. If the clams are sandy, rinse them by dipping 1 at a time into the cooking liquid. Place a clam in each half shell. Generously spoon the filling onto each clam, approximately 1 teaspoon per clam. Sprinkle the tops of the clams with the remaining filling, approximately 4 tablespoons.

PREHEAT THE BROILER Place an oven rack 4 to 5 inches from the broiler heat source. Preheat the broiler.

BROIL THE CLAMS Place the clams on the rack. Broil 1 to 2 minutes, or until browned. Serve hot.

WINE SUGGESTION: KLUGE ESTATE WINES, NEW WORLD BRUT SP, 2002, ALBEMARLE COUNTY, VIRGINIA. *A crisp, clean, sparkling wine made from Chardonnay with aromas of apples, pears, and spiced nuts.*

Peel and Eat Shrimp remind me of the great seafood meals I have enjoyed in Maine. Place them in a bowl in the middle of the table and let everyone help themselves. They are messy to eat, so provide plenty of napkins and plan to serve them to friends who enjoy eating casually—preferably outdoors! | Most shrimp in this country are sold frozen with their heads removed. If you can find them, fresh head-on shrimp are much more flavorful in this recipe. See the Sources (page 274) for suggestions on where to buy them. | SERVES 6

PEEL AND EAT SHRIMP

2 pounds large shell-on shrimp

½ cup Cajun spice blend, such as McCormick Cajun Spice

½ teaspoon Old Bay Seasoning

½ teaspoon Spanish paprika

¼ teaspoon cayenne

8 tablespoons (1 stick) clarified butter (see page 271)

6 tablespoons finely chopped fresh rosemary

3 tablespoons finely chopped garlic

Lime wedges

PREPARE THE SHRIMP Pull off the legs of the shrimp. With a small sharp knife, make a slit along the back of each shell. With the tip of the knife, lift up the vein and pull it out without removing the shell.

SEASON THE SHRIMP In a large bowl, mix the spice blend, Old Bay, paprika, and cayenne. Add the shrimp and butter and toss until coated.

COOK THE SHRIMP Heat a large skillet over medium-high heat. Add half the shrimp and cook, stirring frequently, until they turn pink, about 3 minutes.

Add half the rosemary and garlic and cook until the shrimp are cooked through, about 2 minutes more. Remove the shrimp to a bowl. Cook the remaining shrimp in the same way.

SERVE immediately with lime wedges.

WINE SUGGESTION:
JOHANNESBERG RIESLING, "SEMI-DRY," HERMAN J. WIEMER, 2003, FINGER LAKES, NEW YORK. *An off dry–style Riesling with aromas of fresh peaches, apricots, and minerals.*

When handling raw meat, make sure that everything that will come in contact with it, including your hands, is very clean and the meat is very fresh and cold. Ground meat requires extra caution since the large surface area makes it ideal for the growth of dangerous bacteria. In the BLT kitchens, the cooks always wear latex gloves when working with it. Never use preground meat for Steak Tartare. | The sauce for this appetizer can be made a few hours in advance and then added to the steak just before serving. Try the sauce on grilled steak, too. | I sometimes have Steak Tartare for lunch with a Boston lettuce salad with mustard vinaigrette and French fries. | SERVES 6 TO 8

STEAK TARTARE

Sauce

½ cup mayonnaise

2 tablespoons Dijon mustard

2 tablespoons ketchup

1 teaspoon Worcestershire sauce

1 teaspoon Tabasco sauce

5 tablespoons diced red onion

3 tablespoons chopped cornichons

2 tablespoons rinsed capers, chopped

2 tablespoons chopped fresh flat-leaf parsley

1 anchovy filet, minced

1 teaspoon chopped fresh tarragon

1 teaspoon chopped fresh chives

1 garlic clove, minced

1½ pounds filet mignon, very cold

2 tablespoons extra-virgin olive oil

Fine sea salt and freshly ground black pepper to taste

Country or French bread, sliced and toasted

MAKE THE SAUCE In a medium bowl, combine the mayonnaise, mustard, ketchup, Worcestershire sauce, and Tabasco sauce and mix thoroughly. Stir in the onions, cornichons, capers, parsley, anchovy, tarragon, chives, and garlic.

CHOP THE BEEF Just before serving, remove the beef from the refrigerator; it should be very cold. Using a meat grinder with large holes, grind the beef. Place the ground meat in a bowl set over a larger bowl of crushed ice.

Fold in the mayonnaise mixture and the olive oil just until blended. Do not overwork the mixture. Taste and adjust the seasoning with salt and pepper if necessary.

SERVE immediately on individual plates with toasted bread.

CHEF'S TIP: *If you don't have a meat grinder, have the butcher grind it for you. Don't use a food processor for this recipe; the meat won't have the right texture.*

BEER SUGGESTION: OMMEGANG WITTE, COOPERSTOWN, NEW YORK. *A Belgian-style white ale with aromas of citrus peel and coriander.*

Thinly sliced raw beef is known as carpaccio in Italy. It was invented in 1950 by Harry Cipriani, a Venetian restaurateur, in honor of the Renaissance artist Vittore Carpaccio, who was famous for the brilliant red color he used in his paintings. Though typically made with raw beef dressed with lemon juice and olive oil, my version includes thinly sliced mushrooms, mozzarella, and Parmesan and is served on a bed of arugula. | Another way to present this carpaccio is to melt the mozzarella on top of the mushrooms before placing them on top of the beef. | Follow this appetizer with Baked Black Sea Bass/Tomato/Eggplant/Honey/ Sherry Vinegar (page 138) and Silver Dollars (page 224). | SERVES 6

BEEF CARPACCIO | PORTOBELLO MUSHROOMS | MOZZARELLA

1¾ pounds beef tenderloin or top round

2 medium portobello mushrooms, 3 to 4 ounces each, stems removed

½ cup extra-virgin olive oil

6 sprigs fresh thyme

1 garlic clove, minced

Fine sea salt and freshly ground black pepper to taste

¼ cup freshly squeezed lemon juice

2 teaspoons lemon zest

6 ounces fresh mozzarella cheese, sliced

6 cups baby arugula, trimmed and washed

2 ounces Parmigiano-Reggiano cheese

2 tablespoons Crispy Shallots (page 27)

Toasted or grilled sliced country bread

FREEZE THE BEEF Place the beef on a piece of plastic wrap. Roll the meat in the wrap, forming a cylinder. Twist the ends to tighten the wrap. Place in the freezer until semi-firm, at least 3 hours.

Chill 6 flat salad plates.

PREPARE THE MUSHROOMS Toss the mushrooms with 1 tablespoon of the olive oil, the thyme sprigs, garlic, and salt and pepper

Preheat the oven to 350°F or a grill pan or barbecue grill to medium-high. Bake the mushrooms for 10 to 15 minutes, until tender and cooked through, or grill, turning once, for 5 to 7 minutes. Cool the mushroom caps and slice them thinly on a slight bias.

SLICE THE BEEF Unwrap the beef. Using a sharp knife, cut the meat against the grain into the thinnest slices possible. Arrange the slices slightly over-lapping on the chilled plates. Top each plate with plastic wrap. Very gently pound the meat with a rubber mallet or a rolling pin so that it covers the whole plate. Refrigerate up to 24 hours.

MAKE THE VINAIGRETTE In a large bowl, whisk together the lemon juice, 1 teaspoon of the zest, the remaining oil, and salt and pepper.

TO ASSEMBLE Remove the plastic wrap from each plate. Season the meat with salt, pepper, the remaining 1 teaspoon of the lemon zest, and enough of the vinaigrette to lightly coat the beef. Place a few slices of mozzarella cheese in the center of each plate and place the portobello slices on top.

Toss the arugula with the remaining dressing. Place on top of the mushrooms. With a swivel-blade vegetable peeler, shave the Parmigiano-Reggiano over all and sprinkle with the fried shallots.

SERVE immediately with toasted or grilled white country bread.

WINE SUGGESTION: PINOT NOIR, "MT. JEFFERSON CUVEE," CRISTOM, 2004, WILLAMETTE VALLEY, OREGON. *A medium-bodied red made from Pinot Noir, with notes of fresh strawberries, red flowers, and a hint of spicy earth.*

Honey and balsamic vinegar make a quick and easy marinade for grilled butterflied quail. For a great summer meal, serve these with a green salad, crumbled feta or goat cheese, some Caramelized Walnuts (see page 273), and fresh figs. Tiny quails are usually sold frozen, either whole or partly boned. They cook quickly, so watch them carefully to prevent overcooking. | SERVES 6

GRILLED HONEY-BALSAMIC MARINATED QUAIL

6 semi-boneless quail, thawed if frozen

½ cup honey

½ cup balsamic vinegar

Fine sea salt and freshly ground black pepper to taste

MARINATE THE QUAILS Rinse the quails and pat them dry. Butterfly the quails by cutting them down the back with kitchen shears. Open the quails like a book. Thread a short wooden skewer from the bottom of the leg to the top of the breast on each side so that the quails will hold their shape.

In a shallow dish, combine the honey and vinegar. Add the quails, turning to coat both sides. Cover and refrigerate for at least 1½ hours or up to 3 hours.

MAKE THE GLAZE Remove the quails from the marinade. Pour the marinade into a small pot. Place over medium heat and boil until slightly reduced and thickened, about 10 minutes.

GRILL THE QUAILS Preheat a barbecue or stovetop grill to medium-high heat. Pat the quails dry and season them on both sides with salt and pepper. Grill the quails breast-side down for 4 to 6 minutes, or until crisp and golden. Turn the quails and grill 4 to 5 minutes longer, or until just cooked through, brushing them with the glaze.

TO SERVE Remove the skewers and serve the quails immediately.

WINE SUGGESTION: ROUSSANNE, ALBAN VINEYARDS, 2003, EDNA VALLEY, CALIFORNIA. *A rich, heady white made from the Rhône Valley's Roussanne grape, with aromas of tropical fruits, flowers, and roasted nuts.*

P ort wine simmered with seasonings concentrates and enhances the flavor and complements the sweetness of this chicken liver appetizer. Make sure the livers do not overcook or the spread will be dry. Pink salt, or sel rose, is a combination of potassium nitrate or saltpeter, salt, and food coloring that chefs use to impart a rosy color to pâtés. See the Sources on page 274. Pink salt is optional, though, so if you can't find it, you can substitute sea salt without changing the flavor.

| SERVES 6

WARM CHICKEN LIVER SPREAD

1 bay leaf

7 sprigs fresh thyme

1 cup ruby port

1 shallot, thinly sliced, plus 2 tablespoons chopped shallots

1 garlic clove, thinly sliced, plus 2 teaspoons chopped garlic

1 pound chicken livers, trimmed

1 tablespoon fine sea salt

1¼ teaspoons pink salt (optional)

Freshly ground black pepper to taste

2 tablespoons duck fat or extra-virgin olive oil

3 tablespoons Cognac or brandy

2 tablespoons unsalted butter, softened

Fleur de sel (see Sources, page 274)

2 teaspoons extra-virgin olive oil

6 thick slices country bread, toasted

Cornichons or pickled vegetables

MAKE THE REDUCTION Tie the bay leaf and 2 sprigs of the thyme together with kitchen twine.

In a small, heavy saucepan, bring the port, the herb bundle, sliced shallot, and sliced garlic to a simmer. Cook until the port is reduced to the consistency of a thick syrup. Remove the herb bundle.

COOK THE CHICKEN LIVERS Season the chicken livers with the sea salt and pink salt, if using, and the pepper. Heat 1 tablespoon of the duck fat in a large skillet over high heat. When nearly smoking, add half the livers and brown on 1 side, about 2 minutes. Turn and cook on the other side until golden brown but still pink in the center, about 1 minute more. Stir in half of the chopped shallots and chopped garlic. Pour in 1½ tablespoons of the cognac and heat 1 minute. Scrape the mixture into a bowl. Repeat with the remaining ingredients.

BLEND THE MIXTURE In a food processor, combine the livers and port syrup. Process until smooth. Blend in the butter. Season with salt and pepper. Scrape the mixture into a terrine or glass jar.

(Can be made ahead to this point. Cover and chill up to 3 days. To reheat, place the spread in the top of a double boiler over simmering water. Heat gently, stirring occasionally, until warm.)

TO SERVE Remove the leaves from the remaining thyme sprigs. Garnish the pate with the thyme leaves, a sprinkling of fleur de sel, and the extra-virgin olive oil. Serve warm with grilled country bread and cornichons.

WINE SUGGESTION: ROSÉ, LEWIS CELLARS, 2005, CALIFORNIA. *A crisp, refreshing rosé with aromas of strawberries, orange peel, and spice.*

A crock of this delicious mousse with a basket of toasted French bread is a welcome addition to the table for a casual appetizer or buffet spread. It also makes a fine lunch with a green salad. It is ideal for a party because you can make it several days ahead of serving and the flavor only gets better as it mellows. | If you can't find some of the duck ingredients at your local butcher shop, you can order them either on line or by phone from D'Artagnan (see Sources, page 274). A small amount of prepared foie gras terrine, available in cans at many gourmet markets, gives this mousse extra special flavor. | SERVES 12

DUCK LIVER MOUSSE | PORT GELÉE

⅔ cup dry white wine

1 cup chopped shallots

1 tablespoon chopped garlic

Fine sea salt and freshly ground black pepper to taste

Pinch fresh thyme leaves

2 cups ruby port wine

3 tablespoons vegetable oil

1½ pounds duck liver, tough membranes trimmed

2 tablespoons Cognac

1¾ cups (12 ounces) duck fat (see Sources, page 274), melted and cooled to room temperature

¾ cup heavy cream

2 ounces foie gras terrine

2 tablespoons white wine vinegar

2 teaspoons ground allspice

½ teaspoon unflavored gelatin powder

Sprigs fresh thyme, for garnish

Bay leaves, for garnish

Black peppercorns, for garnish

Country or French bread, sliced and toasted

COOK THE SHALLOTS In a medium saucepan, combine the white wine, ½ cup of the shallots, the garlic, and a pinch each of salt, pepper, and thyme. Bring it to a simmer and cook until all of the liquid is evaporated, 10 to 12 minutes.

REDUCE THE PORT In a small saucepan, simmer 1 cup of the port for 10 to 12 minutes, or until reduced to ⅓ cup.

COOK THE LIVER In large skillet, heat 1½ tablespoons of the oil over medium heat. Add the duck livers, and season them with salt and pepper. Cook until well browned, about 2 minutes. Turn the livers and brown them on the other side, about 2 minutes more. Pour the livers and pan juices into a strainer set over a bowl to stop the cooking.

FLAME THE SHALLOTS Add the remaining 1½ tablespoons of the oil to the skillet. Add the remaining ½ cup shallots and cook on medium-low heat about 5 minutes, or until translucent.

Wearing a heatproof oven mitt, add the Cognac to the skillet. Avert your face and carefully light the Cognac with a long match. Turn off the heat. When the flames subside, scrape the mixture into a food processor with a steel blade.

MAKE THE MOUSSE Add the livers and cooking juices to the processor. Add the white wine mixture, port, and duck fat. Process until very smooth.

Add the cream, foie gras, vinegar, and allspice and process 30 seconds, or just until blended. Season with salt and pepper. (Season generously since chilling will dull the flavor somewhat and make the mousse seem less flavorful.)

STRAIN THE MOUSSE With a rubber spatula, force the mousse through a fine-mesh strainer into a bowl. Scrape the mousse into a 4-cup terrine. Let cool, loosely covered, in the refrigerator.

MAKE THE GELÉE In a small saucepan over medium heat, warm the remaining 1 cup port. Averting your face, light it with a long match. Turn off the heat. When the flames have subsided, stir in the gelatin until it is completely dissolved. Let cool to room temperature.

DECORATE THE TERRINE Pour the gelée over the mousse. Decorate the top with the thyme, bay leaves, and peppercorns. Cover and chill until completely set, at least 4 hours and preferably overnight.

SERVE with toasted French country bread.

CHEF'S TIP: *Flaming is a cooking technique that, when done correctly, allows you to quickly burn off alcohol while adding the flavor of the Cognac or similar liquor to your recipe. Take precautions when doing this. Make sure the cooking area is clear of anything that might easily catch fire and have a heavy pot cover handy to quickly smother the flame if necessary. Protect your hand with a heat-proof mitt, use a long match such as the kind used for lighting a fireplace, and stand back from the pan when you light it. Do not exceed the amount of alcohol called for in the recipe. It will flare up for a moment, but the flames will subside quickly once the alcohol dissipates.*

WINE SUGGESTION: BRUT ROSÉ, IRON HORSE, 2000, GREEN VALLEY, CALIFOR-NIA. *A full-bodied rosé sparkling wine with aromas of framboise, cherries, and tomato skin.*

Here is my version of a classic steakhouse appetizer, grilled thick-sliced bacon in a tangy dressing. Place it in the center of the table for everyone to share. It is a great starter for a hearty steak meal. Bacon smoked over applewood embers is especially aromatic and flavorful. | SERVES 6

GRILLED DOUBLE-SMOKED BACON

Dressing

½ cup extra-virgin olive oil

1 tablespoon sherry vinegar

Fine sea salt and freshly ground black pepper to taste

½ cup chopped fresh parsley

1 tablespoon chopped shallots

1 teaspoon chopped garlic

18 slices applewood smoked bacon (⅛ to ¼ inch thick)

MAKE THE DRESSING In a medium bowl, whisk together the oil, vinegar, and salt and pepper. Stir in the remaining ingredients.

COOK THE BACON Preheat a barbecue or stovetop grill to medium heat. Cook the bacon until browned and crisp on both sides, 5 to 6 minutes. Drain the bacon on paper towels.

TO SERVE Arrange the bacon on a platter. Drizzle with the dressing. Serve hot.

WINE SUGGESTION: SYRAH, "WAHLUKE SLOPE," K VINTNERS, 2002, COLUMBIA VALLEY, WASHINGTON. *A smoky, spicy red made from Syrah with aromas of roasted black fruits, black pepper, and spiced oak notes.*

CHAPTER TWO

Unripe (green) papaya is juicy and crunchy, quite different from the fully ripened fruit. The flavor is mild and only slightly sweet, something like that of the white part of a watermelon. It is a typical ingredient in Thailand, where it is used to make many types of salads. You can sometimes find shredded green papaya in Asian markets. | SERVES 6

GREEN PAPAYA CHICKEN SALAD

Chicken

4 skinless chicken thighs, about 2½ pounds

1 teaspoon ground anise seed

1 teaspoon ground cloves

1 teaspoon fine sea salt

½ teaspoon freshly grated nutmeg

¼ teaspoon ground cardamom

Sweet and Sour Sauce

¼ cup sugar

1 medium carrot, julienned

⅓ cup Thai fish sauce (nam pla)

3 tablespoons rice wine vinegar

1 fresh red Thai chile, chopped

1 lime, juiced

1 garlic clove, minced

Salad

3 cups green papaya, julienned

1½ hothouse or English cucumber, julienned

2 ounces bean sprouts (about 1 cup)

3 scallions, cut into julienne strips

1 cup Thai basil leaves, julienned

⅓ cup fresh mint leaves, julienned

⅓ cup fresh cilantro, roughly chopped

½ cup chopped roasted unsalted peanuts

¼ cup Crispy Shallots (page 27)

ROAST THE CHICKEN Preheat the oven to 400°F. Season the chicken thighs with the spices and salt. Place the pieces on a large sheet of aluminum foil. Fold the ends of the foil over the chicken and fold it several times to seal tightly. Bake for 1 hour, or until the chicken juices run clear when the chicken is pierced with a knife.

Loosen the foil and let the chicken cool. Remove the meat from the bone and cut it into thin slices.

MAKE THE SAUCE In a medium saucepan, combine the sugar and ½ cup water. Bring the mixture to a simmer over medium heat. Stir to dissolve the sugar. Remove the pot from the heat. Stir in the carrot, fish sauce, vinegar, chile, lime juice, and garlic. Allow the carrot to steep for 45 minutes.

ASSEMBLE THE SALAD Combine the chicken, papaya, cucumber, bean sprouts, scallions, basil, mint, and cilantro in a large bowl. Strain the sauce into another bowl. Add the carrot to the chicken mixture. Pour about 1 cup of the sauce over the salad and mix, making sure that everything is well dressed.

TO SERVE Divide the salad equally among 6 dinner plates and garnish with the peanuts and fried shallots.

WINE SUGGESTION: PINOT GRIS, "TIKKA'S RUN," LEMELSON VINEYARDS, 2003, WILLAMETTE VALLEY, OREGON. *A rich and nutty white made from Pinot Gris with aromas of spiced pear and candied apples.*

When I want something light to eat, I always think of this salad. It goes with practically any simply made meat, poultry, or fish. | You can make your own carrot juice with a juice extractor, or buy it freshly made at a health food store. Organic carrots have a good, sweet flavor. I sometimes garnish this salad with toasted pumpkin seeds and a drizzle of pumpkin seed oil. | SERVES 6

CARROT-CILANTRO SALAD | GINGER-ORANGE DRESSING

1 pound carrots, peeled and shredded

1 cup chopped fresh cilantro

½ cup grapeseed oil

2 tablespoons sherry vinegar

1 garlic clove, minced

Fine sea salt and freshly ground black pepper to taste

⅓ cup fresh carrot juice

2 tablespoons finely grated fresh ginger

2 tablespoons mayonnaise

1½ teaspoons toasted sesame oil

MARINATE THE CARROTS Toss the shredded carrots with ½ cup of the cilantro, ¼ cup of the grapeseed oil, the vinegar, garlic, and salt and pepper. Let the carrots marinate for 15 minutes.

MAKE THE DRESSING In a small saucepan, boil the carrot juice over medium heat until it is reduced by half, about 5 minutes. Pour the carrot juice into a bowl and let cool.

Wrap the ginger in a piece of cheesecloth and squeeze it over a small bowl to extract the juice. There should be about ¾ teaspoon juice. Whisk together the carrot juice, remaining ¼ cup of the grapeseed oil, the mayonnaise, sesame oil, ginger juice, and salt and pepper.

ASSEMBLE THE SALAD Strain the marinated carrots and discard the liquid. Add the carrot dressing and remaining ½ cup of the cilantro to the drained carrots and toss well.

Serve immediately.

WINE SUGGESTION: GEWÜRZTRAMINER, STANDING STONE VINEYARDS, 2003, FINGER LAKES, NEW YORK. *A dry and spicy Gewürztraminer with notes of lychee, flowers, and spices.*

Chinese five-spice powder is composed of a mixture of ground spices such as fennel seed, ginger, star anise, cloves, and cinnamon. You can find it wherever spices are sold, or try one of the Sources listed on page 274. | SERVES 6

CHINESE CHICKEN SALAD

4 to 6 boneless, skinless chicken thighs, 2½ pounds

1 teaspoon Chinese five-spice powder

Fine sea salt and freshly ground black pepper to taste

2 tablespoons extra-virgin olive oil

Fried Wonton Strips

Peanut oil for frying

12 wonton skins, cut into thin julienne

Vinaigrette

½ cup rice wine vinegar

¼ cup light sesame oil

2 to 3 tablespoons peanut oil

3 tablespoons soy sauce

2 tablespoons honey

2 teaspoons dry Chinese mustard

Salad

3 cups thinly sliced Napa cabbage

1 cup thinly sliced red cabbage

1 cup thinly sliced romaine lettuce

20 snow peas, cut into julienne strips

½ cup chopped roasted unsalted peanuts

1 medium carrot, julienned

⅓ cup julienned fresh Thai basil

¼ cup julienned fresh cilantro

2 fresh Thai chiles, chopped

1 tablespoon each toasted black and white sesame seeds

1½ tablespoons Vietnamese fish sauce (*nuoc mam*)

PREPARE THE CHICKEN Preheat the oven to 400°F.

Season the chicken thighs with the five-spice powder and salt and pepper. Place the chicken on a large sheet of aluminum foil. Drizzle with the olive oil. Wrap the foil around the chicken, folding the ends over to form a tight seal. Bake 1 hour, or until the chicken juices run clear when they are pierced with a fork.

Remove the chicken from the oven and slit the foil to allow the chicken to cool. Thinly slice the meat.

MAKE THE FRIED WONTON STRIPS Pour about 2 inches of oil into a heavy medium saucepan. Heat the oil to 375°F. Working in batches, fry the wonton strips until golden and crisp, about 1 minute. Using a slotted spoon, transfer the wonton strips to paper towels to drain. Season immediately with salt.

MAKE THE VINAIGRETTE Place all of the vinaigrette ingredients in a bowl. Whisk until smooth. Season with salt and pepper.

ASSEMBLE THE SALAD In a large bowl, combine the chicken, cabbages, romaine, snow peas, peanuts, carrots, basil, cilantro, chiles, and sesame seeds. Add enough vinaigrette to coat the salad evenly and toss well. Season with the fish sauce, and salt and pepper. Top with the fried wonton strips.

WINE SUGGESTION: PINOT GRIS, "CHAMISAL VINEYARD," DOMAINE ALFRED, 2004, EDNA VALLEY, CALIFORNIA. *A spicy, fresh Pinot Gris with notes of tangerines, lime zest, and pears.*

With its creamy oregano dressing, this is a good salad any season of the year. It is substantial enough to serve for a light supper or luncheon with grilled chicken or shrimp. Experiment with other ingredients in this salad using whatever is in season, such as celery or red bell pepper. For example, you can substitute watercress or arugula for the lettuces and use Manchego cheese instead of the feta. | SERVES 6

CHOPPED VEGETABLE SALAD | CREAMY OREGANO DRESSING

Oregano Dressing

3 tablespoons red wine vinegar

2 tablespoons mayonnaise

1½ teaspoons Dijon mustard

3 tablespoons extra-virgin olive oil

3 tablespoons grapeseed oil

1½ teaspoons dried oregano

Fine sea salt and freshly ground black pepper to taste

Salad

1 small head iceberg lettuce, washed and dried

1 small head radicchio, washed and dried

1 small head friseé, washed and dried

2 red radishes, sliced paper thin

1 cup diced feta cheese (6 ounces)

1 small red onion, halved and thinly sliced

1 medium cucumber, peeled and diced

1½ cups corn kernels (see page 272)

¾ cup grape tomatoes, halved

¾ cup thinly sliced scallions (about 6)

¾ cup canned hearts of palm, drained and cut into bite-sized pieces

¼ cup snipped fresh chives

¼ cup pitted and sliced Kalamata olives

1½ teaspoons dried oregano

MAKE THE DRESSING In a medium bowl, whisk together the vinegar mayonnaise, and mustard. Whisking constantly, slowly drizzle in the olive and grapeseed oils until smooth and well blended. Stir in the oregano and salt and pepper.

DRESS THE LETTUCES Chop the lettuce, radicchio, and frisée into bite-sized pieces. Toss them together in a large bowl. Add two-thirds of the vinaigrette and salt and pepper.

MIX THE REMAINING INGREDIENTS Place the remaining vegetables, cheese, and herbs in the mixing bowl and toss with the remaining vinaigrette. Spoon the mixture into the serving bowls.

SERVE immediately.

WINE SUGGESTION: SAUVIGNON BLANC, OJAI, 2004, SANTA BARBARA COUNTY, CALIFORNIA. *A crisp, honeyed Sauvignon Blanc, with aromas of white peaches, citrus, and melons.*

Figs were first cultivated in California by Spanish missionaries, who planted them throughout the state and named a popular purplish-black variety the Mission fig. Calimyrna figs, which are a light golden brown in color, were actually an ancient Turkish variety that was renamed in honor of its new homeland. | The tender, sweet figs are a delightful contrast to the slightly bitter, crunchy greens and creamy, rich Gorgonzola in this salad. | SERVES 6

ENDIVE SALAD | GORGONZOLA | MARINATED FIGS | MUSTARD VINAIGRETTE

Fig Syrup

2 cups ruby port

1 stick cinnamon

1 star anise

12 dried Mission figs

Dressing

¼ cup Dijon mustard

¼ cup whole-grain mustard

3 tablespoons sherry vinegar

2 tablespoons honey

½ cup grapeseed oil

2 tablespoons walnut oil

Fine sea salt and freshly ground black pepper to taste

Salad

3 white endives

3 red endives

1 head frisée lettuce

½ medium Granny Smith apple, peeled and cored

6 ounces Gorgonzola cheese, crumbled

3 tablespoons chopped fresh chives

7 tablespoons Caramelized Walnuts (see page 273)

POACH THE FIGS Heat the port in a small saucepan and add the cinnamon and star anise. Bring to a boil and add the figs. Cover the pot and turn off the heat. Allow the figs to cool in the port. Refrigerate until chilled. Remove the figs from the liquid.

Place the saucepan of port over the heat again and bring to a simmer. Reduce until thick and syrupy. Slice the figs thinly.

MAKE THE DRESSING In a small bowl, whisk together the mustards, vinegar, and honey. Slowly whisk in the oils. Season with salt and pepper.

PREPARE THE SALAD Cut the endives in half lengthwise. Remove the cores from the endives and slice the leaves crosswise on a bias into 1-inch pieces.

Remove the tough outer green parts of the frisée and roughly chop the tender inner leaves Cut the apple into julienne pieces.

TO SERVE In a large bowl, toss the greens with the dressing and season with salt and pepper. Divide among 6 plates. Garnish with the cheese, apple, figs, chives, and walnuts. Drizzle with some of the fig syrup and serve immediately.

WINE SUGGESTION: MARSANNE, "PURISMA MOUNTAIN VINEYARD," BECKMEN VINEYARDS, 2003, SANTA BARBARA, CALIFORNIA. *A rich and nutty wine made from Marsanne, with aromas of honeysuckle, pears, and licorice.*

When fresh fava beans are in season in the spring, I like to use them in as many ways as possible. Their bright green color, bittersweet flavor, and crisp texture make them ideal for salads. Use only the smallest and most tender beans because they are the sweetest. Oversize fava beans taste starchy and have a mealy texture. | I like to serve this salad before a hearty dish like the Osso Buco/ Orange Gremolata (page 179). | SERVES 6

FAVA BEANS | PECORINO | ARUGULA SALAD

2 pounds unshelled fava beans

½ cup freshly squeezed lemon juice

½ cup extra-virgin olive oil

1 tablespoon coarsely chopped fresh mint

1 tablespoon roughly chopped fresh oregano

1 teaspoon crushed red pepper flakes

1 garlic clove, chopped

8 ounces pecorino cheese, diced

Fine sea salt to taste

4 cups baby arugula

SHELL THE FAVA BEANS Remove the fava beans from the pods.

Bring a pot of salted water to a boil. Drop the beans into the boiling water. Cook for 2 minutes, then transfer to ice water immediately. Drain and pat dry. Peel off the skin of each bean.

DRESS THE BEANS In a bowl, whisk together the lemon juice, oil, mint, oregano, red pepper flakes, and garlic. Add the fava beans and pecorino. Add salt.

TOSS THE SALAD Just before serving, add the arugula and toss well. Serve right away.

WINE SUGGESTION: PINOT GRIGIO, "ALISOS VINEYARD," PALMINA, 2003, SANTA BARBARA COUNTY, CALIFORNIA. *A crisp and lively Pinot Grigio with aromas of citrus oil and oranges.*

P ecorino Toscano is a sheep's milk cheese from Tuscany. Known as stagionato, this pecorino is sharper and more flavorful, while fresco, or young pecorino, is milder, sweeter, and has a creamier texture. | I like to serve this salad before Grilled Shrimp/Cauliflower/Soy-Caper Brown Butter Sauce (page 140). | SERVES 6

FENNEL-ARUGULA SALAD | AGED PECORINO

1 large fennel bulb, trimmed and sliced paper thin on a mandoline or in a food processor (about 2 cups)

2 bunches arugula, stems removed (about 6 cups)

7 tablespoons extra-virgin olive oil

3 tablespoons freshly squeezed lemon juice

Fine sea salt and freshly ground black pepper to taste

5 ounces aged pecorino Toscano, shaved into thin flakes

4 radishes, sliced paper thin

2 tablespoons snipped fresh chives

Crispy Shallots (page 27)

MAKE THE SALAD In a large bowl, toss together the fennel and arugula. In a smaller bowl, whisk together the oil, lemon juice, and salt and pepper. Pour the dressing on the salad and toss gently. Mound the salad on serving plates.

ADD THE TOPPING Sprinkle with the cheese, radish slices, chives, and fried shallots.

Serve immediately.

CHEF'S TIP: To get thin shavings of cheese, use a swivel-blade vegetable peeler and pull it slowly across the cut surface of any semi-firm cheese.

WINE SUGGESTION:
CHARDONNAY, "CLONE 76 INOX," MELVILLE WINERY, 2004, SANTA RITA HILLS, CALIFORNIA. An uno-aked, crisp, spicy Chardonnay with aromas of candied green apples, watercress, and slate

Nashi pears are sometimes called "apple" pears since they look like apples, but they taste like crisp, juicy pears. They are also known as Asian pears because they originally come from that continent. They are available all year-round, though mostly in the fall. | Other flavorful oils, such as pumpkin seed, pistachio, hazelnut, or mustard oil can be used in place of the walnut oil in this salad. Each has its own distinctive flavors that will add a different dimension to this salad. |
SERVES 6

FIELD GREENS | MANCHEGO CHEESE | WALNUT VINAIGRETTE

Walnut Vinaigrette

½ cup walnut oil

¼ cup extra-virgin olive oil

5 tablespoons sherry vinegar

2 tablespoons freshly squeezed lemon juice

Fine sea salt and freshly ground black pepper to taste

1 pound mixed baby lettuces, washed and dried

1 firm ripe pear, preferably Nashi variety, very thinly sliced

3 ounces Manchego cheese, shaved thinly with a vegetable peeler

2 tablespoons snipped fresh chives

MAKE THE VINAIGRETTE In a small bowl, whisk together both of the oils, vinegar, lemon juice, and salt and pepper.

MAKE THE SALAD In a large bowl, toss the lettuces with enough vinaigrette to coat evenly.

TO ASSEMBLE Top with the pear, cheese slices, and chives.

CHEF'S TIP: To slice the pears thinly and evenly, use a vegetable peeler or mandoline.

WINE SUGGESTION: ALBARINO, HAVENS, 2003, CARNEROS, CALIFORNIA. A fresh and stony Albarino (native to Galicia in Spain), with aromas of lemons, peaches, and kumquats.

Heirloom tomatoes are unique in color and shape, with remarkably good flavor. They remind me of the tomatoes that my grandmother used to grow in her garden. I like to take full advantage of them when they are in season and use them to make all kinds of delicious and colorful salads, such as this one. | A variation on a classic Russian dressing, made with ketchup and mayonnaise, Thousand Island Dressing was introduced to New Yorkers in the nineteenth century by the famous Oscar Tschirsky, who was a maître d' at the Waldorf-Astoria Hotel. It is great with the tomatoes in this salad, or on crisp lettuce, or even a roast beef sandwich. | SERVES 6

HEIRLOOM TOMATO SALAD | GRILLED ONION VINAIGRETTE

Thousand Island Dressing

½ cup mayonnaise

¼ cup ketchup

3 tablespoons chopped gherkin pickles

2 tablespoons brandy

Fine sea salt and freshly ground black pepper to taste

Grilled Onion Vinaigrette

3 large yellow onions, sliced 1 inch thick

Extra-virgin olive oil

2 tablespoons balsamic vinegar

1 tablespoon sherry vinegar

Salad

6 large heirloom tomatoes (about 3 pounds), cores removed, sliced ½ inch thick

18 fresh basil leaves

1 large red onion, sliced ½ inch thick

6 ounces Stilton or Gorgonzola cheese, crumbled

MAKE THE DRESSING Whisk together the mayonnaise and ketchup until smooth. Stir in the pickles, brandy, and salt and pepper. Cover and refrigerate.

MAKE THE GRILLED ONION VINAIGRETTE Brush the onion slices with oil and sprinkle with salt and pepper. Preheat a barbecue or stovetop grill to high heat. Cook the onions until lightly charred, 3 to 4 minutes per side. Let cool. Chop the onions. There should be about 1 cup.

In a bowl, whisk together the vinegars and ½ cup olive oil. Season with salt and pepper. Stir in the onions.

TO ASSEMBLE Spread about 2 tablespoons of the Thousand Island Dressing on each serving plate. Top with 3 slices of tomato seasoned with salt and pepper, and 3 basil leaves. Spoon some of the vinaigrette over the tomatoes and basil and top with the red onion slices. Sprinkle with the cheese.

Serve immediately.

WINE SUGGESTION: CHENIN BLANC, FOXEN, 2003, SANTA BARBARA COUNTY, CALIFORNIA. *A crisp and clean white made from Chenin Blanc with aromas of fresh flowers, honey, and tropical fruit.*

The original Cobb Salad was invented in 1937 at Hollywood's famous celebrity hangout, the Brown Derby. One night, owner Bob Cobb put together some bits and pieces of things he found in the refrigerator to make a salad for himself and his friend, Sid Grauman, of Grauman's Chinese Theater. Grauman enjoyed the salad so much that the next day he ordered a Cobb Salad, and it soon became a popular specialty. | The original salad was made with chicken, but I like to use lobster instead because it elevates the salad and adds a sophisticated touch. It would also be good with shrimp. The eggs for this salad are cooked just until soft. If you prefer hard-cooked eggs, cook them for 12 to 15 minutes. | SERVES 6

COBB LOBSTER SALAD | RANCH DRESSING

3 eggs

Fine sea salt to taste

1 tablespoon white wine vinegar

Ranch Dressing

¾ cup mayonnaise

½ cup buttermilk

¼ cup roughly chopped fresh tarragon

1 tablespoon chopped scallion (green part only)

1 tablespoon chopped fresh parsley

2 teaspoons chopped garlic

2 teaspoons freshly squeezed lemon juice

1½ teaspoons garlic powder

½ teaspoon dried oregano

¼ teaspoon chili powder

Salad

1 medium head romaine lettuce, sliced ⅛ inch thick (about 4 cups)

2 bunches watercress, tough stems removed (about 2 cups)

COOK THE EGGS Place the eggs and a pinch of salt in a heavy-bottomed pot with cold water to cover. Add the vinegar to keep the eggs from leaking out if the shells crack while cooking. Bring the water to a boil over medium heat, then lower the heat and simmer for 3 minutes. Remove the eggs from the water with a slotted spoon and set aside in ice water. When cold, peel the eggs and cut them in half lengthwise.

MAKE THE DRESSING Combine all ingredients for the ranch dressing in a bowl and whisk until blended.

MAKE THE SALAD In a large bowl, toss together the salad greens, scallions, ¼ cup of the tarragon, and the cheese.

PREPARE THE LOBSTER Remove the lobster meat from the shells. Heat the olive oil in a large skillet over medium heat. Add the lobster and sauté about 2 minutes on each side. Add the remaining ¼ cup of the tarragon and season with salt and pepper. Transfer the lobster to a cutting board. Cut the lobster meat into ½-inch pieces.

TO ASSEMBLE Season the salad with the dressing, salt, and pepper. Toss well. Top with the lobster, avocado, egg halves, bacon, and fried shallots. Serve immediately.

½ small head iceberg lettuce, sliced ⅛ inch thick (about 2 cups)

3 cups sliced arugula leaves (⅛ inch thick)

½ cup chopped scallions (green parts only)

½ cup roughly chopped fresh tarragon

½ cup grated aged Cheddar cheese

3 lobsters (1 pound each), cooked (see page 271)

3 tablespoon extra-virgin olive oil

Freshly ground black pepper to taste

1 avocado, peeled, pitted, and cut into ⅛-inch-thick slices

4 slices bacon, cooked until crisp (see page 43), cut into ½-inch pieces

Crispy Shallots (page 27)

WINE SUGGESTION: SAUVIGNON BLANC, CAKEBREAD CELLARS, 2004, NAPA VALLEY, CALIFORNIA. *A medium-bodied Sauvignon Blanc with aromas of fresh melon, citrus salad, and lemongrass.*

When President Vicente Fox of Mexico visited New York, I was asked to add a French twist to classic Mexican cooking and prepare a dinner in his honor for a group of diplomats. Inspired by the ingredients in guacamole, I came up with this delicious lobster salad. You can also make it with lump crabmeat or boiled shrimp in place of the lobster. | Instead of making fresh mayonnaise for this salad, you can save time by substituting one cup of good-quality jarred mayonnaise and blending it with the pesto. | SERVES 6

POACHED LOBSTER SALAD | AVOCADO | TOMATO VINAIGRETTE

Tomato Vinaigrette

¼ cup plus 1 tablespoon extra-virgin olive oil

½ medium onion, cut into small dice

6 tomatoes, chopped, plus ¼ cup seeded, diced tomato

1 sprig fresh thyme

1 tablespoon sugar

2 tablespoons sherry vinegar

½ teaspoon Tabasco sauce

Fine sea salt and freshly ground black pepper to taste

Pesto Mayonnaise

1 egg

1 tablespoon Dijon mustard

1 tablespoon red wine vinegar

¾ cup grapeseed oil

3 cups fresh basil leaves

½ cup freshly grated Parmigiano-Reggiano cheese

6 garlic cloves

½ cup extra-virgin olive oil

TO MAKE THE TOMATO VINAIGRETTE In a medium saucepan, heat ¼ cup of the oil over medium-high heat. Add the onion and sauté until translucent, about 4 minutes. Add the chopped and diced tomatoes, thyme, and sugar. Stir, cover, and cook a few minutes, until the tomatoes begin to soften. Remove the pot from the heat and transfer the mixture to the bowl of a food processor fitted with the metal blade. Process until well-blended.

Strain the mixture through a fine-mesh strainer set over a bowl. Discard the solids. Add the remaining 1 tablespoon of the olive oil, the vinegar, and Tabasco. Season with salt and pepper. Let cool. Cover and refrigerate for at least 3 hours.

MAKE THE PESTO MAYONNAISE Place the egg in a small saucepan with water to cover. Bring to a boil. Turn off the heat. Cover the pan and let stand 2 minutes.

Scoop out the egg into a food processor or blender. Add the mustard and red wine vinegar. With the motor running, slowly add the grapeseed oil in a thin stream. Blend until creamy and smooth. Transfer to a bowl. Season with salt and pepper.

Put the basil, cheese, and garlic in the blender or food processor. With the motor running, add ¼ cup of the olive oil in a thin stream. Blend or process until thick and smooth.

Gradually add the remaining oil and process until well blended. Scrape the pesto into the bowl with the egg mixture and stir to combine.

Salad

2 Hass avocados, cut into ½-inch dice

2 large tomatoes cut into ½-inch dice

½ small red onion, thinly sliced

2 tablespoons sherry vinegar

2 tablespoons extra-virgin olive oil

3 lobsters (1½ pounds each), cooked and cooled (see page 271), removed from their shells

1 cup baby arugula leaves

MAKE THE SALAD In a bowl, toss the avocados, tomatoes, onion, vinegar, olive oil, and salt and pepper. Arrange the salad on 6 dinner plates.

Place half of a lobster tail and 1 lobster claw on each salad. Spoon the pesto mayonnaise over the lobster. Top with some of the baby greens. Spoon the tomato vinaigrette around the salad.

Serve immediately.

WINE SUGGESTION: PINOT BLANC, "SARALEE'S VINEYARD," ARROWOOD, 2004, RUSSIAN RIVER VALLEY, CALIFORNIA. *A ripe and crisp Pinot Blanc with aromas of pears, white peaches, and orange rind.*

This salad is my interpretation of a steakhouse classic. The original Caesar salad was created in 1924 by Caesar Cardini, an Italian, at his restaurant in Tijuana, Mexico, and was made with romaine lettuce. My version uses full-flavored tender spinach leaves and slightly bitter radicchio instead and includes bacon. I think bacon makes everything taste better. | SERVES 6

SPINACH AND BACON SALAD | CAESAR DRESSING

4 eggs

1 teaspoon salt

2 tablespoons white vinegar

Croutons

½ loaf country bread, crusts removed (about 12 ounces)

½ cup finely grated Parmigiano-Reggiano cheese

¼ cup extra-virgin olive oil

1 teaspoon paprika

1 garlic clove, minced

Fine sea salt and freshly ground black pepper to taste

Caesar Dressing

6 salted anchovy fillets, rinsed and patted dry

2 tablespoons Dijon mustard

2 garlic cloves, peeled

⅔ cup extra-virgin olive oil

¾ cup freshly grated Parmigiano-Reggiano cheese

¼ cup freshly squeezed lemon juice

COOK THE EGGS Place the eggs in a medium saucepan with salted water to cover. Add the vinegar. Bring the water to a boil and reduce the heat to low. Cook for 4 minutes. Remove 2 of the eggs and cool them in a bowl of ice water. They will be lightly cooked. These are for the dressing.

Cook the remaining 2 eggs 8 minutes longer, or until they are hard cooked. Drain and cool to room temperature under running water. Peel the hard-cooked eggs and separate the yolks and the whites. Pass the whites and yolks separately through a sieve.

MAKE THE CROUTONS Preheat the oven to 350°F. Cut the bread into ½-inch cubes. You should have about 2 cups.

Toss the bread with the Parmigiano-Reggiano, olive oil, paprika, garlic, and salt and pepper. Spread the bread cubes in a large pan.

Bake, stirring once or twice, 10 to 15 minutes, or until golden brown.

Let cool.

MAKE THE CAESAR DRESSING Crack the soft-cooked eggs and scoop them into a food processor or blender.

Add the anchovies, mustard, and garlic. Process or blend until smooth. With the motor running, add the olive oil in a thin stream. Blend in the cheese and lemon juice. Season with salt and pepper. You should have about 2 cups dressing.

MAKE THE SALAD Toss the spinach and radicchio with enough dressing to evenly coat the leaves. Divide the salad among 6 plates.

Scatter the croutons and crumbled bacon on top. Sprinkle with the cheese and the sieved eggs.

Salad

1½ pounds baby spinach, washed, trimmed, and well-dried

1 medium head radicchio, washed, trimmed, and well-dried

10 slices double-smoked bacon (about ½ pound), crumbled

1½ cups (12 ounces) crumbled blue cheese, such as Point Reyes

CHEF'S TIP: *Adding vinegar to the water as the eggs cook helps the egg whites to set better.*

WINE SUGGESTION: PINOT NOIR, MELVILLE, 2003, SANTA RITA HILLS, CALIFORNIA. *A spicy and earthy Pinot Noir with notes of forest floor, cherries, and smoke.*

Summer savory adds a lot of flavor to this grilled vegetable salad. It is native to the Mediterranean and has been used for centuries as a culinary herb to flavor meats, vegetables, and beans. The Romans considered savory a powerful aphrodisiac. It has a delicate flavor something like fresh thyme. Many specialty stores carry fresh summer savory, and it is also easy to grow in the garden. If you can't find it, try substituting fresh thyme or oregano instead. | SERVES 6

ZUCCHINI | TOMATO | ONION | RICOTTA SALATA AND BREAD SALAD

Basil Oil

2 cups fresh basil leaves

1 cup extra-virgin olive oil

Salad

½ large sweet onion, sliced ¼ inch thick

1 large red bell pepper, cored, seeded, and sliced ¼ inch thick

1 large yellow bell pepper, cored, seeded, and sliced ¼ inch thick

Extra-virgin olive oil

Fine sea salt and freshly ground black pepper to taste

1 large yellow zucchini, halved lengthwise

1 large green zucchini, halved lengthwise

4 large heirloom tomatoes of mixed colors, cored and cut into large dice

1 loaf ciabatta bread (8 to 10 ounces)

½ medium red onion, thinly sliced (about ½ cup)

¼ cup fresh summer savory

2 ounces ricotta salata

MAKE THE BASIL OIL Bring a large saucepan of salted water to a boil. Add the basil leaves for 15 seconds. With a slotted spoon, transfer the basil to a bowl of ice water to stop the cooking. Drain the leaves. Press the leaves between paper towels to remove excess water. Roughly chop the leaves.

In a blender, combine the chopped basil and oil. Puree 3 to 4 minutes, or until smooth. Set a fine-mesh sieve over a bowl. Line the sieve with a double layer of cheesecloth. Scrape the basil puree into the strainer. Let stand about 1 hour, or until all of the oil has drained into the bowl. Discard the basil.

GRILL THE VEGETABLES In a large bowl, toss the sweet onions and peppers with 1 tablespoon of olive oil. Season with salt and pepper. Brush the zucchini with some of the olive oil and season with salt and pepper.

Preheat a barbecue or stovetop grill to medium-high heat. Place the zucchini halves cut-sides down on the grill. Spread the onions and peppers around the zucchini in a single layer. Grill the vegetables, turning them often, until charred and softened, about 5 minutes for the onions and peppers and slightly longer for the zucchini.

Remove the vegetables and allow to cool down slightly. Cut the zucchini crosswise into 1-inch pieces.

MAKE THE DRESSING In a large bowl, whisk together the oil, vinegar, lemon juice, savory, parsley, and garlic. Season with salt and pepper.

MARINATE THE VEGETABLES Add the grilled vegetables and tomatoes to the bowl with the dressing. Season with salt and pepper and allow to marinate for 1 to 2 hours at room temperature.

Dressing

1 cup extra-virgin olive oil

¼ cup aged sherry vinegar

2 tablespoons freshly squeezed lemon juice

2 tablespoons chopped fresh summer savory

2 tablespoons chopped fresh parsley

1 tablespoon finely chopped garlic

GRILL THE BREAD Just before serving, trim the crust off the bread and cut it into 1-inch-thick slices. Brush each slice with olive oil. Preheat a barbecue or stovetop grill to medium-high heat. Grill the bread, turning once, until browned and crisp on both sides.

TO ASSEMBLE THE SALAD Add the red onion and savory leaves to the marinated vegetables. Place a piece of toast in the middle of each plate. Divide the vegetable mixture evenly among the plates. Shave the ricotta salata over the salad and drizzle with the basil oil. Serve immediately.

WINE SUGGESTION: ROSÉ, TABLAS CREEK, 2004, PASO ROBLES, CALIFORNIA. *A full-bodied Rosé wine with aromas of plums, cherries, and currants.*

Beets and goat cheese are a classic combination. I like to enhance their flavor with a topping of crunchy Caramelized Walnuts flavored with cinnamon. The goat cheese–topped croutons add a salty counterpoint. | This salad is best made with sweet, freshly harvested beets from the farmers' market. Roasting brings out their rich, earthy flavor. After you open a container of walnut oil, make sure you use it up as soon as you can because it has a tendency to go rancid quickly. Store the open container in the refrigerator. | SERVES 6

ROASTED BEETS | GOAT CHEESE CROUTONS | CARAMELIZED WALNUTS

6 small to medium beets (about 1½ pounds), trimmed and scrubbed

2 tablespoons extra-virgin olive oil

Fine sea salt and freshly ground black pepper to taste

Marinade

9 tablespoons extra-virgin olive oil

2 tablespoons red wine vinegar

3 garlic cloves, chopped

3 tablespoons chopped fresh parsley

Goat Cheese Croutons

6 slices crusty bread

6 ounces aged goat cheese

Salad

¼ cup walnut oil

3 tablespoons sherry vinegar

2 bunches watercress, cleaned and stemmed (2 cups)

3 small Belgian endives, trimmed and cut into julienne strips

¾ cup Caramelized Walnuts (see page 273)

ROAST THE BEETS Preheat the oven to 400°F. Rub the beets with the olive oil and sprinkle with salt and pepper. Wrap each beet individually in foil. Roast the beets until tender when pierced with a knife, about 1 hour. Let cool slightly.

MARINATE THE BEETS In a medium bowl, combine the olive oil, red wine vinegar, garlic, parsley, and salt and pepper, and whisk until blended.

While they are still warm, peel the beets and cut them into small dice. Gently fold the beets into the vinaigrette. Cover and refrigerate overnight.

MAKE THE CROUTONS Turn the broiler to high. Place the bread slices on a broiler pan. Brown the bread on both sides. Divide the goat cheese equally between the bread slices and broil them 1 to 2 minutes more, or until the cheese is slightly melted. Cut each slice in half diagonally.

DRESS THE SALAD GREENS In a large bowl, whisk together the walnut oil, sherry vinegar, and salt and pepper. Add the watercress and julienned endive. Toss well.

TO ASSEMBLE Drain the beets, reserving the marinade. Divide the beets among 6 plates. Place the salad on top. Scatter the walnuts over all. Drizzle the marinade around the salads. Serve each plate with 2 pieces of goat cheese croutons.

WINE SUGGESTION: SAUVIGNON BLANC, CROCKER AND STARR, 2004, NAPA VALLEY, CALIFORNIA. *A fragrant, exotic Sauvignon Blanc with notes of citrus zest, honeysuckle, and candied nuts.*

M ost Americans think of a beignet as the sugar-dusted fried doughnut popular for breakfast in New Orleans. But in France, a beignet can be any kind of filled dough, as long as it is fried! These beignets are made with creamy Camembert encased in a crisp and tasty shell of beer batter. | Camembert cheese comes from the Normandy region of France. Napoleon is said to have given the cheese its name in honor of the town where he first tasted it. Camembert is made from cow's milk. It has a soft, white, edible rind and a creamy smooth interior. When buying Camembert, try pressing the cheese in the center. It should be soft and yielding. | SERVES 6

CAMEMBERT BEIGNETS | SMOKED DUCK SALAD

Honey-Mustard Vinaigrette

½ cup grapeseed oil

5 tablespoons sherry vinegar

¼ cup Dijon mustard

¼ cup whole-grain mustard

2 tablespoons honey

2 tablespoons walnut oil

Fine sea salt and freshly ground black pepper to taste

Salad

1 head Boston lettuce, leaves trimmed and roughly chopped

2 bunches watercress, tough stems removed

2 heads frisée, green leaves discarded, tender leaves roughly chopped

½ medium red onion, thinly sliced

2 tablespoons chopped fresh chives

MAKE THE VINAIGRETTE In a large bowl, whisk together the vinaigrette ingredients until well blended.

MAKE THE SALAD In a large salad bowl, combine the salad greens, onion, and chives.

FRY THE CHEESE Fill a deep-fat fryer or heavy saucepan with about 3 inches of the oil. Heat the oil to 375°F.

Dip a few of the Camembert wedges into the beer batter, turning the wedges to coat thoroughly. Carefully slip the pieces into the hot oil, being careful not to crowd the pan. Fry until golden brown, about 2 minutes. With a slotted spoon, remove the wedges from the oil to paper towels to drain. Season with salt. Repeat with the remaining cheese.

TO SERVE In a large bowl, toss the salad with enough vinaigrette to coat evenly. Top with the fried Camembert, sliced duck, and walnuts. Serve immediately while the cheese is still hot.

WINE SUGGESTION: PINOT NOIR, BERGSTROM, 2004, WILLAMETTE VALLEY, OREGON. *A silky and earthy Pinot Noir with aromas of Bing cherries, black raspberries, and smoky oak notes.*

Vegetable or canola oil for frying

1 medium-ripe Camembert cheese (about 8 ounces), cut into 12 wedges

1 recipe beer batter (from Fried Onion Rings, page 214)

18 slices smoked duck breast (about 5 ounces, ⅛ inch thick) (see Sources, page 274)

20 pieces Caramelized Walnuts (see page 273), cut in half

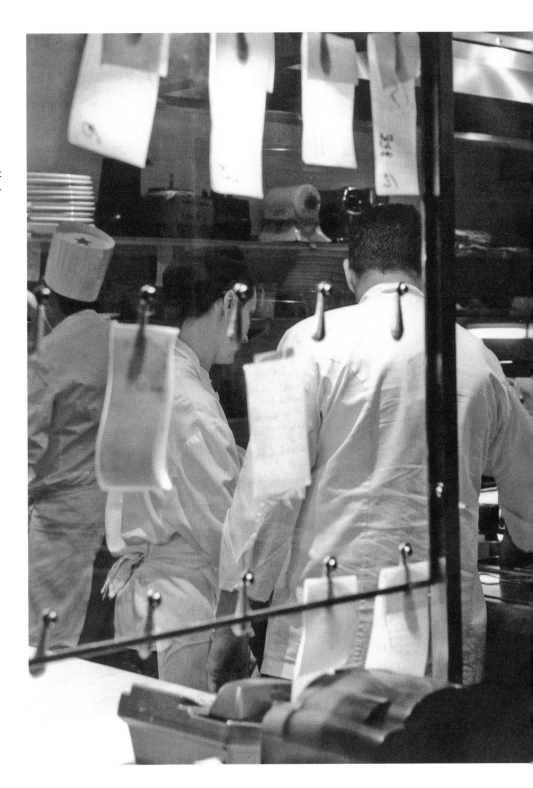

Bergamot is a variety of sour orange that is grown primarily in southern Italy. It is used to flavor Earl Grey tea, and if you have ever had a cup, you are familiar with its slightly floral flavor and aroma. I use oil of bergamot together with orange and lemon zests and juice to create a symphony of citrus flavors in a dressing for tender baby octopus. | As a main dish with Chive-Cheddar Biscuits (page 119) or as an appetizer before Seared Arctic Char/Shiitake-Ginger Vinaigrette (page 142). | SERVES 6

OCTOPUS SALAD | LEMON-BERGAMOT DRESSING

Octopus

4 pounds baby octopus

3 cups dry red wine

½ fennel bulb, chopped

1 carrot, peeled and chopped

1 small red onion, chopped

1 lemon, quartered

3 sprigs fresh thyme

2 tablespoons coarse sea salt

1 teaspoon black peppercorns

1 bay leaf

Marinade

1 cup extra-virgin olive oil

3 garlic cloves, smashed

2 sprigs fresh thyme

1 teaspoon grated orange zest

1 teaspoon grated lemon zest

1 bay leaf

Lemon-Bergamot Vinaigrette

1 cup freshly squeezed blood orange or Valencia orange juice (about 3 oranges)

¼ cup extra-virgin olive oil

COOK THE OCTOPUS In a large pot, combine 6 cups water, the octopuses, wine, fennel, carrot, onion, lemon, thyme, salt, peppercorns, and bay leaf. Bring the liquid to a boil over high heat. Lower the heat and simmer until the octopuses are tender when pierced with a knife, about 1½ hours. Cooking times for octopus varies widely, so test the octopus with a sharp knife about 15 minutes before you expect it to be done. The octopus should feel tender when pierced.

Transfer the octopuses to a bowl with 1 cup of the cooking liquid. Discard the remaining liquid. Let cool. Cut the octopuses into 1-inch pieces.

MARINATE THE OCTOPUS In a large bowl, whisk together all of the marinade ingredients. Add the octopuses. Cover and refrigerate overnight.

MAKE THE VINAIGRETTE In a small saucepan, bring the orange juice to a boil. Cook over medium heat until the juice is reduced to 2 tablespoons. Whisk together the juice with the remaining vinaigrette ingredients.

ASSEMBLE THE SALAD Remove the octopuses from the marinade and drain lightly. Toss the arugula with just enough of the vinaigrette to moisten and coat all the leaves. Toss the octopuses with the remaining vinaigrette. Divide the arugula among 6 serving plates. Top each plate with 1 octopus. Shave some of the Parmigiano-Reggiano over the top.

WINE SUGGESTION: CA'DEL SOLO, CALIFORNIA BIG HOUSE WHITE, BONNY DOON VINEYARD, 2004, SANTA CRUZ, CALIFORNIA. *An exotic white wine blend with aromas of Asian pear, wild mountain honey, and citrus.*

2 tablespoons bergamot oil (see Sources, page 274)

1 tablespoon freshly squeezed lemon juice

1 tablespoon chopped garlic

6 cups arugula, washed, dried, and trimmed

3-ounce chunk Parmigiano-Reggiano cheese

CHAPTER THREE

PASTA AND RISOTTO

This is my favorite Sunday pasta dish. Dried pasta is such a convenient and versatile food, there are many ways to serve it. This idea comes from the many great Italian meals I have enjoyed in New York. Grana Padano is an Italian cow's milk cheese from the northern region of Emilia-Romagna. I like its mellow flavor and the slight creaminess it adds to this pasta. You can substitute Parmigiano-Reggiano, if you prefer. | SERVES 6

MACARONI | TOMATOES | SPICY SAUSAGE

3 tablespoons extra-virgin olive oil, plus more for finishing

1 pound hot Italian sausage, casings removed

1 small onion, finely chopped

3 garlic cloves, finely chopped

½ cup dry white wine

4 medium-ripe tomatoes, cored and cut into large dice

Coarse sea salt and freshly ground black pepper to taste

12 ounces dried rigatoni

1 bunch arugula, tough stems removed and coarsely chopped (1½ cups)

¼ cup chopped fresh basil

¾ cup freshly grated Grana Padano or Parmigiano-Reggiano cheese

COOK THE SAUSAGE In a skillet large enough to hold all of the ingredients, heat the oil over medium heat. Add the sausage meat and cook until lightly browned, stirring the meat to break up the lumps. With a slotted spoon, transfer the meat to a bowl.

Add the onion and garlic to the pan. Sauté until the onion is tender, about 5 minutes. Add the wine and bring to a simmer. Cook 1 minute more.

Add the tomatoes and season with salt and pepper. Simmer for 20 minutes, or until thickened. Stir in the sausage meat and cook until heated through, about 1 minute more.

COOK THE RIGATONI Meanwhile, bring a large pot of water to a boil. Add the rigatoni and plenty of salt. Cook, stirring frequently, until the rigatoni is al dente—tender yet still firm. Drain the rigatoni and add it to the skillet with the sauce.

FINISH THE PASTA Add the arugula and basil and toss well. Drizzle with a little extra-virgin olive oil. Sprinkle with the cheese and serve immediately.

WINE SUGGESTION: BARBERA, RENWOOD, 2002, AMADOR COUNTY, CALIFORNIA. *A classic pasta-friendly red made from Barbera with aromas of plums, spicy cherries, and a tangy finish.*

Republic, owned by a good friend of mine, is a New York City restaurant specializing in Asian noodles. It is one of my favorite places to eat and I was inspired by the flavors of the food there to create these noodles. Boneless, skinless chicken breasts or beef filet can be substituted for the duck, if you prefer. | SERVES 6

SPICY CURRY DUCK NOODLES

Sauce

3 tablespoons canola oil

1½ teaspoons green curry paste

1½ teaspoons red curry paste

4 whole stalks lemongrass, thinly sliced

2½ cups unsweetened coconut milk

1½ cups chicken stock or low-sodium chicken broth

4 Kaffir lime leaves, or a pinch grated lime zest

1½ tablespoons Thai fish sauce (nam plah)

2 teaspoons freshly squeezed lime juice

Duck

3 boneless skin-on duck breasts, (about 2½ pounds)

Fine sea salt and freshly ground pepper to taste

Noodles

2 ounces rice stick noodles

1 tablespoon canola oil

1 medium carrot, cut into julienne strips

1 stalk of celery stalk, cut into julienne strips

2 cups bean sprouts (about 8 ounces)

1½ cups chopped fresh cilantro leaves (approximately one 1 large bunch)

MAKE THE SAUCE In a 2-quart sauce pot, heat the oil and add the curry pastes and lemongrass. Stir until the lemongrass is well coated and slightly softened. Add the coconut milk, stock, and lime leaves. Simmer 3 minutes. Pass the sauce through a fine-mesh sieve into a clean sauce pot. Add the fish sauce and lime juice and bring to a simmer.

COOK THE DUCK Season the duck breasts with salt on the flesh side only. In a medium skillet, sear the duck breasts skin-side down over low heat to render the fat. As the duck cooks, spoon off the excess fat from the pan. When the skin is crisp, about 6 minutes, turn the breasts and brown them on the other side, 2 to 3 minutes. Remove the duck breasts from the pan and let rest 10 minutes.

COOK THE NOODLES In a large pot of boiling water, cook the noodles, stirring occasionally, until al dente—tender yet still firm to the bite—about 5 minutes. Drain and rinse under cold water to stop the cooking.

ASSEMBLE In a large sauté pan or wok, heat the oil over medium- high heat. Add the carrots and celery and sauté until tender, yet still crunchy. Add the noodles, bean sprouts, sauce, and cilantro and toss well. Cook until heated through.

Slice the duck breasts crosswise into thin strips and add them to the noodles. Toss together to coat well

SERVE Divide the salad among 6 bowls. Serve with chopsticks.

WINE SUGGESTION: MARCEL DEISS, "BURG,", 2001, ALSACE, FRANCE *A rich, slightly off-dry white "field blend" from Alsace with aromas of herbal liqueurs, cinnamon, and spicy, super- ripe exotic fruits.*

The filling in these tortellini is flavored with pastis, a sunny yellow, licorice-flavored liqueur. The name in French means "cloudy," a reference to its appearance when mixed with water. Pastis gets its flavor from star anise and a secret blend of herbs and spices. Ricard is the brand name of a similar drink. | These tortellini are so flavorful that they are best when dressed very simply. I like them with just a drizzle of extra-virgin olive oil and some shaved Parmigiano-Reggiano cheese. Wonton wrappers become difficult to handle if they dry out. Keep them covered with a damp cloth as you make the tortellini. The finished tortellini can be made up 24 hours ahead of serving and stored in the refrigerator, covered with plastic wrap. | I like to serve this pasta as a main course with a side dish of Pan-Seared Hen of the Woods Mushrooms (page 223). | SERVES 6

ANISE DUCK TORTELLINI

1 cup milk

¼ zucchini, diced (⅓ cup)

4 button mushrooms, diced

2 teaspoons extra-virgin olive oil, plus extra as needed

1 teaspoon unsalted butter

1 tablespoon chopped onion

1 teaspoon chopped garlic

8 ounces ground duck leg meat

1 tablespoon chopped fresh cilantro

1 tablespoons pastis or Ricard

1 tablespoon cooked egg white, chopped

1 teaspoon ground anise seeds

1 teaspoon whole anise seeds

1 teaspoon harissa paste (see Sources, page 274)

½ teaspoon cracked coriander seeds

BLANCH THE VEGETABLES In a medium saucepan, bring the milk to a simmer. Add the zucchini and mushrooms and cook until tender, about 4 minutes. Drain the vegetables and pat them very dry on a towel. Let cool. Chop them fine.

SAUTÉ THE ONION In a small skillet, heat the oil and butter over medium heat. Add the onion and cook, stirring often, until tender, 2 to 3 minutes. Add the garlic and cook 2 minutes more. Remove the skillet from the heat.

MAKE THE FILLING In a large, chilled bowl set over another bowl filled with ice, combine the duck, zucchini, mushrooms, onion mixture, cilantro, pastis, egg white, ground and whole anise, harissa, and coriander. Season with salt and pepper. Add the heavy cream and stir with a rubber spatula until blended.

MAKE THE TORTELLINI Put 1 tablespoon of the filling in the lower right corner of a wonton wrapper. Brush the edges lightly with water. Fold the upper left corner down over the filling to meet the lower right corner, forming a triangle. Press the edges firmly to seal. Turn the triangle so that the central point faces away from you. Fold the 2 bottom points over the filling so that they overlap, forming a ring. Pinch the ends to seal. Repeat with the remaining wrappers and filling. Arrange the tortellini on lightly floured baking sheets.

Fine sea salt and freshly ground
black pepper to taste

½ cup heavy cream

18 square wonton wrappers

Shaved Parmigiano-Reggiano
cheese

COOK THE TORTELLINI Bring a large pot of water to simmering. Add salt.
Add the tortellini and cook 6 minutes, or until the filling is cooked through.
With a strainer, remove the tortellini from the water and place them in a
warm serving bowl.

TO SERVE Drizzle with a little extra-virgin olive oil and top with shaved
Parmesan.

WINE SUGGESTION: SYRAH, "WYLIE-FENAUGHTY," EDMUNDS ST. JOHN, 2003, EL
DORADO, CALIFORNIA. *An elegant Syrah with aromas of black cherries, licorice,
and Mediterranean spices.*

Gnocchi means "lumps" in Italian and there are many different kinds. Potato gnocchi are the most familiar, but I like this Roman version made with cooked and cooled semolina that is cut into disks, then baked with butter and cheese. These gnocchi are also good baked on a bed of warm tomato sauce and browned as below. I like to have this as a meal with green salad. | SERVES 6

GNOCCHI À LA ROMAINE

2 tablespoons extra-virgin olive oil

1 quart whole milk

Pinch freshly grated nutmeg

1¼ cups instant semolina, Beretta brand recommended

1 teaspoon fine sea salt

Freshly ground white pepper to taste

¾ cup freshly grated Parmigiano-Reggiano cheese

2 eggs

4 egg yolks

2 tablespoons unsalted butter, melted, plus extra for the dish

WINE SUGGESTION: TOCAI FRIULANO, MILLBROOK VINEYARDS, 2004, FINGER LAKES, NEW YORK. A crisp and clean white made from Italy's Tocai Friulano grape, with aromas of peaches, wet stones, and citrus

PREPARE THE PAN Line an 18 x 13-inch baking sheet or tray with parchment paper. Brush the paper with 1 tablespoon of the olive oil.

COOK THE SEMOLINA In a large saucepan, bring the milk and nutmeg to a simmer. Remove from the heat and add the semolina. Stir until smooth and thickened. Season with the salt and pepper. Stir in ½ cup of the cheese. Add the eggs and yolks and stir until well combined.

With a spatula, spread the semolina evenly to about a ¾-inch thickness on the prepared pan. Let the mixture set and brush the remaining 1 table-spoon oil on top to keep a crust from forming. Cover and refrigerate until firm. (This can be prepared up to a day before serving. Cover and refrigerate overnight.)

PREHEAT THE OVEN Butter a large baking dish. Preheat the oven to 350°F.

CUT OUT THE GNOCCHI With a 2-inch round cookie cutter, cut the semolina into crescents or circles. Place the gnocchi overlapping slightly in the prepared dish, and top with the remaining ¼ cup grated Parmigiano-Reggiano and the melted butter.

BAKE THE GNOCCHI Bake for 10 minutes, or until hot.

BROWN THE GNOCCHI Turn the broiler to high. Run the dish under the broiler for 3 minutes, or until the top is lightly browned.

Serve hot.

Tender potato gnocchi in a rosemary-scented sauce are the perfect accompaniment to the Braised Short Ribs (page 163). At BLT, we serve these with a tall crown of grated Parmesan. | SERVES 6

CREAMY ROSEMARY-PARMESAN GNOCCHI

Gnocchi

2 cups coarse sea salt

2¼ pounds baking potatoes, scrubbed

½ cup plus 3 tablespoons all-purpose flour

2 tablespoons extra-virgin olive oil

1 egg

2 pinches freshly grated nutmeg

Fine sea salt and freshly ground black pepper to taste

Sauce

2 cups heavy cream

4-inch sprig fresh rosemary

1 small garlic clove, minced

1 pinch ground nutmeg

White truffle oil

3 tablespoons grated Parmigiano-Reggiano cheese

White truffle (optional)

BAKE THE POTATOES Preheat the oven to 375°F. Mound the coarse salt in the center of a baking sheet with sides. Put the potatoes on the salt and bake until a knife easily pierces to the center of the potatoes, about 1 hour. Remove the potatoes from the oven and let cool.

MAKE THE DOUGH When cool enough to handle, peel the potatoes and pass them through a ricer or food mill into a large bowl, or mash them thoroughly with a potato masher. Add ½ cup of the flour, the oil, egg, nutmeg, and salt and pepper. Mix well. If the dough is too sticky, add a little bit more of the flour.

SHAPE THE GNOCCHI Divide the dough into 6 pieces. On a lightly floured surface, roll each piece into a ¾-inch thick rope. Cut each rope into 1-inch pieces.

COOK THE GNOCCHI Oil a large baking sheet. Bring a large pot of salted water to a boil. Add about one-third of the gnocchi and cook 2 minutes, or until they float to the surface. Remove the gnocchi with a slotted spoon, draining them well. Spread the gnocchi on the prepared baking sheet. Cook the remaining gnocchi in the same way. (These can be made up to 24 hours in advance. Cover with plastic wrap and refrigerate until ready to use.)

MAKE THE SAUCE In a saucepan large enough to hold all of the gnocchi, bring the cream, rosemary, garlic, and nutmeg to a boil. Cook until the mixture thickens and coats the back of a spoon, about 15 minutes. Season with salt and pepper. Strain out the rosemary.

DRESS THE GNOCCHI Add the gnocchi to the saucepan with the sauce. Stir them gently to coat. Cook until the gnocchi are heated through, about 2 minutes.

TO SERVE Spoon the gnocchi into a warm serving bowl. Sprinkle with a little white truffle oil and the Parmigiano-Reggiano. Shave the white truffle on top, if using.

CHEF'S TIP: *To test the dough to see if it has the right consistency, break off a small piece and cook it in a pot of boiling water. If the dough does not hold its shape, knead in a little more flour before shaping the remaining gnocchi.*

WINE SUGGESTION: PINOT GRIGIO, LUNA, 2004, NAPA VALLEY, CALIFORNIA. *A crisp and clean white with aromas of peaches, honeyed pears, and a refreshing finish.*

Ripe, seasonal tomatoes—both roasted and uncooked—are the unusual condiment here for tender squares of pasta filled with a blend of creamy cheeses. Diners at my restaurants love these ravioli and often request them. Sheets of ready-made fresh pasta can be substituted for the homemade to save time. | SERVES 6

GOAT CHEESE RAVIOLI | TOMATO-ANCHOVY VINAIGRETTE

Roasted Tomatoes

3 large Beefsteak or 6 Roma tomatoes, cored and sliced in half horizontally

6 sprigs fresh thyme

3 tablespoons extra-virgin olive oil

3 garlic cloves, crushed

Fine sea salt and freshly ground black pepper to taste

Pinch sugar

Tomato-Anchovy Vinaigrette

6 large ripe Beefsteak or 12 Roma tomatoes, seeded and diced (about 2½ cups)

6 tablespoons extra-virgin olive oil

1 large shallot, minced

2 tablespoons freshly squeezed lemon juice

2 tablespoons capers, rinsed

1 tablespoon chopped fresh chives

1 tablespoon chopped fresh basil

1 tablespoon sherry vinegar

12 white anchovies, coarsely chopped

PREHEAT THE OVEN to 325°F. Line a baking sheet with parchment paper.

ROAST THE TOMATOES Toss the tomatoes with the thyme, olive oil, garlic, salt, pepper, and sugar. Place the tomatoes on the baking sheet cut-side up. Bake 15 minutes or until the skins are loose.

Remove the tomatoes from the oven, and turn the oven down to 275°F. Let the tomatoes cool slightly. Peel off the skins. Return the tomatoes to the oven. Cook for 2 to 3 hours more, or until the tomatoes are almost dry. Let cool, and then chop into a paste.

MAKE THE TOMATO-ANCHOVY VINAIGRETTE Combine the fresh tomatoes, olive oil, shallot, lemon juice, capers, chives, basil, vinegar, and salt and pepper. Let stand for 30 minutes. Add the anchovies just before serving.

MAKE THE RAVIOLI FILLING In a mixing bowl, stir together the cheeses and pepper until evenly blended. Cover and refrigerate.

MAKE THE DOUGH In a large bowl, stir together the flour, semolina, and salt. Make a well in the center.

In a small bowl, whisk together 1 egg yolk and 2 egg whites. Pour the egg mixture and olive oil into the well and use a fork to gradually mix together. When the flour has just been incorporated, turn the dough out onto a lightly floured surface. Work the dough, kneading it and flattening it out, until it forms a smooth elastic ball. This should take about 10 minutes. Dust with flour, wrap in plastic, and refrigerate for at least 30 minutes.

MAKE THE EGG WASH Whisk together the remaining egg yolk with 2 table-spoons water.

MAKE THE RAVIOLI Divide the dough into 2 pieces. With a rolling pin or pasta machine, roll each piece into a thin sheet, about 1/16 inch thick. Cut the sheets into thirty-six 3-inch squares.

Goat Cheese Filling

12 ounces fresh goat cheese, such as Montrachet, crumbled (about 1½ cups)

½ cup Saint André, or other triple-cream cheese

2 teaspoons cracked black pepper

Pasta Dough

¾ cup all-purpose flour

3 tablespoons semolina flour

Pinch fine sea salt

2 eggs, separated

1 tablespoon extra-virgin olive oil

Fresh basil leaves, for garnish

WINE SUGGESTION: SAUVIGNON BLANC, ROCHIOLI, 2004, RUSSIAN RIVER VALLEY, CALIFORNIA. *A crisp, flinty Sauvignon Blanc with notes of lemongrass, melon, and lemon custard.*

Place ¾ tablespoon of the filling in the center of 18 of the squares. Brush the edges lightly with the egg wash. Place the remaining squares on top and seal the edges by pressing them firmly with a fork.

(The ravioli can be made up to 24 hours before serving. Arrange the pieces on a baking sheet dusted with flour and store covered with a towel in the refrigerator. For longer storage, freeze the ravioli in a single layer on a baking sheet. Once frozen, transfer them to a heavy-duty plastic bag. The frozen ravioli will keep for 1 week.)

HEAT THE SAUCE In a small saucepan, heat the roasted tomatoes over low heat.

TO COOK THE RAVIOLI Bring a large pot of salted water to a boil. Add the ravioli and cook until they float, about 4 minutes. Drain.

TO SERVE Divide the tomato sauce among 6 bowls. Place the ravioli on top of the sauce. Drizzle the vinaigrette on top and around the ravioli. Sprinkle with torn basil leaves.

I like to make this risotto in the spring when fresh peas are sweet and tender. In fact, any fresh spring vegetables can be used, such as morel mushrooms, asparagus, ramps, fava beans, or fiddlehead ferns. | SERVES 6

RISOTTO | GREEN PEAS | PANCETTA

2 cups fresh peas

3 tablespoons extra-virgin olive oil

5 ounces pancetta, diced

½ cup chopped onion

3 garlic cloves, chopped

1 sprig fresh thyme

2 cups Arborio or other medium-grain rice

1⅓ cups dry white wine

About 6 cups hot chicken stock or low-sodium chicken broth

Fine sea salt and freshly ground black pepper to taste

3 tablespoons mascarpone cheese

1 tablespoon truffle oil, or to taste

1 large piece Parmigiano-Reggiano cheese

PREPARE THE PEAS Bring a medium saucepan of salted water to a boil. Add the peas and cook until tender, 3 to 4 minutes. Drain the peas. Immediately place ½ cup of them in a bowl of ice water. Place the remaining peas in a blender or food processor and puree until smooth, adding 1 tablespoon of water if needed.

COOK THE RICE In a large, wide saucepan, heat the oil over medium heat. Add the pancetta, onion, garlic, and thyme. Cook, stirring, until the onion is translucent, about 5 minutes. Add the rice and stir to coat it with the oil. Add the wine and simmer until most of the wine has evaporated.

Add 1 cup of the broth to the pan and cook, stirring constantly, until most of the broth is absorbed. Add the remaining broth in 3 more additions. Season with salt and pepper. If the rice seems dry, add a little more broth and stir until creamy and loose.

FINISH THE RISOTTO When the risotto is tender, yet still firm to the bite, stir in the mascarpone and drained whole peas. Add just enough of the pea puree to flavor and color the risotto without making it soupy.

TO SERVE Spoon the risotto into warm shallow bowls. Drizzle with the truffle oil. With a swivel-blade vegetable peeler, shave some of the Parmigiano-Reggiano over each portion.

CHEF'S TIP: *Just before serving the risotto, I like to add an extra splash of white wine to the pot. That bit of acidity lifts and enhances the flavor.*

WINE SUGGESTION: RIESLING, "ADRIA VINEYARD," LEMELSON VINEYARDS, 2004, WILLAMETTE VALLEY, OREGON. *A dry Riesling with aromas of sliced green apples, pears, and flowers.*

The cappuccino in this case is a foamy sauce to pour over the mushroom risotto. I like to have this risotto with pan-seared diver scallops on top. Risotto is typically served as a first course in shallow rimmed soup plates. Any extra garlic butter is great spread on bread or on top of a steak or mashed into potatoes. | Either Braised Short Ribs/Garlic-Thyme Brown Butter (page 163) or Filet and Foie Gras Rossini (page 155) would be good with this risotto. | SERVES 6

WILD MUSHROOM RISOTTO | MUSHROOM CAPPUCCINO

Mushroom Cappuccino

1 pound white mushrooms, wiped clean

⅓ cup heavy cream

Fine sea salt and freshly ground black pepper to taste

Risotto

7 tablespoons extra-virgin olive oil

1 pound assorted wild mushrooms, such as black trumpet, chanterelle, or porcini, cleaned as on page 272, cut into ½-inch pieces

1 tablespoon chopped shallots

2 tablespoons chopped garlic

1 teaspoon fresh thyme leaves, plus extra as needed

½ cup chopped onion

2 cups Arborio or other medium-grain rice

1 cup dry white wine

4 cups hot chicken stock or low-sodium chicken broth

1½ cups freshly grated Parmigiano-Reggiano cheese

1 tablespoon Roasted Garlic Butter (see page 271)

1 tablespoon white truffle oil

MAKE THE CAPPUCCINO Place the white mushrooms and 1 cup water in a blender or food processor and puree in batches, if necessary. Blend until smooth. Pour the mixture into a large pot and bring to a boil. Pour the mixture into a strainer lined with cheesecloth or a lint-free kitchen towel. Let cool slightly. Squeeze out all of the mushroom liquid into a small saucepan. You should have 2 cups liquid.

Bring the liquid to a simmer. Cook, stirring constantly so that it does not burn, until reduced to ¼ cup, 25 to 30 minutes. Add the heavy cream and salt and pepper. Keep the sauce warm.

COOK THE WILD MUSHROOMS In a large skillet, heat 2 tablespoons of the oil over medium-high heat. Add half of the mushrooms and a pinch of salt, making sure not to crowd the pan or the mushrooms will not brown. Cook, stirring, for about 3 minutes, or until the mushrooms are tender and begin to brown. Add half the shallots, 1 teaspoon of the chopped garlic and ½ teaspoon of the thyme. Cook 1 minute more. Remove the mushrooms from the pan and repeat with 2 more tablespoons of the oil, the remaining mushrooms, shallots, 1 more teaspoon of the garlic, and thyme.

COOK THE RICE In a deep, wide saucepan, heat the remaining 3 tablespoons of the oil over medium heat. Add the onion, remaining chopped garlic, and a pinch of thyme leaves. Cook, stirring until the onions are translucent, about 4 minutes.

Stir in the rice until thoroughly mixed. Add the wine and cook until most of the liquid evaporates.

Add about 1 cup of the stock and cook, stirring constantly, until most of the liquid has been absorbed. Add the remaining stock in 3 more additions, stirring well and allowing the liquid to be absorbed after each one. Taste a few grains of rice. They should be tender and creamy. If the rice is not done, or is a little dry, add more stock and stir well. Season with salt and pepper. Stir in the cheese, garlic butter, sautéed mushrooms, and truffle oil.

FINISH THE CAPPUCCINO With a hand-held immersion blender or a whisk, blend the cappuccino until foamy.

TO SERVE Spoon the risotto into warm serving bowls. Pour the mushroom cappuccino around the risotto and serve immediately.

WINE SUGGESTION: PINOT NOIR, HAMACHER, 2003, WILLAMETTE VALLEY, OREGON. *A spice-driven Pinot Noir with aromas of black cherries, tobacco, and cedar.*

When I was cooking at the Four Seasons Hotel in Bangkok, I created this risotto at a special dinner for the Princess of Thailand at the World Gourmet Summit. The rest of the menu was prepared by a group of chefs from around the world. | If rock shrimp are not available, you can substitute another type of shrimp, but be sure to devein them first. Cooked lobster or crab can also be used in this risotto. Fold the meat into the finished risotto to warm it just before you are ready to serve. | Roasted Rosemary-Lemon Chicken (page 183) would be great with this risotto. | SERVES 6

LEMONGRASS ROCK SHRIMP RISOTTO

Topping

1 cup diced fennel

2 garlic cloves, chopped

1 sprig fresh thyme

½ cup extra-virgin olive oil

Fine sea salt and freshly ground black pepper to taste

½ cup small dice zucchini

1 tablespoon Madras curry powder

14 ounces peeled rock shrimp

Lemongrass Sauce

2 tablespoons extra-virgin olive oil

½ cup diced white onion

1 medium, tart green apple, such as Granny Smith, peeled, cored and chopped

1½ stalks lemongrass, cut into 3 or 4 pieces

1 head garlic, halved crosswise

3 tablespoons chopped fresh ginger

COOK THE VEGETABLES Put the fennel in a medium skillet with the garlic and thyme. Add the oil, and salt and pepper. Cook on very low heat until the fennel is very tender, about 15 minutes. Drain off the oil and reserve it. Transfer the fennel and garlic to a plate.

In the same skillet, heat 1 tablespoon of the reserved oil. Add the zucchini and cook, stirring frequently, until golden. Sprinkle with salt and pepper. Transfer to the plate with the fennel.

COOK THE WHOLE SHRIMP In the same skillet, heat 1 more tablespoon of the reserved oil and the curry powder over medium heat. Add the whole shrimp and sauté until just pink on the outside, but still opaque in the center. Season with salt and pepper. Transfer the shrimp to the plate with the vegetables.

MAKE THE SAUCE In a skillet, heat the olive oil over medium heat. Add the onion, apple, lemongrass, garlic, ginger, and thyme and cook, stirring often, until the apple and onion are tender, about 10 minutes. Stir in the curry powder and the curry paste. Add the wine and fish sauce and stir well. Simmer for 5 minutes to reduce slightly. Add the stock and coconut milk and bring to a simmer. Remove from the heat and let cool slightly.

STRAIN THE SAUCE through a fine-mesh sieve, pressing down lightly to extract the liquid.

4 sprigs fresh thyme

2 tablespoons Madras curry powder

1½ tablespoons green curry paste

1 cup dry white wine

2 tablespoons Thai fish sauce (*nam pla*)

3 cups chicken stock or low-sodium chicken broth

1 cup unsweetened coconut milk

3 tablespoons cold unsalted butter

Risotto

4 tablespoons (½ stick) unsalted butter

2 tablespoons extra-virgin olive oil

½ cup diced white onion

2 cups Arborio or other medium-grain rice

1 cup dry white wine

3 cups hot chicken stock or low-sodium chicken broth

12 fresh Thai basil leaves, roughly chopped

WINE SUGGESTION: SAUVIGNON BLANC, SPOTTSWOODE, 2004, NAPA VALLEY, CALIFORNIA. *A ripe, honeyed Sauvignon Blanc with aromas of honeysuckle and citrus.*

COOK THE RISOTTO In a large saucepan, melt 2 tablespoons of the butter with the oil over medium heat. Add the onion and cook, stirring occasionally, until tender. Add the rice and stir to coat with the oil. Add the wine and cook until the liquid is evaporated.

Add 1 cup of the warm chicken stock and cook until the liquid is absorbed. Add 1 more cup of the stock, and stir constantly until absorbed. Cook until the risotto is almost tender, about 12 minutes. Season with salt and pepper.

FINISH THE SAUCE If necessary, gently reheat the sauce. Add the butter and salt and pepper.

FINISH THE RISOTTO Add the remaining 1 cup of the stock to the risotto. Stir in the sautéed zucchini, fennel, and shrimp. Cook, stirring, until the shrimp are cooked through. Stir in the remaining 2 tablespoons of the butter and season.

TO SERVE Spoon the risotto into a large serving bowl or divide it among 6 individual bowls. Remove some of the shrimp and place them on top. Garnish with the chopped basil. With a hand-held immersion blender or with a whisk, blend the sauce until light and frothy. The emulsified sauce can be served on top or on the side. Serve immediately.

CHAPTER FOUR

SOUPS, BREADS AND SANDWICHES

This soup is inspired by the famous potato soup of Vichy, a town near where I grew up in France. It is always served hot, often with a sprinkle of the local blue cheese, bleu d'Auvergne. | I remember eating this soup at my grandparents' country home. Just before finishing it, we would splash in a little red wine as a way of cleaning the plate—and an extra treat—a custom known in French as *faire chabrot.* | Maytag blue cheese was first developed at the University of Iowa in the early 1940s. It is named for Fred Maytag, of household appliance fame, who started the first commercial Maytag Blue Cheese dairy. It is made from cow's milk and I like its mild, creamy flavor. | For a hearty winter meal, serve this soup with Endive Salad/Gorgonzola/Marinated Figs/Mustard Vinaigrette (page 52) or Braised Short Ribs/Garlic-Thyme Brown Butter (page 163). | SERVES 6

POTATO-WATERCRESS SOUP | BLUE CHEESE AND BACON

1 tablespoon olive oil

2 medium onions, thinly sliced

2 leeks, thinly sliced

1 medium potato, peeled and diced

Fine sea salt and freshly ground black pepper to taste

6 cups chicken stock or low-sodium chicken broth

1 cup heavy cream

1 bunch watercress, large stems removed

3 ounces crumbled blue cheese, preferably bleu d'Auvergne or Maytag blue

2 slices crisp cooked bacon (see page 43), chopped

MAKE THE BASE In a 2-quart saucepan, heat the oil over medium heat. Add the onions and leeks and cook until tender but not browned.

Add the potato, sprinkle with salt and pepper, and cover with the chicken stock and cream. Cook over medium-low heat until the potatoes are tender. Let cool slightly.

ADD THE WATERCRESS Blend the soup in batches until smooth. Adjust the seasoning. Pour the soup into a clean pot. Bring the soup to a simmer over medium heat. Stir in the watercress leaves and remove from the heat.

FINISH THE SOUP Divide the blue cheese evenly among 6 bowls. Pour the watercress soup into each bowl and sprinkle with the bacon bits. Serve hot.

WINE SUGGESTION: CHARDONNAY, AU BON CLIMAT, 2003, SANTA MARIA VALLEY, CALIFORNIA. *A rich and creamy Chardonnay with aromas of spiced apples, candied nuts, and hints of vanilla.*

There is nothing like sweet, fresh corn at the height of the summer season. Some people like white varieties and others prefer yellow, but as far as I am concerned as long as it is freshly picked, it will be delicious. Try to buy corn straight from the field at a farmers' market if at all possible. | Serve with Marinated Kobe Skirt Steak (page 157) or Grilled Jerk Chicken (page 185). | SERVES 6

CREAM OF CORN | CORN FRITTERS

14 ears fresh corn, shucked

2 tablespoons unsalted butter

2 tablespoons extra-virgin olive oil

1 Vidalia onion, cut into julienne strips

1 small leek, white part only, thinly sliced

2 garlic cloves, finely chopped

1 cup dry white wine

8 sprigs fresh thyme

1 bay leaf

8 cups chicken stock or low-sodium chicken broth

6 cups heavy cream

Fine sea salt and freshly ground white pepper to taste

Corn Fritters

6 to 7 ears cooked fresh corn, kernels removed (about 2½ cups; see page 272)

2 dried chiles de Arbol, minced

½ cup finely diced white onion

1 tablespoon chopped fresh parsley

2 garlic cloves, minced

PREPARE THE CORN With a large chef's knife, remove the corn kernels from the cobs. Reserve the cobs. You will have approximately 5 cups of corn.

Process 3 cups of the corn in a juicer. If you don't have a juicer, the corn can be put in a blender with just enough water to get it going. Blend until smooth and pass through a fine-mesh sieve. Set aside the remaining 2 cups of kernels, the corn juice, and the corn cobs.

MAKE THE SOUP In large pot over medium heat, heat the butter and oil until the butter foams. Add the onion, leek, and garlic and cook, covered, until soft, about 10 minutes. Check occasionally to see that the vegetables do not brown.

Add the wine and cook, uncovered, until most of the liquid has evaporated.

Tie the thyme and bay leaf together with string so they can be easily removed from the pot after cooking. Add the chicken stock, corn cobs, and herbs to the vegetables and simmer, covered, for 1 hour.

Remove the cobs and herb bouquet from the pot. Add the remaining 2 cups corn kernels and the cream and simmer until the kernels are tender, approximately 20 minutes. Add the corn juice and simmer for an additional 5 minutes.

FINISH THE SOUP Remove the soup from the heat. Puree the soup in batches in a blender until smooth. Taste for seasoning and adjust with sea salt and white pepper. (Soup can be made ahead and refrigerated up to 2 days before serving. Reheat it gently and serve hot with Corn Fritters (recipe follows).

1 cup all-purpose flour

½ cup milk

1 large egg

1 teaspoon salt, plus extra for garnish

1 teaspoon baking powder

1 teaspoon sugar

Freshly ground black pepper to taste

Vegetable oil for frying

Cayenne

WINE SUGGESTION: PINOT BLANC, LIEB CELLARS, 2004, NORTH FORK, NEW YORK. *Crisp, citrusy Pinot Blanc with flavors of tangerines, pears, and minerals.*

MAKE THE BATTER In a large bowl, combine the corn, chiles, onion, parsley, and garlic. In another bowl, whisk together the flour, milk, egg, salt, baking powder, sugar, and ½ cup water. Season with pepper.

Add the corn mixture and stir until well combined. The batter will be slightly runny.

FRY THE FRITTERS Fill a deep, heavy pot or deep fryer with about 4 inches of the oil. Heat to 375°F, or until a small drop of the batter browns quickly in the oil.

Since the batter is very loose, I fry these fritters a spoonful at a time. With a long-handled heatproof spoon, scoop up about 1 tablespoon of the batter. Carefully lower the spoon into the oil and hold it there for about 30 seconds to allow the batter to set up slightly.

With another spoon, push the batter into the hot oil, being careful not to splash. Add additional spoonfuls of batter, but do not crowd the pan. Fry the fritters until golden brown and cooked through, approximately 2 minutes. With a slotted spoon, transfer the fritters to paper towels to drain. Repeat with the remaining batter.

TO SERVE Sprinkle with salt and cayenne and serve immediately.

CHEF'S TIP: *Be very careful when frying these fritters. Wear a heavy, moisture-proof oven mitt to protect your hand.*

If you are looking for the perfect starter to your Thanksgiving or other cold-weather special-occasion menu, look no further. Follow this with roasted turkey, prime rib roast, Roasted Rosemary-Lemon Chicken (page 183), Cornish Hen Diablo (page 188), or Porterhouse/White and Dark Soubise (page 152). | SERVES 6

CHESTNUT | APPLE | CELERY SOUP

1 pound fresh chestnuts, roasted and peeled (see page 272)

2 cups milk

1 sprig fresh rosemary

2 bay leaves

3 ounces thick-sliced bacon, cut into ¼-inch pieces

12 tablespoons (1½ sticks) unsalted butter

2 medium onions, sliced

2 garlic cloves, smashed

2 medium celery roots (about 1½ pounds each), peeled and cut into 1-inch dice

Fine sea salt and freshly ground black pepper to taste

½ cup honey

1 cinnamon stick (3 inches)

1 star anise

1 cup Calvados

4 Golden Delicious apples, peeled, cored, and chopped into 1-inch pieces

About 6 cups chicken stock or low-sodium chicken broth

4 sprigs fresh thyme

1½ cups heavy or whipping cream

Crème fraîche, for garnish

COOK THE CHESTNUTS Chop and set aside a few of the chestnuts for garnish. Place the remaining chestnuts in a large saucepan. Add the milk, rosemary, and 1 of the bay leaves. Bring to a simmer. Cover and cook until the chestnuts are very tender, about 30 minutes. Remove the rosemary and bay leaf. Drain off any liquid remaining and reserve it for thinning the soup later.

COOK THE BACON Place the bacon in a small skillet and cook over medium heat until browned, about 5 minutes. Drain the bacon on paper towels.

COOK THE VEGETABLES Melt 4 tablespoons of the butter in a large pot or Dutch oven with a tight-fitting cover. Add the onions, garlic, and bacon. Cover the pot and cook on medium-low heat, stirring often, until the onions are very tender, about 5 minutes. Do not allow the onions to brown.

Stir in the celery root and salt and pepper. Cover and cook, stirring occasionally, until the celery root is tender, 35 to 40 minutes.

CARAMELIZE THE HONEY In a heavy pot large enough to hold all of the ingredients, combine the honey, cinnamon, and star anise. Cook over medium heat until the honey is caramelized and appears thicker and darker, about 4 minutes.

Add the chestnuts and cook for 5 minutes, stirring. Lower the heat if necessary to avoid burning. Add the Calvados and bring to a boil, scraping the bottom of the pan. Add the apples and cover the pan. Cook on low heat for 10 minutes.

COMBINE THE INGREDIENTS Add the vegetable mixture to the pot. Add 4 cups of the chicken stock, the remaining bay leaf, and the thyme. Bring to a simmer. Cook, uncovered, for 10 minutes, stirring often, until the apples are soft. Add the cream and the reserved cooking liquid. Turn the heat to low and cook, uncovered, 10 minutes more.

PUREE THE SOUP Remove the herbs, cinnamon stick, and star anise. Let the soup cool slightly. Puree it in batches in a blender or food processor.

TO SERVE Gently reheat the soup. If it is too thick, add more stock.

In a small saucepan, cook the remaining 8 tablespoons of the butter over medium-low heat until lightly browned, about 5 minutes. Add the browned butter to the soup and stir well. Taste for seasoning.

Pour the soup into serving bowls. Top each serving with a spoonful of crème fraîche and some chopped roasted chestnuts.

WINE SUGGESTION: CHARDONNAY, "INDIAN WELLS," CHATEAU STE. MICHELLE, 2003, COLUMBIA VALLEY, WASHINGTON. *A medium-bodied lush Chardonnay with aromas of chestnuts, roasted pears, and white flowers.*

Sunchokes are also called Jerusalem artichokes. Though they don't come from Jerusalem and are not really artichokes, they do have a similar flavor to artichokes. They are actually the roots of sunflowers, known in Italy as *girasole*, which somehow was corrupted to Jerusalem. Sunchokes are good roasted, fried, or boiled. They come into season in the fall. | I like to serve this soup before the Sea Salt–Crusted Pink Snapper/Ice Wine Nage (page 133) or Roasted Cod Fish/Herb-Bacon Crust (page 137). | SERVES 6

CREAM OF SUNCHOKE | MELTED PARMESAN

1 tablespoon unsalted butter

4 ounces prosciutto in one piece, cut into ½-inch strips

1 medium leek, white part only, sliced

1 cup diced onion

½ cup diced fennel

1 celery stalk, sliced

3 pounds sunchokes (Jerusalem artichokes), peeled and halved

1 small potato, peeled and diced

4 garlic cloves, peeled

4 cups chicken stock or low-sodium chicken broth

1 bay leaf

3 sprigs fresh thyme

Fine sea salt and freshly ground black pepper to taste

1½ cups heavy cream

6 tablespoons freshly grated Parmigiano-Reggiano cheese

Truffle oil

MAKE THE BASE In a large pot, melt the butter over medium heat. Add the prosciutto and brown the pieces on all sides. Add the leek, onion, fennel, and celery. Cover and cook the vegetables until they are soft, 15 to 18 minutes.

COOK THE SUNCHOKES Add the sunchokes, potato, and garlic to the pot. Cover with the chicken stock and add the bay leaf and thyme. Season the soup lightly with salt and pepper and cook until the sunchokes are tender and can be cut with a spoon, about 20 minutes.

PUREE THE SOUP Remove the prosciutto, bay leaf, and thyme. In 2 batches, blend the soup with the cream, then pass the finished soup through a fine-mesh sieve.

GARNISH THE SOUP Preheat the broiler. Pour the soup into ovenproof bowls, top with the grated cheese and drizzle with truffle oil. Place the bowls under the broiler until the cheese has melted, and then serve hot.

WINE SUGGESTION: DELILLE CELLARS, "CHALEUR ESTATE," 2003, COLUMBIA VALLEY, WASHINGTON. *A Bordeaux-style white blend with aromas of melons, minerals, and almonds.*

This bright orange soup is served cold, so plan to make it a day ahead of serving. It is perfect for a summer meal. Organic carrots are sweeter and more flavorful, so they are my first choice for this. | I like to serve this soup with toasted seven-grain bread spread with cream cheese. Follow it with Green Papaya Chicken Salad (page 47) or Marinated Kobe Skirt Steak (page 157). | SERVES 6

COLD CARROT-COCONUT SOUP

3 shallots, sliced

2 tablespoons grapeseed oil

8 large carrots, preferably organic, peeled and sliced

1-inch piece fresh ginger, peeled and sliced

Fine sea salt and freshly ground black pepper to taste

3 tablespoons Madras curry powder

1¼ cups unsweetened coconut milk

Fresh cilantro leaves, for garnish

WINE SUGGESTION: VIOGNIER, HORTON VINEYARDS, 2003, ORANGE COUNTY, VIRGINIA. *A dry and spicy Viognier with aromas of white peaches and apricots, and hon-eyed flavors.*

COOK THE VEGETABLES In a large soup pot over medium-low heat, cook the shallots in 1 tablespoon of the grapeseed oil until soft, but not browned, about 4 minutes. Add the carrots and ginger and cook for 5 minutes, stirring occasionally. Add enough cold water to cover the carrots by 1 inch. Season lightly with salt and pepper and cook until the carrots are soft.

COOK THE CURRY In a medium saucepan, heat the remaining 1 tablespoon of the oil with the curry powder. Stir well and cook for 1 minute. Stir in the coconut milk. Cook over low heat for 3 to 5 minutes, or until thickened.

PUREE THE SOUP In a blender or food processor, blend the vegetables and the coconut milk mixture in batches until smooth. Pass the soup through a fine-mesh sieve and season.

CHILL THE SOUP Store the soup in a covered container for several hours or overnight.

SERVE COLD garnished with cilantro.

Chili is often attributed to the chuck wagon cooks in the Southwest who had to create hot meals from whatever meats or vegetables they could find when they were on the trails. They added spices and chile peppers borrowed from the local Mexicans and Indians to make a flavorful stew. | A cross between a stew and a soup, this is a hearty meal with chopped jalapeño, shredded Cheddar, and sour cream on top. All you need with it is warm Corn Bread (page 122). | SERVES 6

CORN, BEAN, AND SAUSAGE CHILI

2 tablespoons olive oil

1 onion, diced

1 red bell pepper, diced

6 garlic cloves, chopped

6 sweet Italian pork sausages (about 1 pound), casings removed

2 pounds bulk pork sausage meat

¼ cup chili powder

2 tablespoons ground cumin

2 tablespoons dried oregano

1 bay leaf

Pinch cayenne

1 can (28 ounces) whole peeled tomatoes

1 cup chicken stock or low-sodium chicken broth

1½ cups cooked or canned kidney beans, drained

1 cup cooked corn kernels (see page 272)

½ teaspoon Tabasco Sauce

Fine sea salt and freshly ground black pepper to taste

COOK THE VEGETABLES In a large skillet, heat the oil and cook the onion, pepper, and garlic over medium-low heat until they are soft but not browned, about 10 minutes.

COOK THE SAUSAGE In a large pot, cook both kinds of sausage over medium heat, stirring occasionally, until it is cooked through and lightly browned.

Tip the pan and spoon off the excess fat. Add the vegetables, chili powder, cumin, oregano, bay leaf, and cayenne to the pot. Cook for 1 minute.

FINISH THE SOUP In a blender or food processor, puree the tomatoes until smooth. Do not strain the juices. Add the tomatoes, chicken stock, beans, and corn to the pot. Add the Tabasco and season with salt and pepper. Bring the soup to a simmer and cook for 20 minutes, until thickened. Remove the bay leaf and serve.

BEER SUGGESTION: CORONA, MEXICO *(best served with a lime!). A light, refreshing beer.*

Mushrooms and barley give added flavor to a classic chicken soup. You can also make this soup with leftover roast turkey. | As a variation, stir a spoonful of pesto into the soup just before serving with country bread. This is good served with a bowl of fresh ricotta, a green salad such as the Fennel-Arugula Salad/Aged Pecorino (page 54), and Focaccia (page 120). | SERVES 6

CHICKEN-MUSHROOM BARLEY SOUP

2 tablespoons olive oil

About 14 ounces portobello mushrooms, cut into small dice (about 2 cups)

1 chicken (3 to 4 pounds), preferably organic, cut into quarters

Fine sea salt

1 sprig fresh thyme

1 bay leaf

3 medium carrots, finely diced

1½ cups finely diced onion

1½ cups finely diced celery

1 cup barley, rinsed

1 garlic clove, minced

15 black peppercorns

¼ cup celery leaves, roughly chopped

¼ cup fresh flat-leaf parsley, roughly chopped

COOK THE MUSHROOMS In a large pot, heat the oil over medium heat. Add the mushrooms and sauté until tender, about 5 minutes. Remove the mushrooms to a plate.

ADD THE CHICKEN Add the chicken, 4½ quarts cold water, a pinch of salt, the thyme, and bay leaf to the pot. Bring the liquid to a simmer over medium heat. With a large spoon, skim off the foam that rises to the top.

ADD THE VEGETABLES Add the carrots, onion, celery, barley, garlic, peppercorns, and sautéed mushrooms. When the liquid returns to a simmer, cook for 35 to 40 minutes, until the barley is tender and the chicken is cooked through.

REMOVE THE CHICKEN Remove the chicken from the pot. Let it cool slightly. Remove the skin and bones and cut the chicken into thin slices, then cut it into bite-sized pieces.

REDUCE THE BROTH Strain the liquid, reserving the barley and vegetables. Return the broth to the pot. Bring the broth to a simmer over medium heat. Cook until reduced by about half, about 30 minutes.

FINISH THE SOUP Add the barley, vegetables, chicken, celery leaves, and parsley to the pot. Reheat gently and season with salt and pepper. Serve hot.

WINE SUGGESTION: CHARDONNAY, STONY HILL, 2003, NAPA VALLEY, CALIFORNIA. *A classic Burgundian-style Chardonnay. Clean and crisp with aromas of green apple and a touch of nuttiness.*

Nuoc mam is a Vietnamese sauce made from salted fish. It gives dishes like this whole meal-in-a-bowl soup its distinctive flavor. The best nuoc mam comes from the island of Phu Quoc. A special type of anchovies are packed in wooden vats until they ferment and give off a pungent liquid. The French government recently awarded Nuoc Mam Phu Quoc an *appellation d'origine controlée*, or A.O.C., the same status given to fine wines, to ensure that what you buy is the real thing. | For this hearty soup, chicken can be substituted for the beef. | In Vietnam, this soup is a whole meal served with spicy sriracha chili sauce (see page 13) and pieces of fried bread. | SERVES 6

BEEF CHEEKS PHO | RICE VERMICELLI

Stock

1 medium white onion, halved

One 3-inch piece fresh ginger, halved lengthwise

3 pounds beef cheeks, brisket, or top round, rinsed under cold water

4 garlic cloves

2 tablespoons sugar

1 tablespoon black peppercorns

1 tablespoon Vietnamese fish sauce (nuoc mam)

3 star anise

3 whole cloves

¼ black cardamom pod

Small pinch Chinese five-spice powder

Fine sea salt to taste

Soup

2 tablespoons Vietnamese fish sauce (nuoc mam)

Freshly ground black pepper to taste

MAKE THE STOCK To char the onion and ginger, heat a cast-iron pan over high heat. Add the vegetables, cut-side down, and brown on all sides until blackened but not cooked or soft.

Fill a large pot with 7 quarts of cold water. Add the beef cheeks and bring to a boil, skimming off the foam that rises to the surface.

When the foam stops rising, add the onion, ginger, garlic, sugar peppercorns, fish sauce, star anise, cloves, cardamom, five-spice powder, and a pinch of salt. Bring to a simmer. Cook for 2½ hours, until the meat is tender when pierced with a fork.

Remove the pot from the heat and let cool. Refrigerate overnight.

TO FINISH THE SOUP Remove the beef from the broth and trim off any excess fat. Cut the meat into ⅛-inch-thick slices.

STRAIN THE STOCK Strain the stock into a clean pot. Bring the stock to a simmer. Add the fish sauce and salt and pepper.

COOK THE VERMICELLI In another large pot, bring 3 quarts of salted water to a boil. Add the rice vermicelli, and cook for 3 minutes. Drain the noodles and run under cold water to remove the starch.

8 ounces rice vermicelli

2 cups bean sprouts

½ medium white onion, thinly sliced

¼ cup chopped fresh cilantro

10 fresh mint leaves, roughly chopped

3 scallions, thinly sliced

20 fresh Thai basil leaves, roughly chopped

1 fresh Thai red chile, seeds removed and thinly sliced

3 limes, halved

TO SERVE Divide the vermicelli, meat, bean sprouts, onion, cilantro, mint, scallions, basil, and chile among 6 large serving bowls. Add some of the hot beef stock to each bowl. Serve with the lime halves.

WINE SUGGESTION: SEMI-DRY RIESLING, DR. KONSTANTIN FRANK, 2004, FINGER LAKES, NEW YORK. *An off-dry Riesling with aromas of pineapples, green melon, and Asian pears.*

Brioche rolls, with their delicate flavor and soft texture, are the perfect bread to hold a rich lobster filling. For a cocktail appetizer or a tea party, miniature rolls are ideal. | At BLT Fish, we serve these sandwiches with cole slaw and fries seasoned with Old Bay Seasoning. Cooked crab or shrimp can be substituted for the lobster meat. | SERVES 6

LOBSTER ROLLS

1½ cups mayonnaise

3 tablespoons freshly squeezed lemon juice

2 tablespoons chopped fresh tarragon

2 tablespoons snipped fresh chives

2 tablespoons drained capers

Fine sea salt and freshly ground black pepper to taste

4 cups cooked lobster meat (two 1- to 1½-pound lobsters; see page 271), cut into bite-sized pieces

6 brioche rolls or hot dog buns, split

Unsalted butter

MAKE THE FILLING In a medium bowl, stir together the mayonnaise, lemon juice, herbs, capers, and salt and pepper.

Fold in the lobster meat.

ASSEMBLE THE ROLLS Lightly toast the rolls and spread them with butter. Divide the filling among the rolls. Serve immediately.

BEER SUGGESTION: SHIPYARD BREWING COMPANY, IPA FUGGLES, PORTLAND, MAINE. *An IPA beer from Maine with aromas of grapefruit, hops, and malt.*

Use Kobe beef for these luxury sandwiches, if possible. Its rich flavor is the perfect complement to the foie gras and other ingredients. | I like to serve these sandwiches with the BLT Steak Sauce (page 204) and Rosemary-Parmesan French Fries (page 230). | SERVES 6

STEAK AND FOIE GRAS SANDWICH

3 skirt steaks (12 ounces each)

3 tablespoons unsalted butter, softened

Fine sea salt and freshly ground black pepper to taste

12 slices (about ½ inch thick) ciabatta or other good-quality French or Italian bread

¼ cup olive oil

½ cup mayonnaise

1½ cups baby arugula leaves

3 Beefsteak or other large ripe tomatoes, cut into 12 slices

1 can (9 ounces) terrine of foie gras, cut into 6 slices

12 leaves iceberg lettuce

24 very thin slices bacon, cooked (see page 43)

WINE SUGGESTION: PINOT NOIR, ARCADIAN, 2003, SANTA MARIA VALLEY, CALIFORNIA. *A medium-bodied spicy Pinot Noir with aromas of black cherries, game, and smoky bacon notes.*

PREHEAT a barbecue or stovetop grill to high heat.

GRILL THE STEAK Brush the steak with the butter and season with salt and pepper. Grill about 3 minutes on each side for rare. Remove from the heat and allow to rest.

PREPARE THE BREAD Brush 1 side of each slice of bread with olive oil. Spread some of the mayonnaise on the opposite sides.

MAKE THE SANDWICHES Cut the steak on an angle against the grain into about 30 slices. On the mayonnaise-coated sides of half of the bread, layer 5 slices of steak, some arugula, 2 tomato slices, 1 slice of foie gras, 1 lettuce leaf, and 2 slices of bacon. Place the remaining bread slices mayonnaise-side down on top.

Preheat a large grill pan or 2 large heavy skillets over medium heat.

GRILL THE SANDWICHES Place the sandwiches on the grill or in the pan. Top with a heavy pot cover or other weight to press the sandwiches. (You can use a panini grill if you have one.) Cook until browned, about 2 minutes. Turn the sandwiches, cover with the weight, and grill on the other sides until browned, about 2 minutes more.

TO SERVE Cut the sandwiches in half and serve hot.

CHEF'S TIP: *Make sure the grill is hot before adding the sandwiches so that the foie gras does not melt before the bread is toasted.*

Inspired by the famous *pan bagnat* sandwich of Provence, which is made with canned tuna, I created this version with fresh tuna. It is great for a picnic since you can make it up to several hours in advance. The taste will only improve as the flavors of the ingredients meld together. For a change, substitute pesto for the tapenade. | SERVES 6

BLT GRILLED TUNA SANDWICH

1½ pounds yellowfin tuna, cut into 12 slices, about ⅓ inch thick

Fine sea salt and freshly ground black pepper to taste

½ cup olive oil

4 teaspoons freshly squeezed lemon juice

½ teaspoon chopped garlic

1 large bunch arugula, tough stems removed (about 2 cups)

½ cup mayonnaise

¼ cup Tapenade (page 22)

1 loaf rustic Italian bread, cut into twelve ½-inch-thick diagonal slices, toasted

12 slices applewood-smoked bacon, cooked until crisp (see page 43)

1 medium red onion, sliced

2 ripe tomatoes, sliced

3 hard-cooked eggs, peeled and sliced

6 ounces Parmigiano-Reggiano cheese, thinly sliced with a vegetable peeler or mandoline slicer

1 ripe avocado, preferably Hass

1 bunch fresh basil, tough stems removed

GRILL THE TUNA Preheat a grill pan or barbecue grill to high heat. Sprinkle the tuna on both sides with salt and pepper. Place the tuna on the pan or grill rack and cook 1 to 2 minutes per side, or until rare to medium-rare, depending on your preference.

DRESS THE ARUGULA In a medium bowl, whisk together the oil, lemon juice, garlic, and salt and pepper. Add the arugula and toss well.

ASSEMBLE THE SANDWICHES Spread some of the mayonnaise and tapenade on each slice of bread. Divide the bacon, onion, tomatoes, eggs, cheese, and avocado over half of the slices. Top with the tuna, basil, and the arugula salad. Cover with the remaining bread, coated-sides down.

TO SERVE Cut the sandwiches in half and serve immediately.

CHEF'S TIP: *To make these sandwiches easier to eat, wrap them in butcher paper or waxed paper.*

WINE SUGGESTION: DA RED, DOMAINE ALFRED, 2003, EDNA VALLEY, CALIFORNIA. *A blend of Pinot Noir and Syrah, this wine has both bright fruit and earth tones that show off aromas of red cherries, black pepper, and smoked tomatoes.*

This is my version of *croque monsieur,* a sandwich made famous in Parisian cafés, where it has been a menu staple since the early twentieth century. The name means "crunchy sir" or "mister crunchy" and it is typically a grilled ham and cheese sandwich. A *croque madame* can be made either with ham and cheese or with chicken and cheese, and has an egg on top cooked *à cheval* or sunny-side up. | The truffles aren't essential, but they bring the dish to another level. | SERVES 6

GRILLED HAM AND CHEESE SANDWICH | WHITE TRUFFLE

12 slices Brioche (page 116) or good-quality white bread

6 tablespoons (¾ stick) unsalted butter, softened, plus extra for the eggs

12 tablespoons Béchamel Sauce (page 210)

1 cup grated Gruyère cheese

½ cup freshly grated Parmigiano-Reggiano cheese

6 slices Black Forest ham

6 eggs

1 large white truffle or black truffle (optional)

1 tablespoon white truffle oil

WINE SUGGESTION: MARSANNE, QUPÉ, 2003, SANTA MARIA VALLEY, CALIFORNIA. *A rich, nutty Marsanne with aromas of buttered brioche, nuts, and citrus fruit.*

PREPARE THE BREAD Spread each slice of bread with butter on 1 side. Turn 6 of the slices over and spread each with 1 tablespoon of the béchamel.

MAKE THE SANDWICHES Toss together the 2 cheeses. Divide one-third of the cheese between the béchamel-coated slices of bread and top each with a slice of ham.

Close the sandwiches with the other slices of bread, buttered-sides out. Trim off the bread crusts.

COOK THE SANDWICHES Heat a large nonstick skillet or pancake griddle over medium heat. Cook the sandwiches until golden brown, 2 to 3 minutes on each side. Transfer the sandwiches to a baking sheet.

TOP THE SANDWICHES Turn on the broiler. Spread the rest of the béchamel on top of the sandwiches and sprinkle with the remaining cheese. Broil until the cheese is melted, about 30 seconds.

FRY THE EGGS Reheat the skillet or griddle. Add a little more butter. Break the eggs into the pan and cook them sunny-side up for 2 to 3 minutes, or until the whites are just set.

TO SERVE Transfer the sandwiches to 6 plates. Place 1 egg on top of each sandwich. With a truffle shaver or a swivel-blade vegetable peeler, shave the truffle evenly over the eggs. Drizzle with truffle oil and serve immediately.

Soft-shell crabs are actually blue crabs that have shed their hard shells in preparation for growing larger ones. They come into season in mid-May. | These sandwiches are great with crisp dill pickle spears | SERVES 6

SPICY SOFT-SHELL CRAB SANDWICHES

1 cup mayonnaise

1 tablespoon *sriracha* (Asian red chile sauce; see page 13)

2 cups all-purpose flour

1½ tablespoons chili powder

1½ tablespoons Spanish paprika

1½ tablespoons cayenne

1 tablespoon fine sea salt

12 small soft-shell crabs, cleaned (see page 271)

Vegetable oil for frying

12 slices (½ inch thick) rustic Italian bread such as ciabatta, toasted or grilled

2 or 3 large tomatoes, sliced

1 large red onion, thinly sliced

3 cups baby arugula, washed and trimmed

MAKE THE CHILI MAYONNAISE In a small bowl, stir together the mayonnaise and sriracha.

MAKE THE COATING In a large bowl, stir together the flour, chili powder, paprika, cayenne, and salt.

COAT THE CRABS Dry the crabs with paper towels. Toss the crabs with the flour mixture and shake off the excess.

FRY THE CRABS In a large heavy skillet, heat about ¼ inch of the oil until it reaches 375°F, and a bit of flour added to the hot oil browns quickly. Add the crabs a few at a time without crowding the pan. Be careful, because they may pop and splash oil as they fry. Cook for about 1½ minutes on each side, or until golden and crisp. Drain on paper towels.

ASSEMBLE THE SANDWICHES Spread the mayonnaise on 1 side of each slice of toast. Put 2 slices each of the tomato and onion on half the bread. Top with the arugula and 2 fried crabs. Cover with the remaining bread slices, mayonnaise-side down. Serve immediately.

CHEF'S TIP: *A good fish market will clean and prepare the crabs for you, but it is quite easy to do yourself if you follow the instructions on page 271.*

WINE SUGGESTION: RIESLING, ATWATER ESTATE, 2003, FINGER LAKES, NEW YORK. *A dry and refreshing Riesling with aromas of fresh peaches, honeyed apricots, and wet stones.*

This recipe makes a large batch of dough that you can bake into butter-rich loaves, individual rolls, or the Cinnamon-Pecan Sticky Loaf (page 269). I like to make this into two brioche loaves and one pecan loaf, but the choice is up to you. Brioche is excellent toasted with foie gras, or with butter and jam for breakfast, or use it to make the Dried Apricot Bread Pudding on page 249. | European-style full-fat butter will enhance the flavor and texture of this bread, though it will still taste good made with regular unsalted butter. | Most supermarkets sell fresh cake yeast in the dairy section, or you can ask to buy it at your local bakery. | You will need a heavy-duty mixer to make this recipe. | MAKES THREE 9-INCH LOAVES

BRIOCHE

½ cup milk

1-ounce package (2½ tablespoons) fresh cake yeast

7 cups bread flour

½ cup sugar

¼ cup heavy cream

¼ cup sour cream

1 tablespoon fine sea salt

2 cups eggs (about 10)

2 cups plus 3 tablespoons (4 sticks plus 3 tablespoons) chilled unsalted European-style butter, cut into very small dice

Egg wash: 1 egg yolk mixed with 1 tablespoon water

DISSOLVE THE YEAST Heat the milk until it feels warm to the touch, about 110°F on an instant-read thermometer. Crumble the yeast into the milk and stir until dissolved.

MAKE THE DOUGH In a heavy-duty mixer bowl, combine the flour, sugar, heavy cream, sour cream, salt, and the yeast mixture. With the paddle attachment, mix on low speed until blended. Add the eggs, and stir until the mixture begins to pull away from the sides of the bowl. Gradually add the butter and mix until blended and a sticky dough forms.

LET THE DOUGH RISE Cover the bowl with plastic wrap and refrigerate for 2 hours.

PREPARE THE PANS Butter and flour three 9 x 4½-inch loaf pans. If making Cinnamon-Pecan Sticky Loaf, see page 269.

SHAPE THE DOUGH With your hands, flatten the dough. Cut into 3 equal pieces. Shape each piece into a loaf and place it in a prepared pan. Cover with plastic wrap. Set the pans in a warm, draft-free place and let the dough rise for 1 to 1½ hours, or until doubled in volume.

PREHEAT THE OVEN to 375°F.

BAKE THE BRIOCHE Brush the tops of the loaves with the egg wash. Bake 25 to 30 minutes, or until the top is golden brown and a thin, sharp knife inserted in the center of the loaf comes out clean and warm. Invert the loaves onto racks to cool.

SERVE at room temperature or wrap tightly in foil or plastic wrap and store at room temperature up to 2 days.

At BLT Fish, these hot, cheesy biscuits are served with cold butter sprinkled with sea salt and drizzled with maple syrup. The contrast of flavors, temperatures, and textures makes it difficult to eat just one. A good Cheddar cheese is essential to making these biscuits taste right. I prefer the nutty flavor of sharp Vermont Cheddar. | MAKES 8 BISCUITS

CHIVE-CHEDDAR BISCUITS

1½ cups all-purpose flour

2 teaspoons baking powder

1 teaspoon fine sea salt

¼ teaspoon cayenne

3 tablespoons solid vegetable shortening, at room temperature

3 tablespoons unsalted butter, at room temperature

1 cup grated sharp Vermont Cheddar cheese

1 tablespoon chopped fresh chives

1¼ cups heavy cream

Cold unsalted butter, sea salt, and maple syrup, for serving (optional)

PREHEAT THE OVEN to 375°F.

COMBINE THE DRY INGREDIENTS In a medium bowl, stir together the flour, baking powder, salt, and cayenne.

ADD THE BUTTER Add the shortening and butter to the bowl. With a pastry blender or a fork, blend in the butter and shortening just until they resemble small peas. For tender biscuits, do not overmix. Stir in the cheese and chives.

ADD THE CREAM Stir in the cream just until blended, again being careful not to overmix the dough.

SHAPE THE BISCUITS On a lightly floured surface, roll out the dough to a 1-inch thickness. Cut the dough into 2-inch rounds. Place the biscuits on an ungreased baking sheet at least 1½ inches apart.

BAKE THE BISCUITS 15 to 17 minutes, or until golden brown.

SERVE hot with cold butter sprinkled with sea salt and drizzled with good-quality maple syrup.

CHEF'S TIP: *Bake these biscuits right after you shape them. They reheat well in a low oven.*

Focaccia is an Italian flat bread. Olive oil and sea salt are the principal flavorings, but it can also be topped with herbs, cheese, or vegetables. This is my version of the classic focaccia, followed by some of my favorite variations. I also like to cut focaccia in half and spread it with Pesto Mayonnaise (page 60) or Spicy Aioli (page 21) for a sandwich. | SERVES 8

FOCACCIA

2½ teaspoons active dry yeast

3½ cups unbleached all-purpose flour

⅓ cup dry white wine

⅓ cup plus 2 tablespoons extra-virgin olive oil

2 teaspoons fine sea salt

MAKE THE STARTER In a medium bowl, whisk together the yeast and ⅔ cup warm tap water. Let stand 10 minutes. Stir 1 cup of the flour into the yeast and beat until smooth. Cover with plastic wrap and let rest until large bubbles form, about 30 minutes.

MAKE THE DOUGH Pour the starter into the bowl of a heavy-duty mixer or food processor. Add ⅓ cup plus 1 tablespoon warm tap water, the wine, and ⅓ cup of the oil. Beat until blended. Stir in the remaining 2½ cups of the flour and the salt. Beat until thoroughly mixed.

Continue beating for 4 to 5 minutes, or until the dough is smooth and elastic. Add more flour if necessary so that the dough is not sticky.

LET THE DOUGH RISE Lightly oil a large bowl. Add the dough, turning it once to oil the top. Cover the bowl with plastic wrap and let the dough rest in a warm place for 1 hour, or until doubled in volume.

Remove the dough from the bowl and punch it down to remove the air bubbles. Place the dough in a 12-inch round pizza pan, flattening it out to fit the pan. Cover with a towel and let rise in a warm place for 45 minutes, or until doubled.

Lightly oil a large bowl. Add the dough, turning it once to oil the top. Cover the bowl with plastic wrap and let the dough rest in a warm place for 1 hour, or until doubled in volume.

Remove the dough from the bowl and punch it down to remove the air bubbles. Place the dough in a 12-inch round pizza pan, flattening it out to fit the pan. Cover with a towel and let rise in a warm place for 45 minutes, or until doubled.

PREHEAT THE OVEN to 425°F.

BAKE THE FOCACCIA With your fingertips, make dimples 3 inches apart in the dough. Brush the top with the remaining 2 tablespoons of the olive oil. Add any of the desired toppings now, except the cheese.

Bake for 25 minutes. Turn the oven to broil. Slide the focaccia under the broiler for an additional 2 minutes, until golden brown. Watch carefully so that it does not get too brown.

If adding cheese, do so now, returning the focaccia to the oven just until the cheese begins to melt.

TO SERVE Slide the focaccia onto a cutting board. Cut into squares and serve warm or at room temperature.

CHEF'S TIP: *Focaccia lends itself to many different toppings, but each must be added at the appropriate time. For example:*

BEFORE BAKING:
Sautéed pancetta, and/or onion slices, roasted bell peppers, eggplant slices, and anchovies, sun-dried tomatoes and sliced black olives, minced garlic

AFTER BAKING:
Cheeses, such as mozzarella, Gorgonzola, Parmigiano-Reggiano, or provolone

Corn bread is the perfect accompaniment to a bowl of Corn, Bean, and Sausage Chili (page 105). Of course, it is also good served warm with sweet butter and honey. | SERVES 8

CORN BREAD

Nonstick vegetable oil spray

2½ cups all-purpose flour

1½ cups sugar

1 cup finely ground yellow cornmeal

1 tablespoon baking powder

2 teaspoons fine sea salt

6 eggs

1 cup crème fraîche

1 cup milk

9 tablespoons (1 stick plus 1 tablespoon) unsalted butter, softened

PREHEAT THE OVEN to 350°F. Spray a 12 x 9-inch baking pan with cooking spray.

COMBINE THE INGREDIENTS In a large bowl, stir together all of the dry ingredients. In a medium bowl, beat together the eggs, crème fraîche, and milk. Stir the egg mixture into the dry ingredients until smooth. Add the butter and stir until blended.

Pour the batter into the pan and smooth the top.

BAKE for 35 minutes, or until golden brown and a toothpick inserted in the center comes out clean.

SERVE warm, cut into squares.

CHEF'S TIP: Leftover corn bread can be dried and used for stuffing.

You can bake this stuffing inside the turkey, if you want to, but I like the rich brown crust that forms on the top when I bake it in a pan. | SERVES 6

CHESTNUT TURKEY STUFFING

1 tablespoon extra-virgin olive oil

1 pound pork sausage, casings removed

8 tablespoons (1 stick) unsalted butter

1 large onion, diced

2 celery stalks, diced

9 ounces roasted chestnuts (see page 272), peeled and sliced

4½ cups country-style bread, crusts removed, cut into ¾-inch cubes

2 eggs, beaten

2 tablespoons roughly chopped fresh thyme leaves

2 tablespoons roughly chopped fresh marjoram leaves

2 tablespoons roughly chopped fresh sage leaves

1 tablespoon roughly chopped fresh rosemary leaves

8 ounces hot chicken stock or low-sodium chicken broth

Fine sea salt and freshly ground black pepper to taste

COOK THE SAUSAGE In a large sauté pan, heat the oil over medium heat. Add the sausage meat and sauté, breaking it up with a fork, for 8 to 10 minutes, or until cooked through.

COOK THE VEGETABLES In a large skillet, heat the butter over medium heat until foaming. Add the onion and celery. Cover and cook until soft, but not browned, 12 to 15 minutes.

PREHEAT THE OVEN to 350°F.

MAKE THE STUFFING In a large bowl, mix the cooked vegetables, chestnuts, bread cubes, eggs, thyme, marjoram, sage, and rosemary. Add the hot chicken stock. With a slotted spoon, transfer the sausage to the bowl and mix well. Season with salt and pepper.

BAKE THE STUFFING Butter an 11 x 8-inch baking dish. Transfer the stuffing to the dish and pat it down. Cover with foil. Bake for 30 minutes.

Remove the foil. Turn on the broiler. Slide the dish under the broiler for 1 to 2 minutes, or until the top is browned.

CHEF'S TIP: *For a nice change, serve this stuffing with roasted chicken, duck, goose, or other birds. Leftovers are great reheated the next day with gravy on top.*

Popover pans have deep, narrow cups with sloped sides that help the batter to rise dramatically over the tops of the pan. These popovers turn out golden brown with a thick, cheesy crust. To get the popovers as large as we do at BLT Steak, be sure to pour the batter into the cups so that they are filled level with the tops. Popovers can also be topped with caramelized onions, garlic, and diced bacon instead of the cheese. | MAKES 12

GIANT CHEESE POPOVERS

4 cups all-purpose flour

1 tablespoon plus 2 teaspoons salt

4 cups milk

8 eggs

Nonstick vegetable oil spray

10 ounces grated Gruyère cheese (2¼ cups)

PREHEAT THE PAN Place a popover pan with 12 cups in the oven. Heat the oven and pan to 350°F.

MAKE THE BATTER Place the flour and salt in a fine-mesh sieve and sift it onto a piece of waxed paper.

In a small saucepan, heat the milk until small bubbles appear around the edges.

In a large bowl, whisk the eggs until frothy. Slowly whisk in the hot milk so as not to cook the eggs. Set aside.

Gradually whisk the dry ingredients into the egg mixture, stirring until almost smooth.

FILL THE PAN Remove the popover pan from the oven and spray it with nonstick vegetable oil spray. While the batter is still slightly warm or at room temperature, fill each cup level with the top.

Top each popover with some of the grated Gruyère. Place a baking sheet on the rack below the pan to catch any drips.

BAKE THE POPOVERS Bake for 15 minutes. Rotate the pan 180 degrees so that the popovers will rise evenly. Bake for 35 minutes more, or until golden brown.

TO SERVE Invert the pan and remove the popovers. Serve immediately. The popovers can also be made up to 2 hours in advance. Cool on a wire rack. Reheat in a hot 450°F oven just before serving.

CHAPTER FIVE

FISH AND SHELLFISH

The ingredients in this recipe reflect the flavors, aromas, and colors of Provence. Thick swordfish steaks slowly simmered in a robust tomato sauce turn out fork tender. Be sure to use top-quality canned Italian peeled tomatoes for best flavor. | This recipe makes a lot of sauce. If you don't use all of the sauce with the fish, save it to use another day with spaghetti. | SERVES 6

BRAISED SWORDFISH | TOMATOES, OLIVES, AND CAPERS

½ cup Wondra flour

Fine sea salt and freshly ground black pepper to taste

6 swordfish steaks, about 8 ounces each

¼ cup olive oil

1 red bell pepper, thinly sliced

1 yellow bell pepper, thinly sliced

½ large white onion

6 garlic cloves, finely chopped

1 cup dry white wine

2 cans (28 ounces each) Italian peeled tomatoes, chopped, with their juice

¾ cup pitted green olives, coarsely chopped

3 tablespoons drained capers

Pinch sugar

Pinch crushed red pepper flakes

¼ cup chopped fresh basil

SAUTÉ THE FISH On a piece of waxed paper, mix together the flour, and salt and pepper. Dredge the fish in the flour, shaking the pieces to remove the excess.

In a large skillet, heat the oil over high heat. When it is very hot, add half the fish. Brown it well, about 2 minutes on each side. Remove the fish to a plate. Brown the remaining fish in the same way.

COOK THE VEGETABLES Turn the heat to medium. Stir the peppers, onion, and garlic into the oil in the skillet. Cover and cook until the vegetables are soft, about 15 minutes. Add the wine and cook uncovered, 5 minutes, scraping the bottom of the pan.

MAKE THE SAUCE Add the tomatoes, olives, capers, sugar, and red pepper flakes. Bring the sauce to a simmer and cook for 10 minutes.

FINISH THE COOKING Return the fish to the skillet. Baste the fish with the sauce so that the pieces are completely covered. Simmer 20 to 30 minutes on low heat, or until the sauce is slightly thickened and the swordfish is very tender. Do not overcook or the fish will break apart.

TO SERVE Stir in the chopped basil and serve the fish steaks with the sauce.

WINE SUGGESTION: ROSÉ, OJAI, 2004, CALIFORNIA. *A clean and refreshing rosé with aromas of currants, framboise, and a touch of spice.*

Be sure to read this recipe through to the end and line up all of your ingredients and equipment before starting. You will need a long metal skewer the length of the fish and a very large pot. The pot should be large enough to accommodate the fish and oil with enough headroom for the oil to boil up to two times its depth with the fish in it. If you have a turkey fryer pot, you can use it for this recipe and do the frying outdoors. | Wear mitts to protect your hands when adding and removing the fish and be careful not to splash the oil. | Other fish such as sea bass or black bass can be cooked this way. | Lemongrass Rock Shrimp Risotto (page 92) would be a good first course. | SERVES 4 TO 6

CRISPY RED SNAPPER "CHINESE STYLE"

Sauce

½ cup soy sauce

½ cup Chinese plum wine

¼ cup Vietnamese fish sauce (*nuoc mam*)

2 jalapeños, seeded and minced

2 tablespoons minced fresh ginger

1 tablespoon sugar

2 garlic cloves, minced

Vegetables

2 tablespoons canola oil

2 dried Chinese sausages (about 4 ounces) cut into thin slices (available at Chinese markets)

2 tablespoons sliced fresh ginger

10 fresh shiitake mushrooms, stems removed and caps thinly sliced

1 carrot, cut into julienne strips

1 leek, cut into julienne strips

2 scallions, white parts only, thinly sliced

MAKE THE SAUCE Combine soy sauce, plum wine, fish sauce, jalapeños, minced ginger, sugar, garlic, and 1 cup water in a medium bowl. Stir until the sugar dissolves. Set aside.

COOK THE VEGETABLES Heat the oil in a sauté pan over medium-high heat. Add the sausage and sliced ginger. Cook until the sausage begins to give off its fat, about 3 minutes.

Add the mushrooms and cook until they give off their liquid, about 2 minutes. If the mushrooms are very dry they will absorb the oil, so add more if necessary. Add the carrot, leek, scallions, tomatoes, and chile and cook until just wilted but still crisp. Remove the pan from the heat and keep the vegetables covered and warm.

PREPARE THE POT Measure the length and thickness of the fish. Choose a heavy pot wide enough to hold the fish and deep enough to allow space for the oil to bubble up when the fish is added. The depth should be at least 3 times the thickness of the fish.

Pour enough oil into the pot to completely cover the fish by 1 inch. Heat the oil to 350°F on a frying thermometer.

PREPARE THE FISH With a large chef's knife, cut 4 slashes in the skin on each side of the fish starting about 3 inches behind the head and ending about 2 inches before the tail. Take care just to score the skin and not to cut the flesh of the fish. Dredge the fish in the flour, shaking off any excess. Insert a long metal barbecue skewer through the fish from tail to head.

3 plum tomatoes, seeded and finely diced

1 Thai bird's eye chile, thinly sliced

Fish

1 whole red snapper, 3 to 4 pounds, cleaned and scaled

Canola oil for frying

Wondra flour

Fresh cilantro sprigs

Crispy Shallots (page 27)

COOK THE FISH Protecting your hand with an oven mitt, carefully slip the fish into the hot oil, being careful not to splash. Cook 12 to 15 minutes, turning the fish once for even cooking, until cooked through but still slightly opaque near the bone.

TO SERVE Carefully remove the fish from the oil and drain it on paper towels. Place the fish on a large platter. Spoon some of the sauce on top and around the fish. Reserve the rest to serve on the side.
Top with the vegetables, cilantro sprigs, and Crispy Shallots.

Present the whole fish at the table and then fillet it into individual portions. Serve with the remaining sauce on the side.

WINE SUGGESTION: PINOT NOIR, "THEA'S SELECTION," LEMELSON VINEYARDS, 2003, WILLAMETTE VALLEY, OREGON. *A lighter red wine that combines strawberry and raspberry flavors with smoke and earthy flavors.*

Baking in a spiced salt crust is a gentle way of cooking fish. The meat turns out moist and flavorful and the skin of the fish pulls away when the salt is removed, making it easy to serve. | This fish is served with a *nage*, a light sauce or broth for fish or crustaceans. The word is derived from the French word meaning "to swim." | Ice wine, made from grapes picked during a frost and processed as quickly as possible, is an unusual choice for a nage, and it produces a subtly sweet result. Some of the best ice wines come from Long Island. | Serve with Spring Morel/Vegetable Ragoût (page 226) or Honey/Cumin-Glazed Carrots (page 215). | SERVES 6

SEA SALT-CRUSTED PINK SNAPPER | ICE WINE NAGE

¼ cup juniper berries

1 star anise

10 cups coarse sea salt

3 teaspoons fennel seeds

1 tablespoon grated lemon zest

1 tablespoon grated orange zest

¾ cup egg whites, lightly beaten

1 whole pink snapper or black sea bass, 4 to 5 pounds, cleaned

Extra-virgin olive oil

Nage

12 tablespoons (1½ sticks) unsalted butter

7 to 10 cipollini onions, sliced, or 1 large Spanish onion, sliced

2 heads Belgian endive, cut into julienne strips

2 carrots, thinly sliced

1½ cups ice wine or other sweet white dessert wine, such as Sauternes

1 lemon, juiced

PREPARE THE SALT CRUST With the bottom of a heavy pan, crush the juniper berries and star anise.

In a large bowl, stir together the sea salt, crushed juniper berries and star anise, fennel seed, and zests. Mix well. Add the egg whites and stir until evenly moistened.

Preheat the oven to 350°F. Rub the fish on all sides with oil.

COAT THE FISH Spread 3 cups of the salt mixture on a baking sheet with sides, large enough to hold the fish. Place the fish on top. Mound the remaining salt mixture over the fish, covering it completely. Bake for 30 to 45 minutes for medium to medium-well done. The fish is done when the tip of a knife inserted in the thickest part feels warm to the touch when you remove it.

MAKE THE NAGE Meanwhile, in a large skillet, melt 2 tablespoons of the butter over medium heat. Add the onions and sauté until translucent, about 4 minutes. Add the endive and carrots and cook for 2 minutes more. Add the wine, lemon and orange juices, and saffron. Raise the heat to medium-high and boil 5 minutes, or until the liquid is reduced by about one-third.

With a slotted spoon, transfer the vegetables to a bowl. Whisk the remaining butter 1 or 2 tablespoons at a time into the liquid, just until melted. Season with salt and pepper.

1 orange, juiced

¼ teaspoon saffron threads

Fine sea salt and freshly ground black pepper to taste

2 tablespoons chopped fresh flat-leaf parsley

Return the vegetables to the pan and heat gently just until warm. Do not let the sauce boil or it may break.

TO SERVE With a knife and spoon, break the salt crust and remove it in sections. Lift the fish away from the bones and transfer it to serving plates. Serve with the nage, sprinkled with the parsley.

WINE SUGGESTION: RIESLING, "ESTATE," TREFETHEN VINEYARDS, 2004, NAPA VALLEY, CALIFORNIA. *A dry Riesling with citrus and floral notes and a light spiciness in the refreshing finish.*

Native Americans are said to have taught New England settlers how to make a clam bake. The tradition includes digging a pit on a sandy beach, lining it with stones, and building a fire. When the stones are hot, the pit is filled with seaweed, lobsters, clams, corn, potatoes, sausages, and other good things. The pit is covered with a tarp to keep the steam in and so the flavors can marry. | With this recipe, it's easy to make a clam bake in your own home. It's like a day at the beach! | SERVES 6

CLAM BAKE

2 handfuls of seaweed, available at the fish monger

6 ears fresh corn, shucked, cut into 3 pieces each

6 red potatoes, boiled just until fork tender, quartered

3 lobsters (1½ pounds each), cut in half lengthwise

24 topneck clams, soaked and scrubbed clean

6 bay leaves

1½ cups dry white wine

Melted butter, tartar sauce, lemon wedges, and Tabasco sauce, for serving

COOK Arrange the seaweed evenly across the bottom of a large lobster or canning pot. On top of the seaweed, place layers of the corn, potatoes, and lobster halves. Top with the clams and bay leaves. Pour the wine into the pot. Place the lid on the pot and cook over medium heat for 20 to 30 minutes.

TO SERVE When all of the clams have opened and the lobsters are fully cooked, remove the pot from the heat. Bring the pot to the table. Divide the seafood and vegetables equally among 6 large, shallow bowls. Spoon the liquid over the top and serve immediately. Pass bowls of melted butter and tartar sauce, lemon wedges, and a bottle of Tabasco.

CHEF'S TIP: *You can make a clam bake in individual portions on a barbecue grill. Divide all of the ingredients among 6 large sheets of heavy-duty foil. Seal the foil tightly. Cook on medium-high heat for 15 minutes.*

WINE SUGGESTION: SAUVIGNON BLANC, "HYDE VINEYARD," SELENE, 2004, CARNEROS, CALIFORNIA. *A refreshing white with bright citrus and mineral flavors and clean, crisp finish.*

Here is a quick, easy recipe that's ideal for after work or whenever time is short. Top the cooked fillets with diced lemon, parsley, and capers if you like. Black sea bass, red snapper, or skate are also good cooked this way. This is delicious with roasted potatoes or lemon mashed potatoes. | Curry powder is a blend of many spices and is made in different styles in different regions of India. Curry powder from Madras is moderately spicy and includes turmeric, coriander, cumin, chile, cloves, and fenugreek among its ingredients. | SERVES 6

STRIPED BASS | CURRY BROWN BUTTER

1 cup (2 sticks) unsalted butter

2 teaspoons Madras curry powder

¼ cup freshly squeezed lemon juice

1 teaspoon sugar

6 striped bass filets, 6 to 8 ounces each, with skin on

Fine sea salt and freshly ground black pepper to taste

6 tablespoons extra-virgin olive oil

PREHEAT THE OVEN to 350°F.

MAKE THE SAUCE Melt the butter over medium heat in a small saucepan. When it begins to foam, add the curry powder, stir well and cook until the butter is lightly browned. Stir in the lemon juice and sugar. Remove from the heat. Cover and keep warm.

COOK THE FISH Pat the fish dry with a paper towels. Sprinkle on both sides with salt and pepper.

Heat 2 large, ovenproof nonstick skillets on medium-high heat until a drop of water sizzles when sprinkled on the pan. Add 3 tablespoons of the oil to each pan.

Watch the oil carefully and, just when it begins to smoke, place 3 fillets skin-side down in each pan. Reduce the heat to medium and let the fish cook for 1 minute.

Place the pans in the oven for 6 to 8 minutes, according to the thickness of the fish. The fish is done when a toothpick can be inserted in the flesh without resistance.

TO SERVE Place a fillet of fish skin-side up on each plate and pour the curry butter on top.

WINE SUGGESTION: PINOT BLANC, LAETITIA, 2003, ARROYO GRANDE VALLEY, CALIFORNIA. *A rich, full-flavored white wine with grapefruit and lemon flavors, and integrated oak flavors.*

Crisp, smoky bacon forms the basis of a flavorful crust that is good on white fish fillets. Cod fish fillets are fragile and break easily when they are cooked. Lift them from the pan with a large metal spatula. Hake, a slim-bodied white fish similar to cod, can also be prepared this way. | Sometimes I finish this dish by adding a drizzle of lemon juice and olive oil to the pan juices to lift and enrich the flavor. | SERVES 6

ROASTED COD FISH | HERB-BACON CRUST

1 pound sliced bacon

1 cup Maître d'Hôtel Butter (page 201), softened

2 cups panko bread crumbs

1 cup fresh flat-leaf parsley leaves

Fine sea salt and freshly ground black pepper to tastea

6 skinless cod fillets, 5 ounces each

3 tablespoons unsalted butter

1 tablespoon olive oil

4 garlic cloves, sliced

8 sprigs fresh thyme

2 bay leaves

WINE SUGGESTION: NIEBAUM COPPOLA, "BLANCANEAUX," 2003, NAPA VALLEY, CALIFORNIA. *A savory white Rhône blend with pear and apricot fruit flavors and a smoky, nutty finish.*

PREPARE THE BACON Preheat the oven to 375°F. Line a baking sheet with sides with parchment paper and place strips of bacon on the parchment in a single layer. Bake for 8 to 10 minutes, or until the bacon is crisp. Remove the bacon to a paper towel–lined plate and let cool. Transfer the bacon to a cutting board and chop fine.

MAKE THE CRUST Combine the bacon, Maître d'Hôtel Butter, panko, parsley, and salt and pepper in a food processor. Process until blended.

Scrape the mixture onto a piece of waxed paper. Cover with another sheet and roll the crust out to a ⅛-inch thickness. Place it in the refrigerator for at least 1 hour or until firm.

SAUTÉ THE COD Season the cod with salt and pepper. Heat half of the butter, half of the oil, 2 of the garlic cloves, 4 sprigs of the thyme, and 1 bay leaf in a large sauté pan over medium heat. Place 3 fish fillets in the pan, skinned-side down, and cook for 2 to 3 minutes. Turn the fish over and cook for another 2 minutes, until slightly undercooked and opaque in the center. Leaving the garlic, thyme and bay leaf in the pan, remove the fish and place it skinned-side down on a baking sheet. Cook the remaining fish the same way. With a slotted spoon, remove the garlic and herbs. Keep the pan juices warm while browning the fish.

BROIL THE FISH Preheat the broiler. Cut out and place pieces of the bacon crust on top of the fish. Slide the baking sheet under the broiler and cook until the crust is golden brown, about 1 minute.

SERVE on warm plates, drizzled with the pan juices.

Mediterranean flavors of sherry wine vinegar, olive oil, honey, and thyme enhance the fish and eggplant in this dish. Red snapper and striped bass fillets are also good cooked this way. Long, narrow Japanese eggplants are my choice because they taste sweet and hold their shape well when they are cooked. | To carry the Mediterranean theme throughout the meal, precede this dish with an appetizer of Zucchini/Tomato/Onion/Ricotta Salata and Bread Salad (page 65). | SERVES 6

BAKED BLACK SEA BASS | TOMATO | EGGPLANT | HONEY | SHERRY VINEGAR

6 tablespoons extra-virgin olive oil

5 medium Japanese eggplants, cut into large dice

Fine sea salt and freshly ground black pepper to taste

1 large onion, cut into large dice

6 sprigs fresh thyme

1 bay leaf

3 tablespoons honey

¼ cup sherry vinegar

6 plum tomatoes, peeled, seeded, and diced

2 cups whole canned peeled tomatoes, roughly chopped

1 black sea bass, 4 to 5 pounds, cleaned and dressed

½ cup fresh cilantro leaves

COOK THE EGGPLANT Heat 3 tablespoons of the oil in a large skillet over medium-high heat. Season the eggplant with salt and pepper and sauté until well browned on all sides, about 5 minutes. Remove the eggplant from the pan and set aside.

MAKE THE SAUCE In the same skillet, heat 1 more tablespoon of the oil over medium heat. Add the onion, thyme, and bay leaf. Cook until the onion is tender, but not browned, about 5 minutes. Season with salt and pepper.

Add the honey and cook until the honey begins to bubble. Cook for 2 minutes. Add the vinegar and cook, stirring for 2 minutes more, or until the vinegar has almost evaporated. Add the eggplant and the fresh and canned tomatoes. Season with salt and pepper. Cook 10 to15 minutes over low heat, or until thick.
Remove the bay leaf and thyme.

Preheat the oven to 400°F. Oil a baking dish large enough to hold the fish in a single layer.

COOK THE FISH Season the fish on both sides with salt and pepper and place it in the prepared dish. Drizzle the fish with 1 more tablespoon of the olive oil. Bake for 30 to 35 minutes, or until the fish is cooked through.

TO SERVE Reheat the sauce if necessary and toss in the cilantro leaves. Spoon the sauce into the center of a large platter. Place the whole fish on top of the sauce, and drizzle with the remaining 1 tablespoon of the olive oil. Present the whole fish at the table and fillet it with a knife and fork.

WINE SUGGESTION: PINOT NOIR, LONDER, 2004, ANDERSON VALLEY, CALIFORNIA. *An exotic fruit-forward Pinot Noir with aromas of red cherries, sweet tomatoes, and raspberries.*

Capers are the unopened flower buds of the caper plant, which grows wild all over the Mediterranean. You can buy them both salted or pickled, but the salted ones have better flavor. Either type of caper should be rinsed well before using. | For this recipe, big, juicy shrimp rest on a bed of sweet browned cauliflower slices under a flavorful sauce of brown butter, soy sauce, herbs, and capers. Try this method for Dover sole, lobster, skate, or scallops. | SERVES 6

GRILLED SHRIMP | CAULIFLOWER | SOY-CAPER BROWN BUTTER SAUCE

12 cauliflower florets (2-inch)

8 tablespoons (1 stick) plus 2 tablespoons unsalted butter

Fine sea salt and freshly ground black pepper to taste

18 jumbo shrimp, peeled and deveined

1 tablespoon extra-virgin olive oil

¼ cup plus 2 tablespoons heavy cream

1 tablespoon chopped shallot

1½ teaspoons chopped garlic

3 tablespoons reduced-sodium (lite) soy sauce

3 tablespoons chopped capers

2 tablespoons freshly squeezed lemon juice

1 tablespoon chopped fresh tarragon leaves

1 teaspoon chopped fresh chives

1 teaspoon chopped fresh parsley leaves

COOK THE CAULIFLOWER Cut the cauliflower into ½-inch-thick slices. Heat a large sauté pan over medium heat and add 1 tablespoon of the butter. When the butter is foamy, arrange half of the cauliflower slices in the pan in a single layer. Season with salt and pepper. Cook on both sides until golden brown, 2 to 3 minutes per side. Set aside and keep warm. Repeat with another 1 tablespoon of the butter and the cauliflower.

GRILL THE SHRIMP Season the shrimp with salt, pepper, and the olive oil. Preheat a barbecue or stovetop grill to high heat. Add the shrimp in a single layer. Cook until browned and cooked through, about 2 minutes on each side.

MAKE THE SAUCE Put the cream and remaining 8 tablespoons of the butter in a sauté pan set over high heat. Cook until the butter is melted and browned, about 5 minutes. Stir in the shallot and garlic and cook for another 3 to 4 minutes, until tender. (The sauce can be made ahead to this point. Reheat gently.)

Just before serving, add the soy sauce, capers, lemon juice, tarragon, chives, and parsley.

TO SERVE Arrange the cauliflower slices overlapping slightly on 6 dinner plates. Place the shrimp on top. Drizzle with the sauce. Serve immediately.

WINE SUGGESTION: GEWÜRZTRAMINER, FORIS, 2003, WILLAMETTE VALLEY, OREGON. *An aromatic, dry Gewürztraminer with subtle fruit flavors of lychee and a spicy finish.*

Parchment or foil packages seal in the flavors of the fish, vegetables, and sauce as they cook. Let each guest open their own package, releasing the fragrant aromas. Salmon or flounder are also good cooked this way. | Risotto/Green Peas/Pancetta (page 89) would be a good first course. | SERVES 6

PAPILLOTE OF HALIBUT | CREAMY TOMATO-SORREL SAUCE

1 tablespoon olive oil, plus 6 teaspoons for drizzling over fish

4 shallots, finely chopped

2 garlic cloves, finely chopped

1 can (28 ounces) plum tomatoes, strained and chopped

Fine sea salt and freshly ground black pepper to taste

¼ cup heavy cream

6 sheets 20 x 12-inch parchment paper or foil

4 ounces fresh sorrel leaves, stems removed

6 halibut fillets, 7 to 8 ounces each

6 teaspoons dry white wine

1 egg white, lightly beaten, if using parchment paper

PREHEAT THE OVEN to 450°F.

MAKE THE SAUCE In a medium saucepan, heat 1 tablespoon of the olive oil over medium heat. Add the shallots and garlic and sauté until tender, about 4 minutes

Add the tomatoes and season with salt and pepper. Bring the sauce to a simmer and cook about 20 minutes, or until the sauce is chunky and nearly dry.

Stir in the heavy cream and cook the sauce for 2 minutes. Remove from the heat and let cool.

MAKE THE PAPILLOTES Lay the parchment paper or foil out flat on a countertop. Put 2 large spoonfuls of the prepared sauce in the center of each sheet. Arrange the sorrel leaves over the sauce.

Season the halibut on both sides with salt and pepper, and put 1 fillet on each piece of paper on top of the sorrel. Drizzle the fish with 1 teaspoon each of olive oil and wine.

Fold the long edges of the paper up around the fish until they meet. If using parchment paper, brush 1 outside edge with egg white as glue. Fold the paper over once to seal. Tie the ends with butcher twine. The finished package should look like a giant hard candy in its wrapper.

BAKE THE FISH Arrange the packets on 2 cookie sheets and bake until they begin to puff up, 9 to 10 minutes.

TO SERVE Place the fish in its packages on 6 dinner plates. Serve the fish in the packages. Carefully slit the paper and pull it open.

WINE SUGGESTION: SAUVIGNON BLANC, BRANDER, 2004, SANTA YNEZ VALLEY, CALIFORNIA. *A bright and crisp Sauvignon Blanc with aromas of fresh grapefruits, mango, and hints of spice.*

I created this recipe for *Bon Appétit* magazine's Culinary Classic at Beaver Creek, Colorado. It was judged the best dish in the entire cook-off. The combination of the Asian-accented flavors in the mushroom vinaigrette and the rich taste of the Artic char is sensational. | Sea Salt–Crusted Sunchokes (page 232) go well with this fish. | SERVES 6

SEARED ARCTIC CHAR | SHIITAKE-GINGER VINAIGRETTE

Shiitake-Ginger Vinaigrette

4 cups small shiitake mushrooms (1 pound), stems removed, caps sliced

3 tablespoons plus ½ cup extra-virgin olive oil

2 tablespoons chopped shallots

1 tablespoon chopped garlic

Fine sea salt and freshly ground black pepper to taste

1 cup dry white wine

1 cup chicken stock or low-sodium chicken broth

1 3-inch piece fresh ginger

2 tablespoons low sodium (lite) soy sauce

1 tablespoon roughly chopped fresh tarragon

1 tablespoon roughly chopped fresh cilantro

2 tablespoons extra-virgin olive oil

6 skinless Artic char fillets, 7 ounces each

COOK THE MUSHROOMS In a large skillet, heat 3 tablespoons of the olive oil over medium heat. Add the mushrooms and sauté until softened. Add the shallots and garlic, and season with salt and pepper. Cook until the mushrooms are golden brown, about 4 minutes.

Add the wine, bring to a boil, and cook for 2 minutes. Add the stock and reduce to 1/3 cup liquid. Remove from the heat and allow to cool to room temperature.

MAKE THE VINAIGRETTE Grate the ginger into a kitchen towel and squeeze the towel to extract the juice into a small bowl. You will need 3 tablespoons juice.

Add the soy sauce to the bowl. Whisk in the remaining ½ cup of the olive oil until blended. Stir in the tarragon and cilantro. Add the mushrooms and season with salt and pepper.

COOK THE FISH In a large skillet, heat the 2 tablespoons olive oil. Season the fish with salt and pepper. Sear the fish in batches until warm and opaque in the center, 2 to 3 minutes on each side.

TO SERVE Spoon the vinaigrette and mushrooms onto a large warm platter and top with the fish.

WINE SUGGESTION: PINOT NOIR, "BELLE PENTE VINEYARD," BELLE PENTE WINERY, 2003, WILLAMETTE VALLEY, OREGON. *A spicy, earthy Pinot Noir with notes of fresh picked cherries, raspberries, and smoke.*

Tomatillos are relatives of the tomato family and are frequently used in Mexico, where they are also known as *tomates verdes* because they are eaten while they are still green. Tomatillos have a thin papery husk and a tart flavor. | In this recipe, the refreshing tomatillo sauce is excellent with sweet grilled scallops, but you will find many uses for it, such as on lobster, bass, and shellfish. In fact, it is great on any grilled fish. | I like to serve this with Grilled Corn/Herb Butter (page 217). | SERVES 6

GRILLED SCALLOPS | MEXICAN TOMATILLO SALSA

6 large tomatillos, husks removed

1 small red onion, roughly diced

2 fresh Thai chile peppers, finely chopped

5 tablespoons extra-virgin olive oil

2 tablespoons chopped fresh cilantro

Fine sea salt and freshly ground black pepper to taste

18 large sea scallops

Fresh cilantro sprigs, for garnish

MAKE THE SAUCE Cut the tomatillos into quarters and scrape out the seeds. In a food processor, combine the tomatillos, onion, and chiles. Pulse the blender several times until the sauce is coarsely chopped. Pour the sauce into a bowl and add 3 tablespoons of the oil and the cilantro. Season with salt and pepper and set aside.

COOK THE SCALLOPS Add the remaining 2 tablespoons of the oil to a large grill pan over medium-high heat. Season the scallops with salt and pepper. Add the scallops to the pan and cook for 1 minute. With a metal spatula or pancake turner, rotate the scallops a quarter turn. Cook 1 more minute. Flip the scallops over and repeat the process. Test for doneness by cutting into a scallop. It should be just slightly translucent in the center.

TO SERVE Spoon the sauce into the center of 6 shallow bowls. Arrange 3 scallops on top of each. Garnish with a sprig of cilantro.

WINE SUGGESTION: PINOT GRIS, "VITAE SPRINGS VINEYARD," ST. INNOCENT, 2004, WILLAMETTE VALLEY, OREGON. *A dry Pinot Gris with ripe fruit and orange rind flavors, and a racy, spicy finish.*

D_aurade_ is a kind of sea bream that is similar to the porgy or scup found in America. Sea bass or red snapper can also be cooked this way. | The fish are seasoned with _herbes de Provence,_ a blend of dried herbs typically used in southern France that may include lavender, fennel, savory, rosemary, thyme, basil, tarragon, and marjoram. You can make your own blend or purchase it ready-made. | Poached Artichoke/Goat Cheese/Tapenade (page 22) would be a good starter with this dish. Serve Spring Morel/Vegetable Ragôut (page 226) with the fish. | SERVES 6

HERBES DE PROVENCE–CRUSTED DAURADE

1 cup (8 ounces) unsalted butter, softened

2 cups panko bread crumbs, ground

½ small Vidalia onion, minced

1 ounce _herbes de Provence_

Fine sea salt and freshly ground pepper

3 whole daurade, 1½ pounds each, cleaned and scaled

2 tablespoons canola oil

WINE SUGGESTION: CHATEAU PRADEAUX, 2005, BANDOL, FRANCE. _A rosé from the south of France, made predominantly from the spicy and bold Cinsault grape. Pure and fresh with vibrant red cherry and strawberry, but laced with undertones of pepper and herbs._

MAKE THE CRUST In a medium bowl, combine the softened butter, panko, onion, and _herbes de Provence,_ plus salt and pepper to taste. Spread the mixture between two pieces of parchment paper and, using a rolling pin, roll until the crust is ¼-inch thick. Cut the crust and parchment together into three equally sized strips and then refrigerate them, without removing the paper.

Preheat the oven to 450°F.

COOK THE FISH Heat a large sauté pan over medium-high heat. Season the daurade with salt and pepper. Pour the canola oil into the pan. When the oil begins to smoke, add one fish to the pan. Sear for one to two minutes, until the skin turns brown, then flip the fish over and sear two minutes more. Remove the daurade from the pan to a half-sheet tray or cookie sheet and repeat with the other two fish. When all of the fish have been seared, place them on the sheet in the oven and bake for 5 minutes or until the fish is just slightly opaque when cut near the bone.

BROWN THE CRUST Remove the daurade from the oven and turn on the broiler.

Peel off one layer of paper from each strip of crust. Invert the crust onto the fish and remove the remaining paper. Place the tray of fish under the broiler and cook three to four minutes or until the crust is golden brown. With a large spatula, slide the fish onto a large serving platter and serve immediately.

CHAPTER SIX

MEAT AND POULTRY

My secret burger sauce has a French twist. Green peppercorns, cracked black pepper, and Cognac give it heat and extra flavor. For tender, juicy burgers, use ground beef that has at least 20 percent fat and handle the meat as gently as possible. | Rosemary-Parmesan French Fries (page 230) are perfect with a burger. | SERVES 6

AMERICAN KOBE BURGER | AU POIVRE SAUCE

Sauce

5 tablespoons brined green peppercorns, drained and rinsed

1 tablespoon Cognac

½ cup BLT Steak Sauce (page 204)

½ cup ketchup

½ cup mayonnaise

1 tablespoon cracked black pepper

1 tablespoon fine sea salt

Burgers

2 pounds ground Kobe beef

Coarse sea salt to taste

Cracked black pepper to taste

6 slices sharp Cheddar cheese

6 burger buns with sesame seeds, split

1 red onion, thinly sliced

2 vine-ripe tomatoes, sliced into ¼-inch slices

6 leaves romaine lettuce, ribs removed

MAKE THE SAUCE In a small skillet over medium heat, sauté the green peppercorns until fragrant, 10 to 20 seconds. Add the Cognac and swirl the pan over the heat until the liquid evaporates. Remove the peppercorns from the pan and chop them coarsely. Combine the peppercorns with the remaining sauce ingredients and stir until well blended.

COOK THE BURGERS Season the meat with salt and pepper. Blend well, making sure not to overwork the meat or the burgers will be tough. Gently form the meat into six 6-ounce burgers.

Heat a grill pan over medium-high heat until a drop of water sizzles when flicked on the pan. Grill the burgers for 3 minutes on each side for medium-rare. Do not push down on the burgers while they cook, as this will cause the juices to run out. Place a slice of cheese on top of each burger and cook until slightly melted, about 30 seconds more.

ASSEMBLE THE BURGERS Place the burgers on the bottom halves of the buns. Top with the onion, tomato, and lettuce. Spread the sauce on the top halves of the buns. Serve immediately.

WINE SUGGESTION: ZINFANDEL, D-CUBED, 2003, HOWELL MOUNTAIN, CALIFORNIA. *A juicy, spicy red with aromas of blackberries, anise, and white pepper.*

Smoked salt and pepper give these steaks added flavor. Kobe rib-eye is ideal cooked this way. You can buy smoked salt and pepper at many gourmet shops, but if you have a stovetop smoker, it's easy to make them at home; see Techniques, page 272. | These steaks are great with good mustard or the BLT Steak Sauce (page 204). Accompany them with Creamy Home Fries (page 229), Pan-Seared Hen of the Woods Mushrooms (page 223), or Creamed Spinach (page 210).

| SERVES 6

SMOKED SEA SALT AND BLACK PEPPER–CRUSTED RIB-EYE

3 rib-eye steaks (preferably dry-aged), 30 to 40 ounces each, about 2 inches thick

1 cup Liquid Smoke

4 tablespoons (½ stick) unsalted butter, softened

2 tablespoons Smoked Maldon Sea Salt (see page 272)

2 tablespoons smoked black pepper (see page 272)

MARINATE THE STEAKS With a fork, pierce the steaks all over on both sides. Place the steaks in a shallow dish and pour on the Liquid Smoke. Cover and refrigerate for 48 hours, turning the steaks once.

SEASON THE STEAKS Remove the steaks from the liquid. Do not pat dry. Brush on the butter. Season both sides with the smoked salt and pepper.

GRILL THE STEAK Preheat a barbecue grill or stovetop grill to medium heat.

Cook the steaks, 7 to 10 minutes on each side, until medium-rare. To check for doneness, insert an instant-read thermometer in the thickest part of the meat. The temperature reading should be 130 to135°F for medium-rare. See the chart on page 9 for other cooking temperatures.

TO SERVE Transfer the steaks to a cutting board. Allow to rest 10 to 12 minutes. Cut into 1-inch-thick slices.

WINE SUGGESTION: SYRAH, "CUVÉE D'HONNEUR," NEYERS, 2002, CARNEROS, CALIFORNIA. *A spicy and smoky Syrah with aromas of black cherries, sweet spices like cinnamon and nutmeg, and black pepper.*

*S*oubise is a classic French sauce made with onions. I like to make both a white and dark soubise and serve them on the side of grilled porterhouse steaks. You can also pour the white soubise on top of the sliced meat and run it under the broiler for a minute until the sauce is golden brown on top. | Serve with Creamed Spinach (page 210) and Stuffed Mushroom Caps (page 228). | SERVES 6

PORTERHOUSE | WHITE AND DARK SOUBISE

White Onion Soubise

1 tablespoon extra-virgin olive oil

2 large white onions, sliced thin

1 recipe Béchamel Sauce (page 210)

Freshly grated nutmeg to taste

Fine sea salt and freshly ground black pepper to taste

Dark Onion Soubise

1 tablespoon extra-virgin olive oil

2 large white onions, sliced thin

1 tablespoon sugar

1 cup beef stock or low-sodium beef broth

½ cup BLT Barbecue Sauce (page 195), or store-bought

3 beef porterhouse steaks, 40 ounces each, about 2 inches thick (preferably dry-aged)

4 tablespoons (½ stick) unsalted butter, softened

MAKE THE WHITE SOUBISE In a medium skillet, heat the oil over medium heat. Add the onions and cook until soft, making sure they do not color. Stir in the béchamel, and grated nutmeg, salt, and pepper. Keep warm.

MAKE THE DARK SOUBISE In a medium skillet, heat the oil over medium heat. Add the onions and sugar. Cook, stirring constantly, until the onions are caramelized, about 15 minutes. Regulate the heat so that they do not burn.

Add the beef stock and bring to a simmer. Cook until most of the liquid has evaporated. Add the barbecue sauce and simmer until thickened. Season with salt and pepper. Keep warm.

COOK THE STEAKS Brush the steaks with the butter on both sides.

Sprinkle with the salt and pepper.

Preheat a barbecue or stovetop grill to medium heat. Cook the steaks 8 to 10 minutes on each side for medium-rare. To check for doneness, make a small cut near the bone or better yet, insert an instant-read thermometer in the thickest part of the meat. The temperature reading should be 130 to 135°F for medium-rare. See the chart on page 9 for other cooking temperatures.

TO SERVE Transfer the steaks to a cutting board and cover loosely with aluminum foil. Let stand 10 to 12 minutes. Cut the meat away from the bones. Carve the meat into 1-inch-thick slices. Arrange the meat on a platter. Serve with the white and dark soubise sauces on the side.

WINE SUGGESTION: CABERNET SAUVIGNON, SEQUOIA GROVE, 2002, NAPA VALLEY, CALIFORNIA. *A soft and juicy Cabernet with notes of sweet blackberries, plums, and a touch of spice cabinet.*

The great operatic composer Giocchino Rossini was a renowned gourmet. He particularly loved foie gras and invented many recipes using it. This is my version of one of his most famous creations. | Shaved truffles on top are an elegant touch, but you can leave them out. Try substituting three tablespoons of pâté de foie gras for the foie scraps in the sauce for better flavor. | A simple starter such as Leeks Vinaigrette/Fourme d'Ambert (page 19), would be ideal since this dish has several components. | SERVES 6

FILET AND FOIE GRAS ROSSINI

1½ cups Madeira wine

1½ cups ruby port, such as Warre's Warrior

4 cups veal stock, or 2 cups chicken broth plus 2 cups beef broth

1 fresh Grade A foie gras (see Sources, page 275)

5 tablespoons unsalted butter

6 slices (¾ inch thick) French or Italian country bread

3 filet mignon steaks, 12 ounces each, about 2½ inches thick

Fine sea salt and freshly ground black pepper to taste

2 tablespoons brandy

Truffle oil (optional)

MAKE THE WINE REDUCTION In a medium saucepan, combine the Madeira and port. Bring to a simmer over medium heat. Cook until thick and syrupy and reduced to about ¼ cup. Add the stock and reduce to about 1 cup liquid, about 30 minutes more. Set aside.

PREPARE THE FOIE GRAS With a small sharp knife, divide the foie gras into the 2 natural lobes. Wrap the smaller lobe tightly in foil and refrigerate or freeze it for another use. (Foie gras can be frozen for at least 3 months.)

Slice the larger lobe crosswise into 6 slices. Trim the edges so that the slices will fit on top of the bread. Reserve the trimmings for the sauce.

Preheat the oven 350°F.

BROWN THE BREAD In a large skillet over medium heat, melt 3 tablespoons of the butter. Add the bread slices and cook until browned, 2 to 3 minutes on each side.

COOK THE FILETS Sprinkle the steaks on both sides with salt and pepper. Heat a grill pan or ovenproof skillet over medium-high heat until a drop of water flicked onto the surface sizzles rapidly. Add the filets and brown on both sides, about 2 minutes per side. Transfer the pan to the oven and roast the meat to the desired temperature, about 25 minutes for rare. To check for doneness, insert an instant-read thermometer in the thickest part of the meat. The temperature reading should be 130 to 135°F for medium-rare. See the chart on page 9 for other cooking temperatures.

Remove the steaks to a platter and cover loosely with aluminum foil. Let stand 10 to 12 minutes.

MAKE THE SAUCE Pour the hot reduction mixture into a food processor or blender. With the machine running, add the foie gras scraps a few pieces at a time, until blended and smooth.

Pour the sauce into a saucepan and place it over low heat. Whisk in the remaining 2 tablespoons of the butter and the brandy. Do not allow the sauce to become too hot or it will break.

COOK THE FOIE GRAS While the steaks are resting, return the pan to high heat on top of the stove. Sprinkle the foie gras slices with salt and pepper.

Place 3 of the slices in the very hot pan and cook until browned on 1 side, about 2 minutes. Turn the slices and reduce the heat to medium. Cook until the foie gras is slightly resistant when pressed in the center, 2 to 3 minutes more. Cover loosely with foil and keep warm. Repeat with the remaining foie gras.

TO ASSEMBLE Place a crouton on each dinner plate. Cut each steak into 4 slices. Arrange the slices on the croutons. Top with slice of foie gras. Spoon the sauce over all and drizzle with a few drops of truffle oil, if using.

Serve immediately.

CHEF'S TIP: *To trim the foie gras, carefully cut out any large veins and connective tissues. Ask the butcher to trim the foie gras for you if you have never done it before.*

WINE SUGGESTION: PINOT NOIR, HIRSCH VINEYARDS, 2003, SONOMA COAST, CALIFORNIA. *A full-bodied Pinot Noir with notes of black cherry, berry cobbler, and star anise*

Asian seasonings make a flavorful dressing for tender beef steaks. | I sometimes serve this steak in place of the chicken in the Chinese Chicken Salad (page 49). Flank steak can be substituted for skirt steaks. These are great on an outdoor grill. | Start the meal with Heirloom Tomato Salad/Grilled Onion Vinaigrette (page 57) and serve the steak with Fried Onion Rings (page 212), or Rosemary-Parmesan French Fries (page 230). | SERVES 6

MARINATED KOBE SKIRT STEAK

Marinade

1 cup low-sodium (lite) soy sauce

½ cup toasted sesame oil

½ cup grapeseed oil

½ cup chopped lemongrass

½ cup chopped fresh cilantro

3 tablespoons chopped peeled fresh ginger

2 tablespoons chopped garlic

2 tablespoons chopped carrot

2 tablespoons chopped celery

1 tablespoon honey

6 Kobe skirt steaks, 8 ounces each

6 tablespoons chopped unsalted roasted peanuts

MAKE THE MARINADE In a large bowl, mix together all of the marinade ingredients. Set aside 3 tablespoons of the marinade.

MARINATE THE STEAKS Arrange the steaks in a shallow dish. Pour on the marinade. Cover and refrigerate 2 hours.

COOK THE STEAKS Preheat a barbecue or stovetop grill to medium heat. Drain the steaks. Grill about 3 minutes per side, until medium-rare. To check for doneness, insert an instant-read thermometer in the thickest part of the meat. The temperature reading should be 130 to 135°F for medium-rare. See the chart on page 9 for other cooking temperatures.

Transfer to a cutting board and let rest for 5 minutes.

TO SERVE Carve the steaks into 1-inch slices crosswise against the grain. Arrange the slices overlapping slightly on a platter. Drizzle the steaks with the reserved marinade and sprinkle with the peanuts.

WINE SUGGESTION: PINOT NOIR, TALLEY VINEYARDS, 2003, ARROYO GRANDE, CALIFORNIA. *A fruit-forward, juicy Pinot Noir with notes of bright red fruits and a touch of oak.*

I like these steaks best when they are grilled outdoors over hickory wood, but they also can be cooked indoors. See the Chef's Tip below for an alternate method of cooking them. Steaks on the bone are much more flavorful than boneless, plus you have the bones to nibble on afterward. | The red wine, bacon, and mushroom sauce is delicious, but the steaks are also good with a pat of Maître d'Hôtel Butter (page 201) melted on top. | Spinach and Bacon Salad/Caesar Dressing (page 63) would make a good appetizer. | SERVES 6

GRILLED BLT DOUBLE-CUT STRIP STEAK

2 bottles (750 milliliters each) hearty, full-bodied red wine

8 ounces applewood-smoked bacon, cut into ½-inch strips (about 2 cups)

2 cups ½-inch dice Vidalia onions

2 cups quartered button mushrooms

2 tablespoons finely chopped garlic

12 tablespoons (1½ sticks) unsalted butter

2 cups cherry tomatoes, halved

1 cup watercress, tough stems removed

1 cup fresh parsley leaves, roughly chopped

Fine sea salt and freshly ground black pepper to taste

3 bone-in strip steaks, 32 ounces each, about 3 inches thick

MAKE THE SAUCE In a medium saucepan, simmer the wine over medium heat for 25 to 30 minutes, or until it is reduced to 2 cups.

In a large skillet, sauté the bacon over medium heat until the fat has been rendered, 5 to 6 minutes. Spoon off the fat. Add the onions, mushrooms, and garlic and cook for 3 to 4 minutes, or until soft.

Add the wine mixture to the bacon and slowly whisk in 8 tablespoons of the butter 1 tablespoon at a time, until the sauce is emulsified. Remove from the heat. Add the tomatoes, watercress, and parsley. Cover and keep warm. Taste and adjust the seasoning with salt and pepper if necessary.

COOK THE STEAKS Preheat a barbecue or stovetop grill to medium heat.

Spread the steaks with the remaining 4 tablespoons of the butter. Season them on both sides with salt and pepper. Place the steaks on the grill and cook until browned, about 3 minutes. Turn the steaks and brown on the other side, about 3 minutes more. Transfer the steaks to a cooler part of the grill. Cover and cook for 20 to 25 minutes more for medium-rare. To check for doneness, make a small cut near the bone or better yet, insert an instant-read thermometer in the thickest part of the meat. The temperature reading should be 130 to 135°F for medium-rare. See the chart on page 9 for other cooking temperatures.

TO SERVE Place the steaks on a cutting board and cover loosely with foil. Let rest for 10 to 12 minutes.

Carve the meat off the bone. Cut the steaks crosswise into 1-inch slices. Arrange the slices on 6 plates and serve the sauce on the side. Serve immediately.

CHEF'S TIP: *You can also cook these steaks on your home stove with a combination method that involves pan searing and roasting. To do this, preheat a large skillet, preferably cast iron, until it is very hot and coat the bottom lightly with oil. Add the steaks and cook them until nicely browned, about 2 minutes on each side. Then transfer the steaks to a preheated 350°F oven and cook them until rare to medium-rare, 17 to 20 minutes.*

WINE SUGGESTION: DELILLE CELLARS, "D2," 2002, YAKIMA VALLEY, WASHINGTON. *A big, juicy Bordeaux-style blend with aromas of currants, cherries, exotic spices, and fleshy tannins.*

I borrowed ingredients from several different cultures to create this spicy, citrusy, and full-flavored marinade for beefy hanger steaks. Adobo is a blend of spices that originated in Spain. The word comes from *adobar,* meaning "to stew." | Harissa is a fiery paste of garlic, chiles, and oil typical of North African cooking. Yuzu is a Japanese citrus fruit with a yellow to orange color. Fresh yuzu are not often found in the United States, but you can purchase bottled yuzu juice (see Sources, page 274), or substitute some fresh lime or lemon juice. | Serve with Stuffed Jalapeños (page 214) or Fried Onion Rings (page 212). | SERVES 6

ADOBO-MARINATED HANGER STEAK

Adobo Marinade

1½ cups grapeseed oil

6 tablespoons ancho chile powder

¼ cup chopped shallots

¼ cup chopped fresh thyme

¼ cup chopped fresh oregano

3 tablespoons hot paprika

3 tablespoons rice wine vinegar

2 tablespoons chopped garlic

2 tablespoons harrisa paste

2 tablespoons toasted whole cumin seeds

6 hanger steaks, 10 ounces each

Sauce

1 tablespoon yuzu juice (if not available use an additional ½ tablespoon lime juice)

½ tablespoon freshly squeezed lime juice

2 tablespoons chopped fresh oregano

Fine sea salt to taste

MAKE THE MARINADE Combine the marinade ingredients in a blender. Puree until smooth.

MARINATE THE STEAKS Place the steaks in a shallow glass or ceramic baking dish. Add half of the marinade. Cover and refrigerate the steaks and remaining marinade overnight.

MAKE THE SAUCE Drain about 4 tablespoons of the oil off the remaining marinade into a small bowl. Add the yuzu juice and lime juice and mix thoroughly. Add the oregano. Season with salt. (Cover the remaining sauce and refrigerate it up to 3 days.)

COOK THE STEAKS Preheat a barbecue or stovetop grill to medium-high heat. Remove the steaks from the marinade and pat dry. Add the steaks and cook for 6 to 8 minutes, turning once, or until medium-rare. The temperature reading should be 130 to 135°F for medium-rare. See the chart on page 9 for other cooking temperatures.

TO SERVE Remove the steaks from the grill and allow them to rest for 10 minutes. Cut crosswise into ½-inch slices. Spoon about 1 tablespoon of the adobo sauce on each steak.

WINE SUGGESTION: ZINFANDEL, "MONGA," CAROL SHELTON, 2001, CUCAMONGA VALLEY, CALIFORNIA. *A jammy, juicy, and spicy Zinfandel.*

Beef brisket smoked and slow cooked in barbecue sauce turns out so tender you can cut it with a fork. Plan to smoke the meat one day, and then bake it the next day, since the total amount of time required, mostly unattended, is about fourteen hours. Either an indoor or outdoor smoker can be used with excellent results. | Serve with Grilled Corn/Herb Butter (page 217), or Fried Onion Rings (page 212). | SERVES 8 TO 10

BARBECUED BEEF BRISKET

Dry Rub

6 tablespoons chili powder

3 tablespoons paprika

2 tablespoons dried oregano

2 tablespoons garlic powder

1½ teaspoons freshly ground black pepper

1½ teaspoons sugar

1½ teaspoons dry mustard

1½ teaspoons ground cloves

1½ teaspoons celery seed

1½ teaspoons fine sea salt

½ teaspoon cayenne

5½ pounds beef brisket, trimmed

4 cups hickory or mesquite chips, soaked and drained

4 cups BLT Barbecue Sauce (page 195), or store-bought

BEER SUGGESTION: SHINER BOCK, SPOETZL BREWERY, SHINER, TEXAS. *A full-flavored beer from Texas with aromas of malt, caramel, and a slight hint of hops.*

MAKE THE DRY RUB In a bowl, mix together all of the dry rub ingredients. Place the meat in a roasting pan and rub on all sides with the mixture. Cover and refrigerate at least 4 hours.

SMOKE THE BRISKET In the bottom of a stove-top smoker, arrange the hickory or mesquite chips, mounding them slightly in the center. Place the pan and rack on top, and place the brisket on top of the rack. Cover tightly with the lid and place over low heat for 4 hours. For an outdoor smoker, follow the manufacturer's directions.

Preheat the oven to 325° F.

ROAST THE BRISKET Place the brisket in a large roasting pan. Pour the barbecue sauce on top of the meat. Pour 2 cups of water into the pan around the meat. Cover with aluminum foil, making a tent so that it does not touch the meat. Cook for 5 to 6 hours, basting occasionally, until the brisket is tender when pierced with a fork at the thickest part.

TO SERVE Cut the brisket into thin slices and serve hot.

CHEF'S TIP: *The type of wood chips you add to the barbecue will make a big difference in the flavor of the meat. Hickory is the most popular wood. It has a pungent aroma typical of Southern cooking. Mesquite, typical of Southwestern cooking, has a sweeter and more delicate aroma. The more chips you use, the more pronounced will be their flavor in the meat. Soak wood chips in water for about 30 minutes before using.*

Though it takes a while to cook these short ribs, most of the cooking is unattended, so you can do other things. It is a perfect Sunday project and you can even stop and start the steps over a day or two or make it ahead and reheat it. | Just be sure you have a big enough pot. A big, deep roasting pan, such as a turkey roaster, works great. My mom makes this dish a lot and she likes to add white mushrooms and fingerling potatoes to the simmering sauce about 45 minutes before the end of the cooking. | I like to serve these with Creamy Rosemary-Parmesan Gnocchi (page 84) or garlic mashed potatoes. | SERVES 6

BRAISED SHORT RIBS | GARLIC-THYME BROWN BUTTER

Bouquet Garni

1 thick slice bacon

2 sprigs fresh rosemary

6 sprigs fresh thyme

2 bay leaves

2 celery stalks, trimmed

Ribs

6 beef short ribs, about 9 pounds

Fine sea salt and freshly ground black pepper to taste

¼ cup vegetable oil

3 carrots, peeled and cut into 1-inch pieces

1 large onion, cut into 1-inch pieces

15 garlic cloves, halved and peeled

6 large shallots, peeled and chopped

15 black peppercorns, cracked

¼ cup tomato paste

¼ cup all-purpose flour

2 bottles (750 milliliters each) dry red wine, such as Cabernet Sauvignon

4 cups ruby port

5 cups beef stock or low-sodium beef broth

MAKE THE BOUQUET GARNI Lay the bacon strip on a flat surface. Arrange the rosemary, thyme, bay leaf, and celery on one end of the bacon strip. Roll up the bacon. Tie the bouquet garni with kitchen string.

BROWN THE RIBS AND VEGETABLES Sprinkle the ribs with salt and pepper. Heat the oil in a very large Dutch oven over medium-high heat. Add as many ribs as will fit comfortably in the pot and brown them nicely on all sides, about 10 minutes. Remove the ribs to a plate. Repeat with the remaining ribs. Remove all but ½ cup of the fat from the pan.

Add the carrots, onion, garlic, shallots, and black peppercorns to the pan. Cook, stirring often, until golden brown, about 10 minutes.

Stir in the tomato paste and cook, stirring often, for 2 minutes. Add the flour and stir until blended. Add the bouquet garni, wine, and port. Bring to a boil and cook until the liquid is reduced by two-thirds, about 45 minutes.

Preheat the oven to 350°F.

COOK THE RIBS Return the ribs to the pot. Add the stock and tomatoes and bring the mixture to a simmer. Cover the pot loosely with foil and place it in the oven. Bake for 3½ hours, or until the meat is tender when pierced with a fork.

MAKE THE SAUCE Remove the ribs from the pot. Strain the cooking liquid through a sieve into a clean pot. Discard the solids. Bring the liquid to a simmer and cook until reduced to 1 quart, or until the sauce is thick, rich and glossy, about 1 hour.

6 cups chicken stock or low-sodium chicken broth

5 large (about 1 pound) plum tomatoes, halved

Garlic-Thyme Brown Butter

3 tablespoons unsalted butter

1 tablespoon chopped garlic

2 teaspoons chopped fresh thyme leaves

Taste for seasoning. Return the ribs to the pot and reheat.

MAKE THE BUTTER In a small saucepan, cook the butter and garlic over medium heat, swirling the pan until the garlic is golden brown. Stir in the thyme.

TO SERVE Transfer the ribs and sauce to a serving dish. Drizzle with the butter. Serve hot.

WINE SUGGESTION: PETITE SYRAH, "THOMANN STATION," STEPHEN ROSS, 2002, NAPA VALLEY, CALIFORNIA. *A full-figured Petite Syrah with loads of jammy black fruits, spices, and violets.*

Tapenade, a paste of pureed black olives and other flavorful ingredients, is a typical seasoning for lamb in the Provence region of Southern France. You can buy it ready made, or make it yourself (page 22). This lamb is also good made with a paste of marinated sun-dried tomatoes instead of the tapenade. | Serve the lamb with Oregano-Breaded Tomatoes (page 220). | SERVES 6

TAPENADE-STUFFED LEG OF LAMB

3 to 4 pounds boneless leg of lamb

¼ cup tapenade

3 garlic cloves, sliced

2 tablespoons chopped fresh rosemary leaves

Fine sea salt and freshly ground black pepper to taste

PREHEAT THE OVEN to 350°F. Oil a roasting pan just large enough to hold the lamb. Place a rack in the pan.

STUFF THE LAMB Unroll the lamb and spread the boned-out side with the tapenade. Roll up the lamb tightly. Tie it at 2-inch intervals with kitchen twine. With a small, sharp knife, cut slits 2 or 3 inches apart in the top of the roast. Push the garlic slices into the slits. Sprinkle the roast all over with the rosemary, salt, and pepper.

ROAST THE LAMB for about 1 hour and 15 minutes. To check for doneness, insert an instant-read thermometer in the thickest part of the meat. For medium-rare, the temperature should be 140 to 150°F.

Cover loosely with foil and let the meat rest for at least 30 minutes before slicing.

TO SERVE Cut into thin slices.

WINE SUGGESTION: MOURVEDRE, "THE GRAOSTA," GARRETSON WINE COMPANY, 2003, PASO ROBLES, CALIFORNIA. *A wine made from the great grape of Provence—Mourvedre—with aromas of dark cherries, cloves, and earth.*

Rack of lamb makes any meal a celebration. It can be grilled on a barbecue grill and the crust finished in the oven. Blanching the parsley leaves sets the color and removes any bitterness. | The Spring Morel and Vegetable Ragoût (page 226) would be ideal with this lamb. | SERVES 6

HERB-CRUSTED RACK OF LAMB

½ cup packed fresh curly parsley leaves

4 cups panko bread crumbs

½ cup chopped fresh chives

¼ cup pine nuts, toasted and ground

¼ cup grated Parmigiano-Reggiano cheese

Fine sea salt and freshly ground black pepper to taste

1½ cups (3 sticks) unsalted butter, cut into ½-inch pieces

3 racks of lamb, well trimmed and bones frenched

¼ cup olive oil

WINE SUGGESTION: CABERNET SAUVIGNON, "SLV," ROBERT MONDAVI, 2000, STAGS LEAP DISTRICT, CALIFORNIA. *A classic-style Cabernet Sauvignon from California with notes of blackberry, cassis, violets, and dark chocolate.*

PREPARE THE CRUST Bring a small pot of salted water to boiling. Add the parsley leaves. Drain immediately. Place the leaves in a bowl of ice water. Drain and squeeze out the excess water.

Place the panko in a food processor or blender and process until finely ground. Pour the crumbs into a bowl.

Place the parsley, chives, pine nuts, cheese, and a pinch of salt and pepper in the processor. Chop very finely to form a paste. Add the butter a little at a time, being careful not to overmix it or it will begin to melt.

Transfer the mixture to the bowl and gradually blend in the bread crumbs with a rubber spatula. Scrape the mixture onto a piece of parchment or plastic wrap and top it with another piece. Using a rolling pin, roll the mixture out to a ⅛-inch thickness. Place it in the refrigerator and chill until firm.

PREHEAT THE OVEN to 450°F.

BROWN THE LAMB Season the lamb all over with salt and pepper. Heat the oil in 1 or 2 skillets large enough to hold the lamb. Add the lamb racks fat-side down. Cook until they begin to brown, about 5 minutes.

ROAST THE LAMB Place the lamb racks in the oven bone-side up. Roast 7 minutes. Turn the racks bone-side down and cook the meat for 10 to 15 minutes more for medium-rare. To check for doneness, make a small cut near the bone or better yet, insert an instant-read thermometer in the thickest part of the meat. For medium-rare, the temperature should be 140 to 150°F. Remove the lamb from the oven. Turn on the broiler. Let the lamb rest 5 minutes in a warm place. Transfer the racks to a roasting pan bone-side down.

Unwrap the bread crumb mixture and cut it to fit the meat. Place the crust on top of each rack. Run the meat under the broiler briefly until the crust is lightly toasted, 1 or 2 minutes. Watch it carefully.

TO SERVE Carve the racks and serve immediately.

A tagine is the name of both a Moroccan-style stew and the glazed clay pot with a conical lid in which it is cooked. Tagines can be made with meat, poultry, or seafood mixed with vegetables or fruits and sweet spices. They are typically served from a communal bowl set in the middle of the table. | Chicken is good cooked this way, too. Serve the tagine with couscous and chickpeas. | Serve a starter of Leeks Vinaigrette/Fourme d'Ambert (page 19) and accompany the tagine with plain couscous. | SERVES 6

LEMON-CORIANDER LAMB TAGINE

Spice Bundle

7 green cardamom pods

2 star anise

2 pinches crushed red pepper flakes

Tagine

1 tablespoon coriander seeds

1 tablespoon cumin seeds

4 pounds boneless lamb, preferably neck and breast, trimmed of excess fat and cut into 2-inch cubes

Fine sea salt and freshly ground black pepper to taste

⅓ cup olive oil

2 whole heads garlic, skin left on and cut in half crosswise

4 carrots, cut into ¾-inch pieces

4 celery stalks, cut into ½-inch pieces

2 medium onions, halved and cut into ¾-inch dice

1 cup red wine vinegar

⅓ cup all-purpose flour

5 cups chicken stock or low-sodium chicken broth

3 cups water

PREPARE THE SPICE BUNDLE On a small square of cheesecloth, combine the cardamom seeds, star anise, and red pepper flakes. Tie the cloth into a bundle with a piece of kitchen twine.

TOAST THE SPICES Place the coriander and cumin seeds in a heavy skillet. Toast the spices over medium heat for 2 minutes, shaking the pan continuously so they do not burn. Let cool. In a spice grinder or coffee mill, grind the spices to a powder.

BROWN THE LAMB Season the lamb with salt and pepper. Heat the oil in a large, heavy Dutch oven over high heat. When the oil begins to smoke, add some of the meat in a single layer, making sure not to crowd the pan so that it will brown nicely without releasing too much liquid. Cook about 4 minutes, or until nicely browned. Turn the pieces and continue to brown on all sides. Transfer the browned meat to a bowl. Repeat with the remaining meat.

Add the ground spice mixture and garlic and cook for 1 minute.

Preheat the oven to 350°F.

COOK THE STEW Add the carrots, celery, and onions. Cook until the onions are translucent, about 15 minutes. Add the vinegar and cook, scraping the bottom of the pan, until the vinegar evaporates, about 20 minutes. Sprinkle the flour into the pan and cook for 2 minutes, scraping the bottom of the pan. Add the stock, water, tomatoes, lemon zest, and spice packet. Bring to a simmer.

6 Roma or plum tomatoes, roughly chopped

1 lemon, zest removed with a swivel-blade vegetable peeler

⅔ cup chopped fresh cilantro leaves

2 teaspoons Moroccan preserved lemon peel, finely chopped

½ cup slivered almonds, toasted

BAKE THE STEW Cover the pot loosely with foil and place it in the oven. Cook for 1½ hours, or until the meat is fork tender and the liquid is reduced and somewhat thickened.

Discard the spice bundle and the garlic bulbs. Stir in the cilantro.

TO SERVE Transfer the stew to a serving bowl and sprinkle with the preserved lemon peel. Scatter the almonds on top. Serve hot.

WINE SUGGESTION: SYRAH, "COLSON CANYON," TENSLEY, 2003, SANTA BARBARA COUNTY, CALIFORNIA. *A dark and spicy Syrah with aromas of black cherries, Asian spices, and wildflowers.*

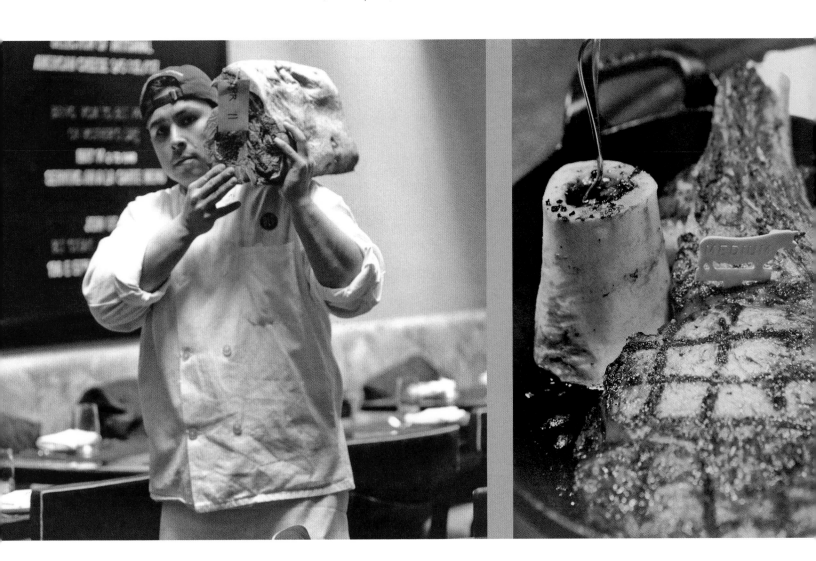

I n this recipe, moist, meaty lamb shanks are braised in a flavorful broth until they are falling off the bone. If you don't have a pot big enough to hold all of the ingredients, you can use two large pots and divide the ingredients between them. | Lamb shanks are good with Potatoes Boulangères (page 222), Creamed Spinach (page 210), or Curried Cauliflower (page 209). | SERVES 6

TOMATO CONFIT LAMB SHANKS

Tomato Confit

6 Roma or plum tomatoes, cut lengthwise into quarters and seeded

2 tablespoons olive oil

1 teaspoon chopped garlic

1 teaspoon fresh thyme leaves

Pinch sugar

Fine sea salt and freshly ground black pepper to taste

Bouquet Garni

8 sprigs fresh thyme

4 sprigs fresh rosemary

2 bay leaves

2 celery stalks

2 thick slices bacon (2 ounces)

Braise

6 large lamb shanks, well trimmed

¼ cup olive oil

8 shallots, chopped

5 carrots, chopped

2 large onions, chopped

8 garlic cloves, skinned

1 teaspoon cracked black peppercorns

¾ cup tomato paste

6 tablespoons all-purpose flour

MAKE THE TOMATO CONFIT Preheat the oven to 300°F.

Toss together all of the ingredients for the confit in a shallow baking pan. Bake for 1½ hours, then remove and cover to keep warm. Increase the oven temperature to 350°F.

MAKE A BOUQUET GARNI Tie the thyme, rosemary, bay leaves, celery, and bacon into a bundle with kitchen twine.

BROWN THE LAMB Sprinkle the lamb with salt and pepper. In a large (10-quart) Dutch oven, heat the oil over medium-high heat. Add the lamb a few pieces at a time without crowding the pan and brown it well on all sides. Remove the lamb to a plate. Pour off all but a couple of tablespoons of the oil.

BROWN THE VEGETABLES Add the shallots, carrots, onions, garlic, a pinch of salt, and peppercorns to the pan. Cook over medium heat, stirring frequently, until the vegetables are golden brown, 10 to 15 minutes. Add the tomato paste and cook, stirring, for 1 to 2 minutes. Stir in the flour and cook 1 minute more.

REDUCE THE WINE Add the red wine, port, and bouquet garni. Bring the mixture to a simmer and cook, stirring occasionally, until it is reduced by about one-third, about 15 minutes. Add the chicken and beef stocks and bring the liquid to a simmer.

Return the lamb to the pot, cover, and transfer the pot to the oven. Cook until the lamb is fork-tender, 2½ to 3 hours. Remove the lamb shanks from the pot and cover to keep warm.

Discard the bouquet garni. Strain the vegetables out of the cooking liquid and discard them. Return the liquid to the pot and simmer until the sauce is thickened and reduced, about 45 minutes. Return the shanks to the sauce and reheat gently.

8 cups dry red wine

4 cups ruby port wine

11 cups chicken stock or low-sodium chicken broth

5 cups beef stock or low-sodium beef broth

TO SERVE Place the lamb shanks in warm shallow bowls and ladle on the sauce. Top each with 4 warmed pieces of tomato confit.

WINE SUGGESTION: TABLAS CREEK, "ESPRIT DE BEAUCASTEL," 2003, PASO ROBLES, CALIFORNIA. *A ripe and spicy Rhône-style blend with aromas of blackberries, blueberries, leather, and spices.*

A lamb T-bone is a flavorful cut that includes a piece of both the loin and the filet. If you can't find T-bones, loin lamb chops are also good prepared this way. | Serve with Honey/Cumin-Glazed Carrots (page 215) and Silver Dollars (page 224). | SERVES 6

GRILLED LAMB T-BONES

2 cups extra-virgin olive oil

1 tablespoon chopped fresh rosemary leaves

1 tablespoon chopped fresh thyme leaves

1 tablespoon chopped fresh parsley

1 teaspoon minced garlic

1 teaspoon coarsely ground pink peppercorns

1 teaspoon black peppercorns, coarsely ground

12 lamb T-bones, 8 ounces each, about 1½-inches thick

Fine sea salt and freshly ground black pepper to taste

MARINATE THE LAMB Combine the oil, herbs, garlic, and peppercorns oil in a shallow dish. Add the lamb. Cover and marinate overnight in the refrigerator.

PREHEAT a barbecue grill or broiler to medium-high heat.

GRILL THE LAMB Remove the lamb from the marinade. Pat the steaks with paper towels to remove excess oil. Season on both sides with salt and pepper.

Grill 5 to 6 minutes on each side for medium-rare. To check for doneness, make a small cut near the bone or better yet, insert an instant-read thermometer in the thickest part of the meat. The temperature should be 140 to 150°F.

TO SERVE Transfer the T-bones to a serving platter. Cover and let rest 5 minutes before serving.

CHEF'S TIP: *To cook meat properly, it is important to use an instant-read thermometer. Check it often for accuracy by measuring the temperature of boiling water. It should read 212°F.*

WINE SUGGESTION: MERLOT, TAMARACK CELLARS, 2003, COLUMBIA VALLEY, WASHINGTON. *A juicy, structured Merlot with aromas of spices, violets, and red cherries.*

This spice rub is good on veal, beef, or poultry. Beef hanger steaks can be substituted for the veal if you prefer. | Serve the skewers with your choice of BLT Barbecue Sauce (page 195), BLT Steak Sauce (page 204), or Chimichurri Sauce (page 198) and Grilled Corn/Herb Butter (page 217). | SERVES 6

SPICED VEAL HANGER SKEWERS

Spice Rub

2 tablespoons garlic powder

1½ tablespoons dried oregano

1½ tablespoons dried thyme

1 tablespoon Hungarian paprika

1 tablespoon coarsely ground black pepper

1 tablespoon fine sea salt

1 tablespoon sugar

12 veal hanger steaks, about 2 pounds, cut into 48 one-inch cubes

12 button mushrooms

12 cherry tomatoes

1 large zucchini, cut in half lengthwise, then cut crosswise into 12 one-inch slices

1 large onion, cut into 12 one-inch squares

1 red bell pepper, seeded and cut into 12 one-inch squares

¼ cup extra-virgin olive oil

Fine sea salt and freshly ground black pepper to taste

SOAK THE SKEWERS Soak 12 long wooden or bamboo skewers in water to cover for at least 30 minutes.

SEASON THE VEAL Stir together all of the spice rub ingredients in a large bowl. Add the veal and toss until coated.

ASSEMBLE THE SKEWERS Arrange the vegetables and meat on the skewers in the following order: onion, veal, tomato, veal, zucchini, veal, mushroom, veal, and red pepper.

PREHEAT a stovetop grill or broiler to medium heat.

GRILL THE SKEWERS Drizzle the skewers with the olive oil. Grill for 6 minutes, or until the veal is pink when cut in the center.

Serve immediately.

WINE SUGGESTION: BARBERA, "SIERRA SERIES," RENWOOD, 2003, SIERRA FOOTHILLS, CALIFORNIA. *A simple red made from Barbera grapes, with aromas of cherry, berry, and spicy oak notes.*

Y ou can find mustard oil in many Indian groceries. One brand that I use is Laxmi (see Sources, page 174). If you don't have any mustard oil, you can substitute good Dijon mustard. | Serve with Creamed Spinach (page 210). | SERVES 6

SMOKY HONEY VEAL PORTERHOUSE

Marinade

1 cup BLT Steak Sauce (page 204), or store-bought

½ cup Worcestershire sauce

½ cup honey

¼ cup chopped fresh parsley

2 tablespoons Tabasco sauce

1 tablespoon chopped fresh thyme

1 tablespoon mustard oil or Dijon mustard

1 teaspoon Liquid Smoke

6 veal porterhouse steaks, approximately 20 ounces each, 2 inches thick

Fine sea salt and freshly ground black pepper to taste

MAKE THE MARINADE In a small saucepan, simmer the steak sauce, stirring occasionally, until reduced by half. Regulate the heat so that the sauce does not scorch. Pour the sauce into a shallow roasting pan. Add the remaining marinade ingredients and whisk until blended.

MARINATE THE VEAL Add the veal in a single layer. Cover and refrigerate at least 6 hours or overnight, turning the meat twice.

GRILL THE VEAL Preheat a barbecue or stovetop grill to medium heat. Remove the veal from the marinade and scrape off the excess. Sprinkle the steaks with salt and pepper. Pour the marinade into a small saucepan.

Grill the steaks over medium heat, about 7 minutes per side, or until pink in the center for medium. To check for doneness, make a small cut near the bone or better yet, insert an instant-read thermometer in the thickest part of the meat. The temperature should be 160°F.

TO SERVE Allow the steaks to rest 10 to 12 minutes before serving. Meanwhile, bring the marinade to a simmer and cook for 5 minutes. Cut the steaks into 1-inch-thick slices. Serve with the sauce.

WINE SUGGESTION: PINOT NOIR, ELVENGLADE, 2003, YAMHILL COUNTY, OREGON. *A smoky and earthy Pinot Noir with aromas of ripe black cherries, dark berries, and spice.*

Thick, juicy veal chops are a steakhouse favorite but easy to make at home. I like to enhance their flavor with a rosemary and Parmesan crust. Veal tastes best and has a better texture when it is cooked to medium-rare. | Serve with Creamy Home Fries (page 229) and Pan-Seared Hen of the Woods Mushrooms (page 223). | SERVES 6

ROSEMARY-PARMESAN-CRUSTED VEAL CHOPS

1 cup (2 sticks) unsalted butter, softened

1½ cups plain dry bread crumbs, preferably Japanese panko

¾ cup freshly grated Parmigiano-Reggiano cheese

⅔ cup finely chopped onion

1 tablespoon chopped fresh rosemary

Fine sea salt and freshly ground black pepper to taste

6 veal chops, about 14 ounces each, 1½ to 2 inches thick

WINE SUGGESTION: SEMILLON, "BARREL FERMENTED," L'ÉCOLE, 2002, COLUMBIA VALLEY, WASHINGTON. *A rich, honeyed Semillon with aromas of spices, melon, and peach.*

PREHEAT THE BROILER Place the broiler rack about 4 inches away from the source of the heat. Turn the heat to high.

MAKE THE CRUST Set aside 3 tablespoons of the butter. In a medium bowl, stir together the remaining butter, bread crumbs, cheese, onion, and rosemary. Add salt and pepper.

COAT THE CHOPS Spread each chop on both sides with some of the remaining 3 tablespoons of the butter. Sprinkle with salt and pepper.

COOK THE CHOPS Place the chops on the broiler rack. Cook, turning them once, about 7 minutes per side, or until medium-rare and pink when cut in the center. To check for doneness, make a small cut near the bone or better yet, insert an instant-read thermometer in the thickest part of the meat. The temperature should be 140 to 150°F for medium-rare.

COAT WITH CRUST Divide the crumbs over 1 side of each chop. Return the chops to the broiler and cook until the crust is golden brown, watching carefully, 1½ to 2 minutes.

Serve immediately.

CHEF'S TIP: *To prevent the bone ends of the chops from burning, wrap them in foil before broiling the chops.*

O sso buco, meaning "bone with a hole," is the Italian name for thick, meaty slices of veal shank. I like to cook them in a savory sauce and top them with a blend of crunchy bread crumbs, orange zest, parsley, and garlic known as gremolata. | Serve with Gnocchi à la Romaine (page 83). | SERVES 6

OSSO BUCO | ORANGE GREMOLATA

Bread Crumbs

½ cup ⅛-inch dice white country bread, or ½ cup fresh bread crumbs

1 teaspoon extra-virgin olive oil

Fine sea salt and freshly ground black pepper to taste

Bouquet Garni

2 celery stalks

2 sprigs fresh rosemary

8 sprigs fresh thyme

2 bay leaves

1 orange, peel removed with a swivel-blade vegetable peeler

Veal

6 meaty slices veal shank, about 12 ounces each, 2¼ inches thick, tied with kitchen twine

3 tablespoons extra-virgin olive oil

2 carrots, trimmed and cut into 1-inch pieces

1 onion, cut into 1-inch pieces

4 shallots cut into 1-inch pieces

10 garlic cloves

1 teaspoon black peppercorns, cracked

3 tablespoons tomato paste

3 tablespoons all-purpose flour

5 cups dry white wine

PREHEAT THE OVEN to 325°F.

TOAST THE BREAD CRUMBS Spread the diced bread, oil, and salt and pepper in a small baking pan. Bake 5 to 10 minutes, stirring occasionally, until golden brown. Let cool.

MAKE A BOUQUET GARNI Tie the celery, rosemary, thyme, bay leaves, and orange peel into a bundle with kitchen twine.

BRAISING THE VEAL Season the veal with salt and pepper. Heat the oil in large Dutch oven over medium-high heat. Add as many pieces of the veal as will fit comfortably without crowding. Brown the veal on all sides, about 15 minutes. Remove the meat from the pan. Repeat with the remaining veal. Pour off all but 2 tablespoons of the oil.

BROWN THE VEGETABLES Add the carrots, onion, shallots, garlic, and peppercorns. Cook over medium heat, stirring occasionally, until browned. Add the tomato paste and cook for 1 to 2 minutes. Stir in the flour and cook for 1 minute more.

Add the wine and cook until it is reduced by one-third. Add all of the stock and the bouquet garni. Bring the liquid to a simmer. Return the veal to the pot, overlapping the pieces slightly. Cover the pot.

BAKE THE VEAL Transfer the veal to the oven. Cook until fork tender, about 3 hours. Check the veal from time to time to be sure that the liquid is never boiling. If it is, reduce the temperature slightly.

MAKE THE GREMOLATA Bring a small pot of water to boiling. Add the orange zest and blanch for 5 seconds. Drain and immediately transfer the zest to a bowl of ice water. Drain the zest and repeat the process 2 more times. Let cool, then chop the zest very fine. You should have about 1½ teaspoons.

In a small bowl, mix the parsley, chopped zest, cheese, and toasted diced bread.

4 cups veal stock, or a combination of half beef and half chicken broth

4 cups chicken stock or low-sodium chicken broth

Gremolata

2 strips (2 inches) orange zest, removed with a swivel-blade vegetable peeler

½ cup chopped fresh flat-leaf parsley

¼ cup freshly grated Parmigiano-Reggiano cheese

FINISH THE SAUCE Remove the veal. Strain the liquid and return it to the pot. Bring the liquid to a boil over high heat and cook until thickened. Return the veal to the pot to reheat. Baste with the sauce.

TO SERVE Place 1 slice of veal in each serving bowl. Spoon on the sauce and sprinkle with a little of the gremolata.

WINE SUGGESTION: NEBBIOLO, "STOLPMAN VINEYARD," PALMINA, 2003, SANTA YNEZ VALLEY, CALIFORNIA. *A "Cal-Ital" wine made from Nebbiolo grapes, with notes of sweet cherries, tobacco leaf, and smoke.*

Savory pies made with meat, fish, or poultry originated in Northern Europe, but they have long been an American favorite. In this recipe, a classic chicken pot pie gets an Asian makeover. | One brand of red and green curry paste that I recommend is Mae Ploy. | Begin your meal with the Carrot-Cilantro Salad/ Ginger-Orange Dressing (page 48). Simple steamed jasmine or white rice goes best with the pie. | SERVES 6

CURRY-KAFFIR LIME CHICKEN POT PIE

1 tablespoon peanut oil

4 to 5 large boneless, skinless chicken breast halves, about 2 pounds, cut into 1½-inch cubes

2 tablespoons red curry paste

1 tablespoon green curry paste

2 tablespoons finely chopped peeled fresh ginger

½ medium white onion, chopped

1 can (13.5 ounces) unsweetened coconut milk

1 cup chicken stock or low-sodium chicken broth

7 Kaffir lime leaves, torn

1 tablespoon Vietnamese fish sauce (*nuoc mam*)

1 teaspoon sugar

Fine sea salt and freshly ground black pepper to taste

2 carrots, sliced ⅓ inch thick

1 large potato, peeled and cut into 1-inch dice

10 fresh Thai basil leaves, roughly chopped

½ cup fresh green peas

1 egg yolk

1 sheet all-butter frozen puff pastry (half of a 17-ounce package), thawed according to package directions

MAKE THE FILLING Heat the oil in a large skillet and brown the chicken on all sides. Add both curry pastes and cook for 2 minutes.

Add the ginger and onion and cook for 2 minutes. Add the coconut milk and bring to simmer.

Add the stock, lime leaves, fish sauce, and sugar. Bring the sauce to a simmer. Season with salt and pepper. With a slotted spoon, remove the chicken to a plate.

Add the carrots and potato. Cook until tender, 15 to 18 minutes. Stir in the basil. Let cool. Return the chicken and stir in the peas.

Preheat the oven to 375°F.

ASSEMBLE THE PIE Pour the stew into a 6-cup ovenproof casserole. Brush the rim and outer edge of the casserole bowl with the egg yolk.

Measure the diameter of the top of the casserole and cut out the pastry ½ inch larger. Cover the casserole with the pastry and press the edges to secure it. Brush the pastry with the remaining yolk.

BAKE THE PIE for 20 to 25 minutes, or until the pastry is golden brown and the sauce is bubbling.

WINE SUGGESTION: VIOGNIER, "SANDFORD AND BENEDICT," COLD HEAVEN, 2003, SANTA BARBARA COUNTY, CALIFORNIA. *An aromatic and floral Viognier with hints of apricots, almonds, and spiced flowers.*

Moroccan preserved lemons, along with bread crumbs and seasonings, are stuffed under the skin of this chicken for added flavor. The lemons are pickled in salt and spices and are widely available in Middle Eastern markets, or check the Sources on page 274. | Fingerling potatoes come in many varieties, but they are all thin-skinned and creamy inside. They are ideal for roasting in this recipe since they absorb the flavors of the chicken. | My friend Francis Staub, of the famous Staub cookware company, says this is the best-tasting chicken he has ever eaten in the world. It was originally my great-grandmother's recipe. | Serve with Honey Caramelized Brussels Sprouts/Roasted Chestnuts (page 233). | SERVES 6

ROASTED ROSEMARY-LEMON CHICKEN

3 pounds fingerling potatoes, cut in half lengthwise

2 large onions, sliced, plus 3 tablespoons chopped onions

8 large garlic cloves, chopped

¼ cup plus 1 tablespoon olive oil

2 tablespoons chopped fresh rosemary

Fine sea salt and freshly ground black pepper to taste

12 tablespoons (1½ sticks) unsalted butter, softened

½ cups fresh bread crumbs

¼ cup rinsed and chopped preserved lemon (about 1 lemon; see Sources, page 274)

1 chicken, or 2 smaller chickens, 6½ to 7 pounds total

PREHEAT THE OVEN to 375°F. Oil a large baking pan.

PREPARE THE VEGETABLES In a large bowl, toss together the potatoes, sliced onions, garlic, ¼ cup of the oil, 1 tablespoon of the rosemary, and salt and pepper. Spread the vegetables out in the pan.

MAKE THE STUFFING In a bowl, combine the butter, bread crumbs, lemon, chopped onion, remaining 1 tablespoon of the rosemary, and salt and pepper. Mix well to form a thick paste.

PREPARE THE CHICKEN With a chef's knife or cleaver, cut off the chicken wings at the joint closest to the breast. Push the vegetables to the sides of the pan. Place the wings in the center. Place the chicken on top.

Gently work your fingers between the skin and flesh of the chicken. Stuff the bread crumb mixture under the skin, distributing it evenly to cover the flesh. Brush the skin with remaining 1 tablespoon of the oil.

ROAST THE CHICKEN Put the chicken in the oven and baste occasionally, 1 to 1½ hours according to the size of the chicken, or until the skin is golden brown and crisp and the juices run clear when the chicken is pierced with a knife at the joint of the leg. Transfer the chicken to a platter, cover loosely with foil, and keep warm.

BROWN THE VEGETABLES Toss the potatoes again and turn the broiler to high. Cook until the potatoes are well browned and tender, 5 to 10 minutes more, stirring and turning them over once or twice.

TO SERVE Carve the chicken, making sure each portion includes some of the skin and stuffing. For a large chicken, cut each breast into 3 pieces and separate the legs and thighs at the joint. Serve with the vegetables.

WINE SUGGESTION: CHARDONNAY, FORMAN, 2004, NAPA VALLEY, CALIFORNIA. *A crisp and clean Chardonnay with aromas of apples, white peaches, lemon blossoms, and a crisp acidity and a touch of oak.*

The origin of the word "jerk" for this Jamaican way of cooking meats is uncertain. Some say it refers to your reaction when you taste the spicy meat, while others claim it refers to the motion of turning the food on the fire as it cooks. It may also be derived from the Spanish word *charqui*, used for dried meats, which eventually became "jerky" in English. | Scotch Bonnet chiles are one of the hottest of all varieties. Always wear rubber or disposable plastic gloves when handling them. To adjust the spice level, remove some or all of the seeds from the chiles before adding them to the marinade. | Start this recipe at least 3 days before you plan to serve the chicken so that the marinade has a chance to flavor the meat. This chicken is great cold. | Serve with Curried Cauliflower (page 209). | SERVES 6

GRILLED JERK CHICKEN

Marinade

8 scallions, chopped

1 small onion, diced

½ cup white vinegar

4 garlic cloves, chopped

2 Scotch Bonnet chiles, chopped

¼ cup packed dark brown sugar

¼ cup soy sauce

¼ cup freshly squeezed lime juice

¼ cup vegetable oil

¼ cup freshly squeezed orange juice

3 tablespoons chopped fresh thyme

2 tablespoons ground allspice

1 tablespoon fine sea salt

1¼ teaspoons freshly grated nutmeg

1 teaspoon ground cinnamon

2 whole chickens cut into 8 pieces each

Fine sea salt and freshly ground black pepper to taste

Lime wedges, for serving

MAKE THE MARINADE Combine the marinade ingredients and store them in an airtight container in the refrigerator overnight.

MARINATE THE CHICKEN Loosen the skin on the chicken pieces so that the marinade can get underneath. Place the chicken and marinade in a bowl. Cover and refrigerate for 2 days, turning the pieces occasionally.

PREHEAT a barbecue or stovetop grill to medium-high heat.

COOK THE CHICKEN Remove the chicken from the marinade and season with salt and pepper. Grill the chicken for 10 minutes, skin-side up. Turn the chicken and grill, skin-side down, for an additional 10 minutes, or until the juices run clear when the chicken is cut near the bone.

SERVE immediately with lime wedges.

WINE SUGGESTION: GEWÜRZTRAMINER, HANDLEY, 2004, ANDERSON VALLEY, CALIFORNIA. *A spicy, citrusy white made from Gewürztraminer with aromas of orange blossoms, roses, and sun-warmed melon.*

I named this stew for the Basque region of Spain, where *espelette* peppers are grown. The mature peppers are tied in braids and hung to dry outdoors. The ground peppers have a smoky and mildly hot flavor stronger than paprika, but not quite as hot as cayenne. | Chorizo is a sausage from the Catalonia region of Spain. Though there are several different varieties, it is typically made from ground pork, garlic, red bell peppers, paprika, and dried chiles. | Serve with Field Greens/Manchego Cheese/Walnut Vinaigrette (page 55) as an appetizer and nothing more complicated than steamed rice as an accompaniment. | SERVES 6

CHICKEN-CHORIZO BASQUAISE

¼ cup plus 1 teaspoon olive oil

6 ounces prosciutto or bacon, diced

2 chickens, about 3½ pounds each, both cut into 8 pieces

Fine sea salt and freshly ground black pepper to taste

1 large white Spanish onion, sliced

1 sprig fresh thyme

Pinch ground espelette pepper or crushed red pepper flakes

2 green bell peppers, sliced

2 garlic cloves, finely chopped

2 cups dry white wine

1 can (28 ounces) chopped tomatoes

1 small chorizo (about 3 ounces), thinly sliced

¼ cup Arbequina or Niçoise olives

COOK THE PROSCIUTTO Heat the oil in a large Dutch oven over medium heat. Add the prosciutto and cook, stirring frequently, until golden brown, 6 to 8 minutes. Remove the prosciutto to a plate with a slotted spoon.

BROWN THE CHICKEN Season the chicken with salt and pepper. Add the chicken to the pan skin-side down. Cook until golden brown, about 5 minutes on each side. Remove the chicken.

COOK THE VEGETABLES Return the prosciutto to the pan and add the onion, thyme, and espelette pepper. Cook until the onion is soft. Add the bell peppers and garlic and cook 2 minutes more.

MAKE THE SAUCE Add the wine and bring it to a simmer. Cook until the wine is reduced by half.

Add the tomatoes and bring the sauce to a boil. Add the chicken. Cover and cook 20 minutes on medium heat, turning the pieces occasionally, until the juices run clear when the chicken is pierced with a knife.

COOK THE CHORIZO In a small skillet, heat the remaining 1 teaspoon of the olive oil. Add the chorizo and cook 3 to 4 minutes, or until lightly browned on both sides.

FINISH THE DISH Remove the chicken from the heat. Add the chorizo and olives. Season with salt and pepper.

TO SERVE Place the Dutch oven in the center of the table and serve immediately.

WINE SUGGESTION: TEMPRANILLO, "VINO TINTO," PAGOR, 2002, CALIFORNIA. *A Tempranillo (the famous grape of Rioja, Spain) with notes of red cherries, tobacco, and hints of spices and leather.*

In French cuisine, many recipes containing mustard are called "diablo," meaning "devil-style," because they are spicy. This treatment works on chicken, too. Leftovers make great sandwiches spread with mayonnaise flavored with cornichons. | Cornish hens are readily available in most grocery stores. However, you can make this recipe with chicken or even chicken parts. | Hens or chicken prepared this way are good even without the sauce. Serve with Rosemary-Parmesan French Fries (page 229). | SERVES 6

CORNISH HEN DIABLO

Sauce

6 anchovy fillets, finely chopped

1 egg yolk

2 tablespoons red wine vinegar

1 tablespoon Dijon mustard

½ cup extra-virgin olive oil

2 tablespoons chopped fresh parsley

1 tablespoon chopped fresh tarragon

Fine sea salt and freshly ground black pepper to taste

Coating

2 cups plain dry bread crumbs, preferably Japanese panko

2 tablespoons finely chopped garlic

2 tablespoons finely chopped fresh rosemary

6 Cornish hens

6 tablespoons Dijon mustard

3 tablespoons extra-virgin olive oil

TO MAKE THE SAUCE In a bowl, whisk together anchovies, egg yolk, vinegar, and mustard. Slowly whisk in the oil. Add the herbs, salt and pepper.

PREPARE THE COATING Mix the bread crumbs, garlic, and rosemary together.

PREPARE THE CORNISH HENS With kitchen shears or a sharp, heavy knife, split the hens down the center of their backs. Open the hens like a book. Pat dry with paper towels. Thread a short wooden or bamboo skewer from the bottom of each leg to the top of the breast on each side so that they will keep their shape.

COAT THE HENS Sprinkle the hens with salt and pepper and brush them with the mustard on both sides. Cover both sides with the bread crumb mixture and drizzle with the olive oil.

GRILL THE HENS Preheat a barbecue or stovetop grill to medium-high heat.

Add the hens and cook, turning them about halfway through the cooking time, until cooked through and golden brown, about 20 minutes, or until the juice runs clear when the legs are pierced with a knife near the bone. If the hens begin to brown too rapidly, move them to a cooler part of the grill.

TO SERVE Remove the skewers, carve the hens into pieces, and serve immediately with the sauce.

Acacia honey is my first choice for this recipe. It has a delicate aroma that suggests vanilla and flowers. Because it has a high concentration of fructose, it remains liquid longer than most other kinds of honey. If you can't find it, use orange blossom honey, which is always available and the flavor is great. | Honey and soy sauce give the duck skin a rich brown color and crisp texture while the meat inside remains juicy and medium-rare. | Pekin ducks, also know as Long Island ducks, are originally from China. They were first brought to this country by a Connecticut merchant who bred and raised them. | Serve the duck with Potatoes Boulangères (page 222). | SERVES 6

5-SPICE CARAMELIZED LONG ISLAND DUCK

Duck

1½ cups honey

1 tablespoon Chinese five-spice powder

3 tablespoons low-sodium (lite) soy sauce

2 tablespoons freshly squeezed lemon juice

6 skin-on, boneless Pekin duck breasts

1 tablespoon vegetable oil

Apple Puree

1 cup (2 sticks) plus 2 tablespoons unsalted butter

2 tablespoons olive oil

6 Honey Crisp or Macintosh apples, peeled, cored, and cut into 6 pieces

4 sprigs fresh rosemary

4 tablespoons sliced fresh ginger

⅓ cup apple juice

Fine sea salt and freshly ground white pepper to taste

MAKE THE MARINADE In a medium saucepan, combine the honey and five-spice powder. Bring to a simmer over medium heat. Cook until the honey is dark brown, about 10 minutes.

Add the soy sauce and cook until thickened, about 3 minutes. Carefully add the lemon juice. The honey will bubble up. Pour the marinade into a shallow glass or earthenware pan and let cool to room temperature.

MARINATE THE DUCK Add the duck breasts to the marinade and turn them over to coat completely with marinade. Cover and refrigerate, turning the pieces occasionally, at least 4 hours or preferably overnight.

MAKE THE APPLE PUREE Heat 2 tablespoons of the butter and the olive oil in a large sauté pan over medium heat. Add the apples and cook until soft and golden brown, about 30 minutes.

In a small saucepan over high heat, combine the remaining 1 cup of the butter, the rosemary, and ginger. Cook until the butter begins to brown, 4 to 5 minutes. Remove from the heat. Let stand 20 to 25 minutes to allow the rosemary and ginger flavors to infuse the butter.

Strain the butter. In a blender or food processor, puree the butter, apple juice, and apples until smooth. Adjust the seasoning with salt and white pepper. Keep warm.

COOK THE DUCK In a large skillet, heat the oil over medium heat.

Add the duck breasts skin-side down. Cook until the skin is crisp and golden brown, lowering the heat if necessary, 4 to 5 minutes. Watch carefully so that they do not burn. Turn the duck breasts and spoon the pan liquid over the top. Cook until the duck breasts are medium-rare, 5 to 6 minutes more, or until an instant-read thermometer reads 130°F when inserted in the thickest part.

SERVE immediately with the warm apple puree.

CHAPTER SEVEN

SAUCES

SAUCES	GOES WITH
BLT Barbecue Sauce	Barbequed Beef Brisket (page 162) Spiced Veal Hanger Skewers (page 175)
Béarnaise Sauce	Herb-Crusted Rack of Lamb (page 168) Grilled BLT Double-Cut Strip Steak (page 159) Smoked Sea Salt and Black Pepper–Crusted Rib-Eye (page 151)
Blue Cheese Sauce	Grilled BLT Double-Cut Strip Steak (page 159) Smoked Sea Salt and Black Pepper–Crusted Rib-Eye (page 151) Smoky Honey Veal Porterhouse (page 176)
Chimichurri Sauce	Sea Salt–Crusted Pink Snapper (page 133) (instead of the Ice Wine Nage) Any grilled meat or chicken Spiced Veal Hanger Skewers (page 175) Grilled Lamb T-bones (page 174)
Cranberry Sauce	Cornish Hen Diablo (page 188) Roasted Rosemary-Lemon Chicken (page 183)
Curry Lemongrass Sauce	Sea Salt–Crusted Pink Snapper (page 133) (instead of the Ice Wine Nage) Grilled Shrimp (page 140) (instead of the Soy-Caper Brown Butter Sauce) Striped Bass (page 136) (instead of the Curry Brown Butter)
Maître d'Hôtel Butter	Grilled BLT Double-Cut Strip Steak (page 159) Marinated Kobe Skirt Steak (page 157) Grilled Corn (page 217) (instead of the Herb Butter) Sea Salt–Crusted Sunchokes (page 232)
Peppercorn Sauce	Cornish Hen Diablo (page 188) (instead of the Diablo Sauce) Herb-Crusted Rack of Lamb (page 168) Grilled Lamb T-Bones (page 174) All Steaks
Red Wine Sauce	Grilled BLT-Double Cut Strip Steak (page 159) Smoked Sea Salt and Black Pepper–Crusted Rib Eye (page 151) Tapenade-Stuffed Leg of Lamb (page 167)
BLT Steak Sauce	Grilled Lamb T-Bones (page 168) All Steaks Spiced Veal Hanger Skewers (page 175) Smoky Honey Veal Porterhouse (page 176)

BLT BARBECUE SAUCE

MAKES ABOUT 5½ CUPS

15 garlic cloves, peeled (about 1 whole head)

1 tablespoon olive oil

Fine sea salt to taste

3 cups ketchup

3 celery stalks, chopped

1½ medium, sweet onions, such as Vidalia or Bermuda, chopped

1½ cups water

¾ cup packed dark brown sugar

12 tablespoons (1½ sticks) unsalted butter

¾ cup Worcestershire sauce

¾ cup apple cider vinegar

3 tablespoons chili powder

1 tablespoon instant espresso powder

¾ teaspoon cayenne

¾ teaspoon crushed red pepper flakes

¾ teaspoon ground cloves

ROAST THE GARLIC Preheat the oven to 375°F. In a small baking pan, toss the garlic cloves with the oil and a pinch of salt. Roast for 30 minutes, or until very soft and beginning to brown.

COOK THE SAUCE Combine the roasted garlic, the remaining ingredients, and ¾ teaspoon salt in a large, heavy saucepan. Bring to a simmer over medium heat. Cook the sauce, stirring it frequently to prevent it from scorching, for 45 minutes, or until the vegetables are soft and the sauce looks dark and rich.

BLEND THE SAUCE Let cool slightly. Pour the sauce into a blender or food processor. Blend until completely smooth. Taste for seasoning.

STORE the sauce in a jar in the refrigerator for up to one month.

BÉARNAISE SAUCE

MAKES 1¾ CUPS

½ cup white wine vinegar

¼ cup dry white wine

3 tablespoons chopped shallots

1 tablespoon chopped fresh tarragon stems

1½ teaspoons cracked black peppercorns

5 egg yolks

1¼ cups (2½ sticks) clarified butter (see page 271), at room temperature

2 tablespoons chopped fresh tarragon leaves

Fine sea salt and freshly ground black pepper to taste

COOK THE SHALLOTS In a small saucepan, bring the vinegar, wine, shallots, tarragon stems, and peppercorns to a boil over high heat. Cook until the liquid is reduced by one-third, about 4 minutes. Strain the liquid into the top of a double boiler or small heatproof bowl that will fit comfortably over a saucepan.

MAKE THE SAUCE Add the egg yolks to the vinegar and whisk until blended. Place the bowl over another pot half full of simmering water. The bottom of the bowl should not touch the water. Do not allow the water to boil. Continue whisking, moving the bowl on and off the heat so that the eggs do not overheat and curdle. The eggs are ready when the mixture thickens and forms a thin ribbon when the whisk is lifted, about 5 minutes.

ADD THE BUTTER Remove the bowl from the heat and let the mixture cool until it is about the same temperature as the butter. In a thin stream, slowly whisk the butter into the egg mixture. Stir in the chopped tarragon leaves and season with salt and pepper.

TO SERVE This sauce can be made up to 1 hour before serving it and kept warm over a pan of hot water.

CHEF'S TIP: *If the sauce gets too hot, whisk in 1 teaspoon of cold water. If the sauce becomes too cold, whisk in 1 tablespoon of hot water.*

BLUE CHEESE SAUCE

MAKES ABOUT 1¼ CUPS

8 ounces heavy or whipping cream

6 ounces Maytag blue cheese, crumbled

1 teaspoon Worcestershire sauce

½ teaspoon Tabasco sauce

Fine sea salt and freshly ground black pepper to taste

MAKE THE SAUCE Pour the cream into a medium saucepan. Bring to a boil over medium heat and cook until thickened and reduced to about ⅔ cup, 3 to 4 minutes.

Using a hand-held immersion blender or whisk, blend in 4 ounces of the cheese.

FINISH THE SAUCE Add the Worcestershire and Tabasco and cook until the mixture is thick and coats the back of a spoon, 3 to 4 minutes more. Season with salt and pepper.

TO SERVE Just before serving, stir the remaining 2 ounces of the cheese into the sauce. Serve immediately.

CHIMICHURRI SAUCE

MAKES 2 CUPS

½ cup canola oil

½ cup extra-virgin olive oil

2 tablespoons white wine vinegar

Fine sea salt and freshly ground black pepper to taste

½ cup chopped fresh cilantro

½ cup chopped fresh parsley

⅓ cup chopped jarred piquillo or roasted red peppers

2 tablespoons chopped garlic

2 tablespoons minced Spanish onion

2 teaspoons crushed red pepper flakes

1 tablespoon freshly squeezed lime juice

MAKE THE SAUCE In a medium bowl, whisk together both oils, the vinegar, and salt and pepper. Stir in the remaining ingredients except the lime juice.

MARINATE Let stand 1 hour at room temperature or cover and refrigerate up to overnight. Add the fresh lime juice just before serving.

SERVE at room temperature.

SPICED CRANBERRY SAUCE

MAKES 1–1 1/2 CUPS

4 cups (about 2 pounds) fresh or frozen cranberries

2 cups freshly squeezed orange juice

¼ cup honey

2 star anise

2 cinnamon sticks

1 teaspoon sherry vinegar

Fine sea salt and freshly ground black pepper to taste

COOK THE CRANBERRIES In a medium saucepan, combine the cranberries, orange juice, honey, star anise, and cinnamon sticks. Bring to a simmer and cook over low heat until the cranberries are soft but still whole, about 20 minutes. Do not overcook.

REDUCE THE LIQUID With a slotted spoon, remove the cranberries, star anise, and cinnamon from the liquid. Discard the spices.

Place the saucepan over medium heat and simmer the liquid until it is thick and saucy. Add the vinegar, and salt and pepper.

TO SERVE When ready to serve, return the cranberries to the sauce and reheat gently. If the sauce is too thick, stir in a little water.

Serve hot.

CURRY-LEMONGRASS SAUCE

MAKES 1 QUART

2½ tablespoons canola oil

3 shallots, diced

1½ stalks lemongrass, cracked and chopped

Fine sea salt to taste

1½ tablespoons Madras curry powder

1½ cups dry white vermouth

½ cup diced ripe mango (about ½ medium mango)

1 cup peeled and diced pineapple

1 cup peeled and diced celery root

Pinch saffron threads

1 can (14 ounces) unsweetened coconut milk

1 cup heavy cream

½ tablespoon freshly squeezed lime juice

1 to 2 Kaffir lime leaves, torn in half

COOK THE VEGETABLES In a large saucepan, heat the oil over medium heat. Add the shallots and the lemongrass and season with salt. Cover and cook on medium-low heat until the vegetables are soft, stirring often to make sure that the vegetables do not brown. Add the curry powder and cook for 1 minute more.

Add the vermouth and cook for 1 minute, stirring. Add the mango, pineapple, celery root, and saffron. Bring to a simmer and let cook over medium heat until the liquid is reduced slightly, about 2 minutes.

MAKE THE SAUCE Add the coconut milk and cream. Bring to a simmer and cook for 30 minutes, or until slightly thickened. Strain the sauce through a fine-mesh strainer into a clean saucepan. (The sauce can be made to this point and refrigerated up to 24 hours before serving.)

FINISH THE SAUCE If the sauce has been refrigerated, place the chilled sauce in a small saucepan and bring to a simmer over low heat. About 15 minutes before serving, add the lime juice and torn lime leaves. Remove the leaves before serving. Taste for seasoning.

Serve warm.

MAÎTRE D'HÔTEL BUTTER

MAKES ABOUT 1 CUP

1 cup (2 sticks) European-style unsalted butter

2 tablespoons finely chopped fresh parsley

1 tablespoon finely chopped shallot

1 tablespoon snipped fresh chives

½ teaspoon minced garlic

½ teaspoon chopped fresh sage

Fine sea salt and freshly ground black pepper to taste

MAKE THE BUTTER In a medium bowl, beat together all of the ingredients until blended. Place on a sheet of plastic wrap and roll it into a sausage shape. Store in the refrigerator up to 3 days or in the freezer up to 2 weeks.

TO SERVE Cut the butter into slices.

PEPPERCORN SAUCE

MAKES 1½ CUPS

2 tablespoons unsalted butter

2 large shallots, finely chopped

Fine sea salt to taste

1½ teaspoons black peppercorns

½ teaspoon white peppercorns

⅓ cup dry white wine

1½ teaspoons red wine vinegar

1½ teaspoons sugar

½ cup brandy

2 cups chicken stock or low-sodium chicken broth

2 cups veal stock or low-sodium beef broth

1¼ cups heavy cream

¼ cup green peppercorns, rinsed and drained

COOK THE SHALLOTS In a small, heavy-bottomed saucepan, melt the butter. Add the shallots with a pinch of salt and cook gently, covered, over low to medium heat for 5 to 7 minutes, or until the shallots are soft and translucent. Raise the heat to medium-high and add the black and white peppercorns. Stir them for 1 minute.

MAKE THE SAUCE Add the wine, vinegar, and sugar. Over medium-high heat, reduce the mixture until most of the liquid has evaporated and it begins to caramelize slightly, 3 to 5 minutes.

Set aside 1 tablespoon of the brandy. Add the remainder to the pot and cook until reduced by about one-third, 3 to 5 minutes.

Add the chicken and veal stocks. Bring the mixture to a boil and cook over medium-high heat until reduced to 1 cup liquid, about 40 minutes.

Stir in the cream and bring to a boil. Cook 15 minutes, or until the sauce thickens.

FINISH THE SAUCE Just before serving, stir in the green peppercorns and the remaining 1 tablespoon of the brandy. Taste for seasoning.

CHEF'S TIP: *Peppercorn Sauce keeps well in the refrigerator up to 3 days. If you are making it ahead, do not add the green peppercorns and tablespoon of brandy until the sauce is reheated.*

RED WINE SAUCE

MAKES ABOUT 3 CUPS

1 tablespoon grapeseed oil

3 small shallots, finely chopped

1 garlic clove, finely chopped

1 sprig fresh thyme

1 bay leaf

¾ cup (about 3 ounces) chopped button mushrooms

½ cup red wine vinegar

1 tablespoon plus ½ teaspoon sugar

1 bottle (750 milliliters) dry red wine

6 tablespoons ruby port wine

1 quart veal stock or 2 cups each low-sodium beef broth and chicken broth

3 tablespoons unsalted butter

Fine sea salt and freshly ground black pepper to taste

MAKE THE SAUCE In a medium saucepan over medium heat, warm the oil. Add the shallots, garlic, thyme, and bay leaf. Cover and cook until the shallots are translucent, 4 to 5 minutes.

Add the mushrooms and cook covered, for 1 to 2 minutes, or until most of the liquid has evaporated.

Add the vinegar and sugar and reduce until almost dry, about 5 minutes more. Add the wine and port and reduce until syrupy, 15 to 20 minutes.

Add the stock and simmer until reduced by half and thickened slightly, about 20 minutes more.

Strain the sauce through a fine-mesh sieve; discard the solids. (The sauce can be refrigerated at this point up to 4 days or frozen for up to 3 months.)

FINISH THE SAUCE Over low heat, gently stir in the butter and season with salt and pepper. Do not allow the sauce to boil or it may break.

CHEF'S TIP: *Do not whisk the butter into the sauce. Whisking adds air and makes the sauce seem cloudy when it should be shiny. Stir it in with a spoon.*

BLT STEAK SAUCE

MAKES 4 CUPS

2 cups ketchup

1¼ cups packed light brown sugar

1 cup chopped onion

1 cup water

½ cup freshly squeezed lemon juice

½ cup white wine vinegar

½ cup Worcestershire sauce

¼ cup low-sodium (lite) soy sauce

¼ cup unsulphured molasses

2 tablespoons Dijon mustard

2 garlic cloves, chopped

1 teaspoons Liquid Smoke

1 teaspoon Hungarian paprika

1 teaspoon chili powder

½ cup prepared horseradish (do not drain)

Fine sea salt and freshly ground black pepper to taste

COOK THE SAUCE In a large saucepan, combine all of the ingredients except the horseradish and salt and pepper. Bring to a simmer. Cook until thick, 35 to 45 minutes.

BLEND THE SAUCE Pour the sauce into a blender jar or use a hand-held immersion blender to mix the sauce until completely smooth. Add salt and pepper. Let cool.

FINISH THE SAUCE Stir in the horseradish. Taste and adjust seasoning with salt and pepper.

STORE the sauce in a covered container in the refrigerator up to 2 weeks.

CHAPTER EIGHT

VEGETABLES

The dark color of the mushroom caps outlines the bright green broccoli filling, making these especially attractive. Serve them as a side dish, or as an appetizer with an arugula salad dressed with lemon vinaigrette. | For a fancier presentation, cut the baked mushroom caps into ½-inch-thick slices and arrange them overlapping slightly on a platter. | To serve them as an hors d'œuvre, cut the mushrooms into wedges. | Serve with a starter of Fennel-Arugula Salad/ Aged Pecorino (page 54), followed by Roasted Rosemary-Lemon Chicken (page 183) or as a side dish with Striped Bass/Curry Brown Butter (page 136). | SERVES 6

BROCCOLI-STUFFED PORTOBELLO MUSHROOMS

4 cups panko bread crumbs

6 medium (about 2 pounds) portobello mushrooms

1½ pounds broccoli, trimmed into florets

2 cups freshly grated Parmigiano-Reggiano cheese

2 garlic cloves, chopped

Fine sea salt and freshly ground black pepper to taste

¾ cup heavy cream

GRIND THE BREAD CRUMBS Place ½ cup of the bread crumbs in a blender. Blend on high speed until very finely ground.

PREPARE THE MUSHROOMS Wipe the mushrooms clean with damp paper towels. Snap off the stems and reserve them for another use.

COOK THE BROCCOLI Bring a large pot of salted water to a boil. Add the broccoli and cook until tender, about 8 minutes. Drain the broccoli and wrap in a kitchen towel. Squeeze the towel to extract the liquid.

MAKE THE STUFFING In a food processor, blend 1½ cups of the cheese with the garlic and a pinch of salt and pepper until the mixture is finely ground. Add the broccoli and puree.

Add the remaining 3½ cups of the bread crumbs and process until blended. With the machine running, slowly add just enough of the cream until the mixture forms a ball. You may not need all of the cream.

Preheat the oven to 400°F. Oil a baking pan just large enough to hold the mushroom caps in a single layer.

STUFF THE MUSHROOMS Generously season the mushroom caps with salt and pepper. Divide the broccoli mixture into 6 balls. Spread the broccoli mixture evenly in the caps, filling them to the top. Sprinkle with the ground panko and remaining ½ cup of the cheese.

BAKE THE MUSHROOMS Bake for 20 minutes, or until the tops are golden brown and the mushrooms caps are tender.

Serve hot.

Cauliflower is at its best from September to March—the peak growing season. Crisp and spicy, these are great as a side dish or serve them in a basket with the mayonnaise served in the Spicy Soft-Shell Crab Sandwiches (page 115). | Sometimes I use this cauliflower to dress up a simple fish dish. I cut the fried cauliflower into ¼-inch-thick slices and lay the slices on top of the grilled fish fillets. | Serve with Grilled Shrimp/Cauliflower/Soy-Caper Brown Butter Sauce (page 140) or Grilled Jerk Chicken (page 185), or any of the lamb recipes. | SERVES 6

CURRIED CAULIFLOWER

1 large cauliflower, about 2 pounds, trimmed and cut into 2-inch florets

¾ cup all-purpose flour

5 tablespoons Madras curry powder

1 teaspoon fine sea salt

1¼ cups panko bread crumbs

3 eggs

Canola or grapeseed oil for frying

COOK THE CAULIFLOWER Bring a large pot of salted water to a boil. Add the cauliflower and cook for 6 minutes, or until cooked through but still firm. Drain and place in a bowl of ice water to cool. Drain well.

PREPARE THE INGREDIENTS In a small bowl, stir together the flour, 2½ tablespoons of the curry powder, and the salt. In another bowl, stir together the remaining 2½ tablespoons curry powder and the panko. Beat the eggs until frothy.

COAT THE CAULIFLOWER Roll a piece of cauliflower in the flour, then in the eggs, coating it well on all sides. Roll the cauliflower in the panko mixture. Place the pieces on a tray or baking sheet without letting them touch. Repeat with the remaining florets.

FRY THE CAULIFLOWER Fill a large, heavy pot about 3 inches deep with the oil or fill a deep fryer following the manufacturer's directions. Heat the oil until the temperature reaches 375°F on a frying thermometer. Add the cauliflower pieces a few at a time, being careful not to crowd the pan. Fry 3 to 4 minutes, or until golden brown.

Remove the cauliflower with a slotted spoon. Transfer the pieces to paper towels to drain. Taste for salt. Fry the remaining cauliflower in the same way.

SERVE immediately on a folded paper towel.

love this enriched version of the classic steakhouse side dish—creamed spinach. I could eat it every day. The cheese in the mixture makes it special. A small amount of creamy béchamel sauce gives this spinach an added richness and body. | When my mom makes it, she sometimes spreads the creamed spinach in a buttered gratin dish, makes indentations in the spinach, fills them with poached eggs, sprinkles the dish with additional grated cheese, and browns it lightly under the broiler. | Serve with Smoked Sea Salt and Black Pepper–Crusted Rib-Eye (page 151), Grilled BLT Double-Cut Strip Steak (page 159), Braised Short Ribs/Garlic-Thyme Brown Butter (page 163), Grilled Lamb T-Bones (page 174), Smoky Honey Veal Porterhouse (page 176), or Roasted Rosemary-Lemon Chicken (page 183). | SERVES 6

CREAMED SPINACH

Béchamel Sauce

1½ cups milk

4 tablespoons (½ stick) unsalted butter

¼ cup all-purpose flour

Fine sea salt and freshly ground black pepper to taste

Freshly grated nutmeg

Spinach

4 pounds spinach, washed and trimmed

2 tablespoons unsalted butter

2 teaspoons chopped garlic

1 cup heavy cream

1 cup grated Gruyère cheese

MAKE THE BÉCHAMEL In a small saucepan, heat the milk until small bubbles form around the edge.

In a medium saucepan over medium heat, cook the butter until melted and foamy. Add the flour and whisk constantly for 1 minute.

Slowly whisk in the warm milk until blended. Season with salt, pepper, and nutmeg. Cook about 2 minutes, whisking constantly, until smooth and thick. Pay attention to the corners of the pan so the sauce doesn't stick.

Transfer the sauce to a bowl. You should have about 1½ cups. Place a piece of plastic wrap directly on the surface. Cover and chill up to 3 days.

COOK THE SPINACH Bring a large pot of salted water to a boil. Add the spinach. Cook 3 minutes, then drain the spinach. Place it in a bowl of ice water to stop the cooking.

Wrap the spinach in a lint-free towel and squeeze it until it is very dry. Place the spinach on a cutting board and chop it fine. (It can be refrigerated overnight at this point.)

MAKE THE CREAMED SPINACH Place the butter in a medium saucepan over medium heat. Swirl the pan until the butter is browned. Add the garlic and cook, stirring, for 1 to 2 minutes, until golden.

Add the spinach, 3 tablespoons of the béchamel, the cream, and cheese. Season with salt, pepper, and nutmeg. Cook, stirring frequently, until heated through.

Serve immediately.

CHEF'S TIP: *The remaining béchamel can be stored in the refrigerator up to 3 days. Use it for Grilled Ham and Cheese Sandwich/White Truffle (page 114 or the White Onion Soubise (page 152).*

Rings of sweet onion fried in a crisp, puffy beer batter, are ideal with steaks, burgers, or even as a snack. At BLT Steak, we serve these in tall stacks for maximum effect. I like to serve these with a sprinkle of cayenne. | Serve with any of the beef or veal recipes, the Lobster Rolls (page 110), or BLT Grilled Tuna Sandwich (page 112). | SERVES 6

FRIED ONION RINGS

1½ cups all-purpose flour

1 tablespoon plus 1 teaspoon baking powder

1½ teaspoons fine sea salt, plus extra for garnish

12 ounces beer, preferably lager

1 egg, lightly beaten

Vegetable or canola oil for frying

3 large sweet onions, such as Vidalia, cut crosswise into ½-inch slices

MAKE THE BATTER In a large bowl, whisk together the flour, baking powder, and salt. Stir in the beer and egg just until smooth. Do not overmix or the batter will become tough.

HEAT THE OIL Pour about 3 inches of oil into a deep, heavy saucepan or fill a deep fryer according to the manufacturer's directions. Heat the oil to 375°F on a deep-frying thermometer or until a small drop of the batter dropped into the batter turns golden brown in about a minute.

COAT THE ONION RINGS Separate the onion slices into rings. Dip the rings into the batter, lifting them out with tongs. Tap the onion rings gently on the side of the bowl to let the excess batter drip off.

FRY THE ONION RINGS Carefully slip the rings into the oil without crowding the pan. Cook for about 1½ minutes, turning the onion rings over once, until golden brown.

Remove the onion rings with a slotted spoon. Drain on paper towels. Fry the remaining onion rings in the same way. Season with salt.

SERVE immediately on paper towels.

CHEF'S TIP: *If the batter becomes too thick, stir in a little more beer.*

Beer-battered jalapeños stuffed with cream cheese are a big seller at BLT Fish as a bar snack. Serve them with a good beer, such as Brooklyn Lager. I sometimes eat these with a sprinkle of Tabasco sauce. | Serve with Grilled Jerk Chicken (page 185), Adobo-Marinated Hanger Steak (page 161), BLT Grilled Tuna Sandwich (page 112), or Grilled Scallops/Mexican Tomatillo Salsa (page 144). | SERVES 6

FRIED STUFFED JALAPEÑOS

15 large fresh jalapeño chiles, cut in half lengthwise, seeds and white membranes removed

8 ounces cream cheese, at room temperature

2¼ cups all-purpose flour

1½ teaspoons fine sea salt to taste

1½ teaspoons baking powder

12 ounces beer, preferably lager

1 egg, lightly beaten

Canola or grapeseed oil for frying

Old Bay Seasoning, for serving

STUFF THE CHILES Stuff each jalapeño half with about 1 tablespoon of the cream cheese, mounding it slightly and pressing it in firmly. Refrigerate for 20 minutes.

MAKE THE BATTER In a large bowl, whisk together 1¾ cups of the flour, 1½ teaspoons salt, and the baking powder. Whisk in the beer and egg just until smooth. Do not overbeat or the batter will become tough.

HEAT THE OIL Pour about 3 inches of the oil into a deep, heavy saucepan or fill a deep fryer according to the manufacturer's directions. Heat over medium heat until the oil reaches 375°F on a deep-frying thermometer or until a small drop of the batter dropped into the batter turns golden brown in about a minute.

FRY THE JALAPEÑOS Roll a jalapeño half in the remaining ½ cup of the flour. Dip it in the batter, and then tap it against the side of the bowl to remove the excess. Carefully place the jalapeño in the oil. Repeat with the remaining jalapeños. Add as many as will fit comfortably without crowding. Fry 2 minutes, or until nicely browned. Remove the jalapeños with a slotted spoon and drain on paper towels.

TO SERVE Sprinkle with salt or Old Bay Seasoning and serve immediately.

Carrots were not my favorite vegetable when I was a child, but now I love to eat them this way. | Serve with 5-Spice Caramelized Long Island Duck (page 190), Striped Bass/Curry Brown Butter (page 136), Sea Salt–Crusted Pink Snapper/Ice Wine Nage (page 133), or Braised Short Ribs/Garlic-Thyme Brown Butter (page 163). | SERVES 6

HONEY | CUMIN-GLAZED CARROTS

Broth

1 medium white onion, chopped

1 tablespoon fine sea salt

1 tablespoon sugar

½ teaspoon fennel seeds

¼ teaspoon coriander seeds

1 star anise, chopped

1 bay leaf

2 sprigs fresh thyme

6 to 8 medium carrots, peeled and trimmed

¼ cup acacia honey

1 teaspoon cumin seeds

2 limes, zested and juiced

3 tablespoons unsalted butter

PREHEAT THE OVEN to 375°F.

MAKE THE BROTH In a large pot, combine 4 cups water and the broth ingredients. Bring the liquid to a simmer. Turn off the heat and let steep for 1 hour. Strain the liquid and discard the solids.

BAKE THE CARROTS Arrange the carrots in a baking dish just large enough to hold them. Add enough of the broth to cover the carrots. Cover with foil. Bake for 1½ hours, or until the carrots can easily be pierced with a knife.

Cool the carrots in the baking dish. Remove them carefully from the liquid. Strain the liquid and set aside.

MAKE THE GLAZE In a medium skillet, heat the honey and cumin seeds until the honey is boiling and begins to brown slightly. Remove the honey from the heat. Carefully add the lime juice (it may sputter and splash), butter, and ½ cup of the reserved liquid. Bring the mixture to a simmer and cook for 2 minutes on medium heat, until thick and reduced by one-third. Add the carrots and turn them gently to coat with the glaze.

TO SERVE Sprinkle the carrots with the lime zest. Serve immediately.

Grilling fresh corn in the husk keeps the kernels tender and moist while infusing it with flavor from the butter and seasonings. This is perfect for a summer barbecue or with steamed lobster. If you can't find corn in the husk, prepare the corn in the same way, but wrap and grill it in aluminum foil. | Serve with Grilled Shrimp/Cauliflower/Soy-Caper Brown Butter Sauce (page 140), Grilled Scallops/Mexican Tomatillo Salsa (page 144), Adobo-Marinated Hanger Steak (page 161), Grilled Jerk Chicken (page 185), or Barbecued Beef Brisket (page 162). | SERVES 6

GRILLED CORN | HERB BUTTER

6 ears fresh corn, husks on

12 tablespoons (1½ sticks) unsalted butter, softened

Fine sea salt and freshly ground black pepper to taste

2½ tablespoons finely chopped fresh parsley

1 finely chopped shallot

1½ tablespoons chopped fresh chives

¼ teaspoon finely chopped garlic

PREPARE THE CORN Pull the husks back from the corn, leaving them attached at the base. Pull off and discard the silks.

MAKE THE BUTTER Beat together the butter and remaining ingredients. Spread 2 tablespoons on each ear of corn. Sprinkle the corn with salt and pepper. Pull the husk up around the corn and tie tightly with kitchen twine.

GRILL THE CORN Preheat a barbecue or stovetop grill to medium heat. Grill the corn 6 minutes, turning once. Close the cover on the grill and cook 5 minutes more.

SERVE immediately.

My grandmother liked to serve these hash browns with soft, creamy St. Nectaire cheese melted on top and a green salad on the side. We called it *tartiflette*. | Serve with Cornish Hen Diablo (page 188), Smoked Sea Salt and Black Pepper–Crusted Rib-Eye (page 151), Grilled BLT Double-Cut Strip Steak (page 159), Porterhouse/White and Dark Soubise (page 152), or Herb-Crusted Rack of Lamb (page 168). | SERVES 6

LEEK-POTATO HASH BROWNS

2 medium leeks, white part only, cut into ¼-inch slices (about 2 cups)

2 medium baking potatoes (about 2 pounds), peeled

1 small sweet onion, such as Vidalia, thinly sliced

Fine sea salt and freshly ground black pepper to taste

¼ cup plus 2 tablespoons canola oil

1 tablespoon unsalted butter

PREPARE THE VEGETABLES Place the leek slices in a colander under cold running water. Rinse well to eliminate any grit. Drain and pat very dry with paper towels.

Grate the potatoes on the large holes of a box grater or in a food processor.

In a bowl, mix together the potatoes, leeks, and onions. Add salt and pepper.

COOK THE POTATOES In a 12-inch nonstick skillet, heat ¼ cup of the oil over medium-high heat. Add the potato mixture. Flatten the vegetables with a spatula and smooth the edges. The cake should be about 1 inch thick. Reduce the heat to medium and cook until the cake is crusty and golden brown on the bottom, about 15 minutes. Drain off the excess oil.

Place a baking sheet on top of the pan. Invert the pan onto the sheet. Place the pan back on the heat and add the remaining 2 tablespoons of the oil. Slide the hash browns back into the pan, uncooked-side down. Cook until the bottom is golden brown, about 7 more minutes. Turn the heat up to medium-high and add the butter on top. Cook 2 minutes more.

TO SERVE Slide a spatula under the hash browns to be sure that they are not sticking. Slide the cake onto a platter and sprinkle with salt. Cut into wedges. Serve hot.

CHEF'S TIP: *A nonstick skillet does the best job of browning these potatoes.*

These tomatoes go well with a wide variety of dishes. Zucchini, onions, and other vegetables can also be prepared this way. Raw sausage meat can be added to the bread crumb mixture. Sprinkle a little white wine on top and bake until the sausage is cooked through, about 30 minutes. | Serve with Tapenade-Stuffed Leg of Lamb (page 167), Herb-Crusted Rack of Lamb (page 168), Roasted Cod Fish/Herb-Bacon Crust (page 137), Cornish Hen Diablo (page 188), Smoky Honey Veal Porterhouse (page 176), Smoked Sea Salt and Black Pepper–Crusted Rib-Eye (page 151), or Grilled BLT Double-Cut Strip Steak (page 159). | SERVES 6

OREGANO-BREADED TOMATOES

1 cup panko bread crumbs

5 tablespoons extra-virgin olive oil

3 tablespoons chopped fresh parsley

2 tablespoons chopped fresh oregano

1 tablespoon finely chopped garlic

Fine sea salt and freshly ground black pepper to taste

6 large vine-ripened tomatoes, halved lengthwise

PREHEAT THE OVEN to 350°F. Oil a small baking pan.

MAKE THE STUFFING In a bowl, stir together the bread crumbs, oil, parsley, oregano, garlic, salt, and pepper.

FILL THE TOMATOES Sprinkle each tomato half with salt and pepper and place them in the pan, cut-side up. Top with the bread crumb mixture.

BAKE THE TOMATOES 30 minutes, or until the crumbs are golden brown. Serve hot.

Thick slices of potato are poached first in cream until tender but still whole, then browned with cheese under the broiler. These are great with a plain steak or chops. | Serve with Roasted Cod Fish/Herb-Bacon Crust (page 137), Papillote of Halibut/Creamy Tomato-Sorrel Sauce (page 141), Smoked Sea Salt and Black Pepper–Crusted Rib-Eye (page 151), Grilled BLT Double-Cut Strip Steak (page 159), Braised Short Ribs/Garlic-Thyme Brown Butter (page 163), Tapenade-Stuffed Leg of Lamb (page 167), Herb-Crusted Rack of Lamb (page 168), Grilled Lamb T-Bones (page 174), or Smoky Honey Veal Porterhouse (page 176). | SERVES 6

SCALLOPED POTATOES GRATIN

2½ pounds small baking potatoes, peeled and cut crosswise into ⅓-inch-thick slices

5 cups heavy cream

4 sprigs fresh thyme

1 tablespoon minced garlic

¼ teaspoon freshly grated nutmeg

Fine sea salt and freshly ground black pepper to taste

1 cup grated Gruyère cheese (3 ounces)

SIMMER THE POTATOES In a large pot, combine the potatoes, cream, thyme, garlic, and nutmeg. Season with salt and pepper. Bring the liquid to a simmer over medium heat. Cook very gently, shaking the pan occasionally so that the potatoes do not stick, 20 to 25 minutes, or until tender when pierced with a knife.

Place a flat strainer or a cake rack over a saucepan. Strain the cream into the saucepan. Let the potatoes cool slightly.

REDUCE THE CREAM Bring the strained cooking liquid to a simmer. Cook until it is reduced to 2 cups.

BROWN THE POTATOES In a 10-inch gratin or baking dish, arrange the potato slices overlapping slightly. Pour on the cream. Sprinkle the potatoes with the cheese.

Place the broiler rack very close to the heat source. Turn the heat to high. Place the pan under the broiler. Broil until golden brown. Serve hot.

CHEF'S TIP: *Be sure that the broiler is turned to high and the potatoes are very close to the heat so that they brown quickly and the cream does not break.*

Named for the baker's wife, who would slip a pan of these potatoes into the hot bread oven beneath a roasting leg of lamb to catch all of the delicious meat juices, these potatoes are good with just about any roast. | My mother sometimes browns pork tenderloins and places them to finish cooking on top of the potatoes when they are almost done. | Serve with Tapenade-Stuffed Leg of Lamb (page 167), Striped Bass/Curry Brown Butter (page 136), or Rosemary-Parmesan–Crusted Veal Chop (page 177). | SERVES 6

POTATOES BOULANGÈRES

3 ounces double-smoked bacon, cut into ½-inch pieces

1 medium white onion, chopped

1 garlic clove, chopped

5 juniper berries, crushed

6 sprigs fresh thyme

2 bay leaves

2 tablespoons chopped fresh sage

2 tablespoons chopped fresh parsley

3 large baking potatoes (about 3 pounds), peeled and sliced ⅛ inch thick

Fine sea salt and freshly ground black pepper to taste

About 2 cups beef stock or low-sodium beef broth

About 2 cups chicken stock or low-sodium chicken broth

3 tablespoons unsalted butter, cut into bits

PREHEAT THE OVEN to 425°F. Butter a 2-quart casserole dish that is at least 3 inches deep.

COOK THE BACON In a skillet, cook the bacon over medium heat until lightly browned, about 5 minutes. Add the onion, garlic, and juniper berries. Cook until the onion is soft, about 5 minutes more. Stir in the thyme, bay leaves, sage, and parsley.

ASSEMBLE THE DISH Layer the potato slices in the pan. Top with the bacon mixture. Season with salt and pepper. Add enough of the broth to almost cover the potatoes. Dot with the butter.

BAKE THE POTATOES Loosely cover the dish with foil. Bake for 20 minutes. Reduce the oven temperature to 350°F and uncover the potatoes. Bake for 1 hour more, or until the potatoes are very tender when pierced with a knife.

Serve hot.

Hen of the Woods mushrooms are also known as *maiitake.* Wild mushrooms, which appear in October, can grow to enormous size, though much of them are then too woody to eat. Cultivated Hen of the Woods mushrooms are available year-round. They are about the size of a fist and their color ranges from beige to brown or gray. | I like to use this two-step cooking method of poaching the mushrooms first to tenderize them, and then pan-searing them for added flavor. This technique is also good because you can steam them ahead of time and finish them when you are ready to serve. | Serve with Spicy Curry Duck Noodles (page 78) or Smoked Sea Salt and Black Pepper–Crusted Rib-Eye (page 151). | SERVES 6

PAN-SEARED HEN OF THE WOODS MUSHROOMS

1 pound Hen of the Woods mushrooms

1 teaspoon fine sea salt

1 sprig fresh thyme

1 bay leaf

3 tablespoons extra-virgin olive oil

4 tablespoons (½ stick) unsalted butter

2 tablespoons chopped fresh parsley

1 teaspoon freshly squeezed lemon juice

1 garlic clove, minced

Freshly ground black pepper to taste

PREPARE THE MUSHROOMS Brush the mushrooms gently with a soft brush or cloth. Divide them into 2-inch pieces by gently pulling them apart.

POACH THE MUSHROOMS In a medium saucepan, combine 1 cup water, the salt, thyme, bay leaf, and mushrooms. Cover and bring to a simmer over medium low heat for 5 minutes. Drain the mushrooms, discarding the thyme and bay leaf. Gently pat dry with a paper towel.

SAUTÉ THE MUSHROOMS In a large skillet, heat the oil over medium heat. Add the mushrooms and brown on all sides. Tip the pan and spoon out the excess oil. Add the butter, parsley, lemon juice, and garlic. Cook, stirring frequently, until the mushrooms are nicely browned, about 5 minutes. Add salt and pepper.

Serve immediately.

When we first made these potatoes, we baked them in 2-inch-diameter ovenproof espresso cups. You can use cups, or you will need twelve 4-ounce rigid foil cups, found at most grocery stores. | These potatoes are good with any meat or fish, but they are also great served with a green salad on top. | Serve with Baked Black Sea Bass/Tomato/Eggplant/Honey/Sherry Vinegar (page 138), Braised Swordfish/Tomatoes, Olives, and Capers (page 128), or Papillote of Halibut/Creamy Tomato-Sorrel Sauce (page 141). | SERVES 6

SILVER DOLLARS

2 cups (4 sticks) unsalted butter

6 large baking potatoes (about 6 pounds), peeled

Fine sea salt to taste

CLARIFY THE BUTTER In the top half of a double boiler set over simmering water, melt the butter. Refrigerate the butter until firm, about 1 hour.

Remove the solid clarified butter from the surface and place it in a small saucepan. Discard the milky liquid.

Melt the clarified butter over low heat. Pour it into a large bowl. Cover and keep warm so that the butter remains liquid.

PREPARE THE POTATOES With a large heavy chef's knife, trim the potatoes to flatten the sides and form a rectangular shape. With a 2-inch round cookie cutter, cut 2 cylinders out of each potato. On a mandoline slicer, cut the potato cylinders into ⅛-inch slices.

Bring a medium saucepan of salted water to a boil.

Drop some of the slices into the boiling water and cook for 1 minute, or until they become transparent. With a slotted spoon, drain the slices and transfer them to the bowl with the clarified butter. Stir the potatoes to coat them well with the butter. Repeat with the remaining potato slices.

ASSEMBLE THE MOLDS Place twelve 4-ounce rigid foil molds on a large baking sheet. Stack 12 slices of potato in each mold. Fill each container with additional butter, covering the top of the potatoes.

Preheat the oven to 400°F.

BAKE THE MOLDS Place the molds on a baking sheet. Bake for 1 hour to 1 hour and 15 minutes, or until the potatoes are crisp and brown around the edges. (The potatoes will already be tender from the blanching process.)

TO SERVE Protecting your hands with potholders, tip the molds to drain off the excess butter. (This can be refrigerated or frozen and reused.) Spread the potato slices out on a warm serving platter and sprinkle them with sea salt. Serve hot.

This recipe uses many of the ingredients that appear in the spring: morel mushrooms, asparagus, fiddlehead ferns, peas, and fava beans. Make it during those few weeks in early May when they are all available at the same time. | A word about wild mushrooms: There is so much talk about foraging for them these days that you might be inspired to try it yourself. But I would warn you against it. Because it can be very difficult to tell an edible variety from a poison one, it is a job best left to the experts. | Don't make the same mistake I made as a young cook when I ruined a terrine of lobsters and morels. Morels can hold a lot of sand, so be sure to clean them thoroughly with a soft brush. | For a perfect spring meal, serve with Sea Salt–Crusted Pink Snapper (page 133) or Tapenade-Stuffed Leg of Lamb (page 167). You can also toss the ragoût with freshly cooked fettuccine. | SERVES 6

SPRING MOREL AND VEGETABLE RAGOÛT

11 ounces small fresh morels (about 2 cups)

Fine sea salt to taste

½ cup shelled fresh peas

1 cup fiddlehead ferns

18 medium asparagus tips

1 bunch ramps (about 24), trimmed and rinsed but left whol

2 pounds fava beans, shelled (about 1 cup shelled beans)

6 tablespoons (¾ stick) unsalted butter

4 heads garlic, cloves separated, peeled, and chopped

½ cup dry white wine

1 medium spring onion, white and green parts chopped separately

CLEAN THE MORELS Rinse the morels in a bowl of cold water. Drain and repeat 2 times or until there is no trace of sand left in the bottom of the bowl.

BLANCH THE VEGETABLES Bring a pot of salted water to a boil over high heat. Add the peas and cook for 3 minutes. Scoop out the peas with a strainer and transfer them to a bowl of ice water.

Repeat with the fiddlehead ferns, cooking them for 5 minutes. Cool the ferns in a bowl of ice water. Cook the remaining vegetables in the same way, changing the water after each vegetable. Cook the asparagus for 4 minutes, the ramps for 4 minutes, and the fava beans for 1 minute. Peel each fava bean. Drain the vegetables and pat them dry with paper towels.

COOK THE MORELS Melt 1 tablespoon of the butter in a large skillet over medium heat. Add three-quarters of the garlic, the wine, white parts of the onion, thyme, and morels. Bring the wine to a boil over high heat, and cook for 2 minutes.

Add the chicken stock and a pinch of salt and cook over medium heat until the morels are cooked through, 12 to 15 minutes more.

1 sprig fresh thyme

1 cup chicken stock or low-sodium chicken broth

Freshly ground black pepper to taste

COOK THE FIDDLEHEAD FERNS In another skillet melt 1 more tablespoon of the butter over medium heat. Add the fiddlehead ferns and remaining garlic. Cook, stirring often, for 2 minutes.

COMBINE THE VEGETABLES Add the ferns and the other vegetables to the pan with the morels. Add the remaining 4 tablespoons of the butter. Raise the heat to high and cook, stirring, until the butter is melted. Stir in the green parts of the onions and season with salt and pepper.

Serve hot.

Use small mushrooms if you want to serve these tasty caps as hors d'oeuvres. Cremini or portobello mushrooms can be substituted for the button mushrooms if you prefer. | Serve with Grilled BLT Double-Cut Strip Steak (page 159), Smoky Honey Veal Porterhouse (page 172), or Filet and Foie Gras Rossini (page 155).

| SERVES 6

STUFFED MUSHROOM CAPS

24 very large button mushrooms

Fine sea salt and freshly ground black pepper to taste

⅓ cup extra-virgin olive oil

3 tablespoons unsalted butter, softened

2 sprigs fresh thyme

3 whole unpeeled garlic cloves plus 2 tablespoons chopped garlic

1 tablespoon chopped shallot

1¾ cups panko bread crumbs

⅔ cup plus 1 teaspoon chopped fresh flat-leaf parsley

CLEAN THE MUSHROOMS Wash the mushrooms thoroughly under cold water. Set the caps aside and chop the stems finely. Season the caps with salt and pepper.

SAUTÉ THE CAPS In a large skillet, heat the olive oil and 1 tablespoon of the butter. Add the mushroom caps, rounded-side down. Scatter the thyme and whole garlic cloves between the caps. Cook on low heat, turning the mushrooms once, until the mushrooms are tender, about 5 minutes. Remove the caps to a roasting pan with a slotted spoon. Discard the whole garlic cloves and thyme.

MAKE THE FILLING Add the chopped mushroom stems, chopped garlic, and shallot to the skillet with a pinch of salt and pepper. Cook, stirring frequently, for 4 minutes, or until the vegetables are soft.

Remove the mixture to a bowl and add the panko, the ⅔ cup parsley, and remaining 2 tablespoons of the butter. Add salt and pepper. Mix well.

Preheat the oven to 325°F.

BAKE THE MUSHROOMS Spoon the bread crumb mixture into the mushroom caps. Bake 10 minutes.

BROWN THE TOPS Run the mushrooms under the broiler until golden brown, about 2 minutes.

TO SERVE Sprinkle with the remaining 1 teaspoon of the parsley and serve immediately.

These home fries first appeared on the menu for the opening of BLT Prime. The potatoes are cooked in a creamy sauce tangy with mustard and herbs. You can bake the potatoes a day before serving them and they will be ready to cook the next day for brunch with eggs, or with steak or chops. | Serve with Grilled Lamb T-bones (page 174), Porterhouse/White and Dark Soubise (page 152), and Cornish Hen Diablo (page 188). | SERVES 6

CREAMY HOME FRIES

3 pounds baking potatoes

2 tablespoons unsalted butter

2 tablespoons olive oil

Fine sea salt and freshly ground black pepper to taste

2 tablespoons diced shallot

1 tablespoon finely chopped garlic

1 cup heavy cream

2 tablespoons Dijon mustard

2 tablespoons whole-grain mustard

1 tablespoon chopped fresh sage

PREHEAT THE OVEN to 400°F.

BAKE THE POTATOES With a small, sharp knife, pierce each potato. Bake 45 minutes, or until fork tender. Let cool slightly, then refrigerate until cold. Peel the potatoes and cut and into ½-inch cubes.

SAUTÉ THE POTATOES Heat a large sauté pan over medium-high heat. Add half of the butter and oil. When the butter is melted, add half of the potatoes or as many as will fit comfortably in a single layer. Season with salt and pepper. Cook until the potatoes are golden brown, 8 to 10 minutes. Add half of the shallots and garlic and cook for 30 seconds more. Transfer the potatoes to a plate. Cover and keep warm.

Add the remaining butter and oil to the pan and brown the second half of the potatoes in the same way, adding the second half of the shallots and garlic at the end.

STIR TOGETHER the cream and mustards until blended.

FINISH THE POTATOES Return the first batch of potatoes to the skillet. Stir in the cream mixture and bring it to a simmer. Remove the skillet from the heat and stir in the sage. Adjust the seasoning to taste.

Serve immediately.

Crisp, brown *frites,* or French fries, are one of my mom's specialties. I decided to enhance them with cheese, garlic, and rosemary and asked one of the BLT cooks to come up with a recipe. This was the delicious result. When preparing potatoes for French fries, be sure to cut all of the pieces into the same thickness so that they will cook and brown evenly. | Serve with American Kobe Burger/au Poivre Sauce (page 148), Cornish Hen Diablo (page 188), Smoked Sea Salt and Black Pepper–Crusted Rib-Eye (page 151). | SERVES 6

ROSEMARY-PARMESAN FRENCH FRIES

3 large baking potatoes (about 3 pounds), peeled

8 tablespoons (1 stick) unsalted butter

2 tablespoons chopped garlic

4 tablespoons chopped fresh rosemary

Peanut oil for frying

2 cups freshly grated Parmigiano-Reggiano cheese

Fine sea salt to taste

PREPARE THE POTATOES Using a mandoline, French fry cutter, or chef's knife, cut the potatoes into ¼-inch-thick sticks. Soak the sticks in cold water for several hours or overnight. Drain the potatoes and pat them dry with paper towels.

MAKE THE SAUCE In a small saucepan, slowly brown the butter. Add the garlic and 2 tablespoons of the rosemary. Remove from the heat and allow the garlic and rosemary to infuse the butter.

FRY THE POTATOES Pour the oil into a large, heavy pot or deep fryer to a depth of 3 inches. Heat the oil to 300°F on a deep-frying thermometer. Carefully add enough of the potatoes so they fit without crowding. Blanch the fries for 3 to 4 minutes, until soft and only very slightly colored. With a slotted spoon, remove the potatoes and transfer them to paper towels to drain. This step can be completed an hour or 2 before you plan to serve the fries.

Increase the temperature of the oil to 375°F. Fry the potatoes in batches until golden brown, 1 to 2 minutes. Remove to paper towels to drain.

TO SERVE In a large bowl, toss the French fries with the cheese and flavored butter. Season with sea salt. Garnish with the remaining 2 tablespoons of the rosemary. Serve immediately.

Sunchokes, also known as Jerusalem artichokes, are good sautéed or baked, but my favorite way to cook them is to roast them coated with salt, the way we do potatoes in my family. Their flavor seems more concentrated and the texture is great. When buying Jerusalem artichokes, look for large, firm ones with few knobs. | Serve with Roasted Cod Fish/Herb-Bacon Crust (page 137) or Porterhouse/White and Dark Soubise (page 152). | SERVES 6

SEA SALT-CRUSTED SUNCHOKES

12 medium to large sunchokes (Jerusalem artichokes), about 2 pounds

1¼ cups coarse sea salt or kosher salt

1 tablespoon chopped fresh rosemary

1 tablespoon chopped fresh thyme

1 tablespoon cracked black peppercorns

3 egg whites, at room temperature

½ cup crème fraîche

½ cup grated Parmigiano-Reggiano cheese

2 tablespoons truffle oil, or to taste

PREHEAT THE OVEN to 400°F. Brush a baking sheet with vegetable oil.

PREPARE THE VEGETABLES Scrub the sunchokes gently with a brush and dry thoroughly with paper towels.

PREPARE THE SALT CRUST Combine the salt, rosemary, thyme, and peppercorns. In an electric mixer, beat the egg whites until they are frothy but are not yet holding peaks. Stir in the salt mixture to form a paste.

BAKE THE ARTICHOKES On the prepared baking sheet, spread the paste evenly around the artichokes, pressing it into them to form a crust. Try to coat them as much as possible.

Bake 1½ hours, or until the sunchokes are very soft when pierced with a sharp knife.

MAKE THE TOPPING Spoon the crème fraîche into a small serving bowl. Top with the grated cheese and truffle oil.

TO SERVE Remove the salt crust and spread it on a serving platter. Cut the sunchokes in half. Place them cut-side up on top of the salt. Provide spoons to scoop out the flesh and dip in the sauce.

My grandfather wasn't really a cook, but he had one specialty—this combination of Brussels sprouts and roasted chestnuts with a caramelized honey glaze. He would make this dish for us on Sundays and we would eat them with roast leg of lamb. | Serve with Roasted Rosemary-Lemon Chicken (page 183) or Tapenade-Stuffed Leg of Lamb (page 167). | SERVES 6

HONEY CARAMELIZED BRUSSELS SPROUTS | ROASTED CHESTNUTS

12 ounces chestnuts, roasted and peeled (see page 272)

2 pounds Brussels sprouts, stems trimmed

2 tablespoons unsalted butter

1 tablespoon minced garlic

1 tablespoon minced shallots

1 cup honey

10 ounces prosciutto, cut into ½-inch strips

1 tablespoon sugar

Fine sea salt and freshly ground black pepper to taste

1 cup chopped fresh parsley leaves

PREPARE THE CHESTNUTS Cut the peeled chestnuts into thin slices.

BLANCH THE BRUSSELS SPROUTS Bring a large pot of salted water to a boil. Add the Brussels sprouts and cook 5 minutes. Drain and transfer the sprouts to a bowl of ice water to cool. Drain well.

SAUTÉ THE BRUSSELS SPROUTS In a large sauté pan over medium heat, melt the butter until it begins to foam. Add the garlic and shallots and sauté for 2 to 3 minutes, or until the shallots are tender. Add the Brussels sprouts and chestnuts. Stir until well combined. Cook for 2 to 3 minutes.

Add the honey, prosciutto, and sugar. Turn up the heat to medium-high. Cook, without moving the pan, for about 2 minutes to allow the Brussels sprouts to caramelize and the prosciutto to crisp.

Season with salt and pepper. Stir in the parsley.

Serve immediately.

CHAPTER NINE

Pecan
Pie

Panna cotta literally translates to "cooked cream" in Italian. However, in this recipe, the cream is barely brought to a simmer and the silky smooth consistency is achieved by using sheets of gelatin. These desserts are ideal for a dinner party because they can be made a day in advance and kept in the refrigerator.

| SERVES 6

GOAT CHEESE PANNA COTTA | PORT-HUCKLEBERRY REDUCTION

¾ cup Montrachet or other fresh goat cheese

⅓ cup sugar

¼ cup plain whole milk yogurt

1 teaspoon vanilla extract

3½ sheets gelatin (not granulated; see Sources, page 274)

2 cups heavy cream

Port-Huckleberry Sauce

3 cups tawny port

2 tablespoons sugar

3 tablespoons frozen huckleberries or wild blueberries

Honey Sauce

½ cup honey

1 tablespoon julienned dried fig

1 tablespoon julienned dried date

1 tablespoon dried cranberries

1 tablespoon julienned dried apricot

3 tablespoons chopped roasted skinned hazelnuts

1 teaspoon water

MAKE THE PANNA COTTA In a large mixer bowl, beat the goat cheese, sugar, yogurt, and vanilla for 2 to 3 minutes, or until blended.

Soften the gelatin sheets in a bowl of warm water for 2 to 3 minutes.

In a small saucepot, bring the cream to a simmer. Drain the gelatin sheets and stir them into the cream until dissolved.

Pour the cream into the goat cheese mixture. Beat until smooth.

Pour into six 4-ounce ramekins. Allow to set in the refrigerator for a minimum of 4 hours.

MAKE THE PORT-HUCKLEBERRY SAUCE In a medium saucepan, bring the port to a simmer over medium heat. Cook until reduced to 1 cup. Add the sugar and continue to simmer until reduced to 2 tablespoons of liquid. Stir in the huckleberries. Remove from the heat.

MAKE THE HONEY SAUCE In a small pot over low heat, warm the honey with the dried fruit and 1 tablespoon of the hazelnuts. Just before serving, add the water and stir to combine.

TO SERVE Dip a ramekin of panna cotta in warm water for 30 seconds. Invert the panna cotta onto a serving plate. Repeat with the remaining ramekins.

Pour the honey sauce over the panna cottas. Sprinkle the remaining roasted hazelnuts on top and drizzle some of the port reduction and huckleberries around the sides. Serve immediately.

WINE SUGGESTION: ICEWINE, SELAKS, 2004, MARLBOROUGH, NEW ZEALAND (BLEND OF GEWÜRZTRAMINER AND RIESLING). *An ice wine with aromas of passion fruit, honeyed melon, and spring flowers.*

At the restaurant, we flame these rich custards with a blowtorch to get an even crunchy topping. Many cookware stores sell blowtorches for this purpose, but you can just as easily do this in the broiler. | Dutch-process cocoa powder is more subtle than regular cocoa powder. It still gives a strong chocolate flavor and a rich dark color, but with less bitterness. | SERVES 6

CARAMEL CRÈME BRÛLÉE | DOUBLE CHOCOLATE CHUNK COOKIES

Custard

4 cups milk

1¼ cups heavy cream

¾ cup plus ⅓ cup sugar

2 whole eggs

6 egg yolks

Double Chocolate Chunk Cookies

8 ounces milk chocolate, preferably Valrhona

1 cup (2 sticks) unsalted butter

1 cup all-purpose flour

½ cup unsweetened Dutch-process cocoa powder

½ teaspoon baking soda

½ teaspoon fine sea salt

1½ cups sugar

2 eggs

1 teaspoon vanilla extract

2 tablespoons superfine sugar

MAKE THE CUSTARD In a medium pot, heat the milk and cream until small bubbles appear around the edge. In a medium saucepan over medium heat, cook the ¾ cup sugar, swirling the pan occasionally until it is a dark amber color, about 8 to 10 minutes. Remove the pan from the heat. Slowly pour the hot milk mixture into the caramel carefully so that the mixture does not bubble up and splatter. Whisk until all of the caramel is dissolved.

In a large electric mixer bowl, beat the whole eggs and yolks with the ⅓ cup sugar until frothy and pale yellow. Still beating, slowly add ¼ cup of the warm milk. Whisk the egg mixture into the remaining milk.

BAKE THE CUSTARD Preheat the oven to 325°F. Pour the custard into six 8-ounce ramekins or coffee cups. Place them in a large roasting pan and place the pan in the oven. Carefully pour hot water to a depth of ½ inch into the pan.

Bake for 30 to 40 minutes, or until the middle of the custard jiggles just slightly when a cup is shaken.

COOL THE CUPS Remove the cups from the pan. Let cool slightly, then cover and refrigerate for at least 4 hours or overnight.

CHOP THE CHOCOLATE FOR THE COOKIES With a large heavy chef's knife, chop half of the chocolate into ¼-inch chunks. Set aside.

Chop the remaining chocolate coarsely.

MELT THE CHOCOLATE Place the coarsely chopped chocolate and the butter in the top half of a heatproof bowl or double boiler. Set the bowl or boiler top over a saucepan of slowly simmering water.

MAKE THE DOUGH In a medium bowl, whisk together the flour, cocoa, baking soda, and salt.

Scrape the chocolate mixture into a large mixer bowl. Add the sugar, eggs, and vanilla and mix on medium speed until combined.

Reduce the speed to low. Gradually add the dry ingredients, scraping the sides of the bowl with a rubber spatula until blended. Fold in the chocolate chunks.

BAKE THE COOKIES With a 1¼-inch ice cream scoop, or using 2 large spoons, shape the dough into balls about the size of a large walnut. Place the balls 2 inches apart on the prepared baking sheets.

Bake until the cookies are flat and the surface begins to crack, but the cookies are still soft, about 15 minutes. Let the cookies set on the pans for about 1 minute. Transfer to wire racks to cool.

STORE Place the cookies in airtight containers. They keep well up to 3 days.

GLAZE THE CUSTARD When ready to serve, heat the broiler and place the rack about 2 inches from the heat source. Sprinkle the superfine sugar on top of the custards, making sure that they are completely covered.

Place the cups on a baking sheet. Broil until the sugar just starts to caramelize, rotating the sheet for even browning, about 2 minutes.

COOL THE CUPS Remove the cups from the pan. Let cool slightly, then cover and refrigerate for at least 4 hours or overnight.

SERVE immediately with the Double Chocolate Chunk Cookies.

WINE SUGGESTION: VIOGNIER DOUX, BONNY DOON VINEYARD, 2004, SANTA CRUZ, CALIFORNIA. *A late-harvest wine with aromas of dried apricots, caramel, and violets.*

I like all kinds of cookies, but these are my favorite kind. They are great plain, especially when warm, but I also like to use the cooled cookies to make ice cream sandwiches. | This makes extra-large cookies, but you could make them smaller if you prefer. | MAKES ABOUT TWENTY 4-INCH COOKIES

CHOCOLATE-ESPRESSO COOKIES

1½ tablespoons instant espresso powder

1 tablespoon hot water

2 cups all-purpose flour

1¼ teaspoons baking soda

¼ teaspoon fine sea salt

1 cup (2 sticks) unsalted butter, at room temperature

¾ cup packed light brown sugar

¾ cup granulated sugar

1 egg

1¼ teaspoons vanilla extract

1½ cups semisweet chocolate chips

PREHEAT THE OVEN to 325°F. Line 3 large baking sheets with parchment paper.

MAKE THE DOUGH In a cup, stir together the espresso powder and water until dissolved. On a piece of waxed paper, stir together the flour, baking soda, and salt.

In a large bowl with an electric mixer, beat the butter and both sugars until smooth and creamy. Add the coffee, egg, and vanilla and beat until blended.

Stir in the flour mixture. Fold in the chocolate chips.

SHAPE THE COOKIES Scoop up about ¼ cup of the dough with a small ice cream scoop or dry measuring cup. Drop the dough 3 inches apart onto the cookie sheets.

BAKE 18 minutes or until slightly puffed but still soft in the center.

COOL the cookies for 1 minute on the baking sheets. Transfer the cookies to wire racks to cool.

SERVE warm or let cool completely, then store in an airtight container.

CHEF'S TIP: *For bar cookies, press the dough out on a parchment-lined baking pan to an even ½ inch thickness. Cut into bars while still warm.*

WINE SUGGESTION: ZINFANDEL PORT, ROSENBLUM CELLARS, 2003, SAN FRANCISCO BAY, CALIFORNIA. *A port-style wine made from Zinfandel grapes, with aromas of jammy red berries, dried cherries, and spice.*

My mom made this cake, from my grandmother's recipe, for my thirty-ninth birthday. It makes a beautiful presentation in a footed glass bowl served like a trifle, or you can make it in a charlotte mold and unmold it like a cake onto a platter. If you do unmold it, first dip the mold briefly in warm water to loosen the cake. Pour the crème anglaise on top and garnish with the chocolate curls. | *Strega,* meaning "witch" in Italian, is a yellow liqueur made from a blend of herbs and spices including saffron, which gives it its color. | The key to the crème anglaise is cooking it until just right: One way to test it is to dip a spatula in the cream and run your finger through it. If your finger makes a trail rather than causes all of the custard to run off, it's done. | SERVES 6

MOM'S BLACK AND WHITE CHOCOLATE CAKE | CRÈME ANGLAISE

Mousse

7 ounces semisweet or bittersweet chocolate

1 tablespoon instant espresso powder

⅓ cup Strega, kirsch, or rum

¼ cup heavy cream

5 eggs, separated

6 tablespoons sugar

¾ cup Simple Syrup (see page 273)

½ cup Strega, kirsch, or rum

20 to 25 ladyfingers, cut in half

Crème Anglaise

2 cups milk

1 vanilla bean, split and scraped

½ cup plus 2 tablespoons sugar

5 egg yolks

Chocolate curls

MELT THE CHOCOLATE Break the chocolate up and place it in the top half of a double boiler set over simmering water. Add the espresso powder and ⅓ cup Strega and let stand uncovered until the chocolate is softened. Stir until blended. Transfer the chocolate to a large bowl.

WHIP THE CREAM In a large chilled bowl with chilled beaters, whip the cream on high speed for 4 minutes, or until soft peaks form.

BEAT THE YOLKS With an electric mixer on medium speed, beat the egg yolks with 2 tablespoons of the sugar until pale, about 3 minutes.

WHIP THE WHITES In a large mixer bowl with clean beaters, beat the whites on medium speed until frothy. Gradually add the remaining 4 tablespoons of the sugar and increase the speed to high. Whip until soft peaks form.

ADD THE CREAM Add the egg yolk mixture to the chocolate and stir to combine. Gently fold in the whipped cream. Gently fold the whites into the chocolate mixture.

ASSEMBLE THE CAKE Mix together the simple syrup and ½ cup Strega.

Dip half the ladyfingers in the syrup until slightly softened.

In a 2-quart glass serving bowl, make alternate layers of the mousse and ladyfingers, finishing with the mousse. Cover and chill at least 8 hours or up to 2 days.

COOK THE CRÈME ANGLAISE In a large saucepan, bring the milk, vanilla bean and seeds, and ½ cup of the sugar to a simmer over medium-low heat, stirring occasionally. Immediately remove the pot from the heat and discard the vanilla bean.

ADD THE EGG YOLKS In a bowl, whisk the egg yolks until thick and well blended. Gradually add about ½ cup of the hot mixture into the eggs and whisk until well incorporated. Pour the egg mixture into the saucepan with the remaining milk mixture. Add the remaining 2 tablespoons of the sugar. Cook over low heat, stirring constantly in a figure-8 motion, until thickened slightly and the mixture coats the back of a spoon, about 5 minutes.

STRAIN AND COOL Remove from the heat and strain the custard through a fine-mesh strainer. Cool in a bowl set over a bowl of ice.

Cover with plastic wrap and refrigerate for at least 2 hours, or overnight.

SERVE scoops of the cake with crème anglaise and chocolate curls.

CHEF'S TIP: *If the custard separates after it's done, transfer it to a heatproof jar with a tight cover. Shake the jar vigorously until the sauce is blended.*

WINE SUGGESTION: BLACK MUSCAT, "GALLAGHER RANCH," ROSENBLUM CELLARS, 2003, CALIFORNIA. *A sweet red wine with aromas of creamy cherries, ripe berries, and chocolate.*

At home I like to serve sabayon with fresh raspberries and grated lime zest. It is also good layered with meringue like a Pavlova or over poached pears as a winter dessert. | SERVES 6

ORANGE BLOSSOM SABAYON WITH BERRIES

4 eggs yolks

⅓ cup Simple Syrup (see page 273)

1 tablespoon kirsch

1 cup heavy cream

2 tablespoons honey

1 teaspoon orange blossom water

18 ounces berries, like raspberries, strawberries, or blueberries (about 5 cups)

MAKE THE SABAYON In a microwave-safe bowl, whisk the egg yolks with the syrup and kirsch until frothy. Cook 8 to 10 seconds on high heat in the microwave. Remove from the oven and whisk until smooth.

Repeat 9 to 10 times, until the sabayon is cooked and thick. Let cool for 10 to 15 minutes.

BEAT THE CREAM In a large chilled bowl, beat together the cream, honey, and orange blossom water until soft peaks form.

FINISH THE SABAYON Fold the whipped cream into the sabayon. Cover and refrigerate up to 2 hours.

TO SERVE Scoop the fruits into 6 shallow bowls or plates. Top with the sabayon. Serve immediately.

CHEF'S TIP: *I make this sabayon in the microwave oven, but if you don't have one, you can whisk it in the top of a double boiler over simmering water until light and fluffy.*

WINE SUGGESTION: MUSCAT VIN DE GLACIÈRE, BONNY DOON VINEYARD, 2004, SANTA CRUZ, CALIFORNIA. *A wine made from Muscat grapes with aromas of lime sorbet, pineapple, and orange blossoms.*

Two crunchy praline layers and a soft creamy filling make an easy and impressive dessert. It is made with *feuilletine,* a flaky blend of chocolate and hazelnuts frequently used by pastry chefs to give a crunchy texture to desserts. Don't use a peanut butter that separates at room temperature. | You can find information on where to buy feuilletine, the ring molds, and a kitchen blowtorch, in the Sources section on page 274. | I like this cake best with banana ice cream and the chocolate sauce that follows. | SERVES 6

PEANUT BUTTER-CHOCOLATE PARFAIT

Feuilletine Layer

5 tablespoons creamy peanut butter, preferably Skippy

2½ ounces milk chocolate

2 ounces feuilletine (see Sources, page 274)

Mousse

7½ ounces milk chocolate (35 percent cocoa)

⅓ cup plus 1 tablespoon creamy peanut butter

Pinch fine sea salt

½ cup plus 1 tablespoon milk

¾ cup heavy cream

Chocolate Sauce

1⅓ cups sugar

1¾ cups water

1 cup unsweetened cocoa

1 cup heavy cream

MAKE THE FEUILLETINE LAYERS Line 2 large baking sheets with parchment paper.

Put the peanut butter and chocolate in a microwave-safe bowl. Microwave on medium high heat until melted. Stir in the feuilletine.

Spread the mixture evenly into a 10 x 12 x ⅛-inch-thick square on 1 sheet of parchment paper. Freeze 30 minutes, or until firm. Using a 3-inch ring mold as a template, cut out 12 rounds. Place the rounds back in the freezer on the baking sheet until ready to use.

MAKE THE MOUSSE Break up the chocolate and place it in a large heat-proof bowl. Add the peanut butter and salt.

Bring the milk to a simmer and pour it into the bowl. With a whisk, stir until the chocolate is melted and the mixture is blended. Beat with an electric mixer until light.

In a large chilled bowl with chilled mixer beaters, whip the cream until it begins to form soft peaks. With a rubber spatula, fold the cream into the warm chocolate mixture.

Place 6 ring molds on the second parchment-lined baking sheet. Fill the molds 1¼ inches deep with the mousse. Freeze until set, about 2 hours or overnight.

MAKE THE SAUCE In a medium saucepan, bring the sugar and water to a boil. Whisk in the cocoa until smooth and bring the mixture back to a boil. Stir in the cream and reduce the heat. Simmer 40 minutes, or until the sauce is thick and syrupy.

Use immediately or pour into a container and let cool. Cover and chill for up to 2 weeks. To reheat, place the sauce in the top of a double boiler over simmering water and stir gently.

ASSEMBLE THE PARFAITS Remove the molds from the freezer and place each one on top of a feuilletine layer. Using a blowtorch, slightly warm the outside of the ring mold and gently lift it off from around the frozen mousse. Top each mousse with the remaining feuilletine layers.

TO SERVE Place each portion on a dessert plate. Allow the mousse to thaw at room temperature for at least ½ hour before serving. Drizzle the chocolate sauce over the top and serve immediately.

WINE SUGGESTION: PETITE SYRAH, "ESSENCE," RIDGE VINEYARDS, 2001, SONOMA COUNTY, CALIFORNIA. *Serve a late-harvest Petite Syrah with aromas of dried red berries, spices, and prunes.*

first had this delicious bread pudding when I lived in England. When fresh blueberries are in season, I like to use them instead of the dried fruit. The pudding is also good made with fresh raspberries in the summer, or cranberries and pears for Thanksgiving. I like to serve these individual bread puddings with Crème Anglaise (page 243) or ice cream. | SERVES 6

DRIED APRICOT BREAD PUDDING

8 ounces (about ½ loaf) Brioche bread (page 116) or challah

1 Earl Grey tea bag

¼ cup dried apricots, cut into small pieces

2 eggs

1 egg yolk

1 cup milk

1½ cups heavy cream

¾ cup sugar

1 teaspoon grated orange zest

½ teaspoon grated lemon zest

1 teaspoon vanilla extract

PREPARE THE BREAD Remove the crusts from the brioche. Cut the bread into 1-inch cubes. You should have about 4 cups.

SOAK THE APRICOTS Pour 1 cup hot water into a small bowl with the tea bag. Add the apricots. Let stand 10 minutes, or until soft. Remove the tea bag. Strain the apricots and discard the liquid.

MAKE THE PUDDING In a large heatproof bowl, whisk together the eggs and egg yolk and ¼ cup of the milk until blended.

In a medium saucepan bring the cream, remaining ¾ cup of the milk, sugar, zests, and vanilla to a boil. Stir until the sugar is dissolved. Gradually pour the hot liquid over the egg mixture, whisking constantly. Pass the egg mixture through a fine-mesh strainer into a large bowl. Gently stir in the brioche and soaked apricots, being careful not to break up the bread. Cover and refrigerate at least 2 hours or overnight.

Preheat the oven to 325°F. Butter six 6-ounce ramekins or charlotte molds.

BAKE THE PUDDING Spoon the brioche mixture into the prepared cups. Bake 30 minutes, or until golden brown.

Serve warm.

CHEF'S TIP: *You can make these little puddings up to a day ahead of serving them. To reheat, place them in a 325°F oven for 10 to 15 minutes, or until warmed throughout. They can also be reheated in the microwave.*

WINE SUGGESTION: VIOGNIER DESSERT, CALERA, 2004, MOUNT HARLAN, CALIFORNIA. *A sweet and floral Viognier with aromas of dried apricots, honeysuckle, and orange peel.*

have been making these feather-light crêpes since 1994, when I was the executive chef at CT, Claude Troisgros' New York City restaurant. The food there was unique, with an exotic cross between French and Brazilian flavors. | You will need a kitchen blowtorch, the kind used to make crème brûlée, to caramelize the tops of these crêpes. If you have a second sauté pan, you can make these crêpes two at a time. | Passion fruits grow in the tropics. The fresh fruits are mostly available in the spring and early summer. You can tell they are ripe when the skin is wrinkled and they give slightly when pressed. | SERVES 6

PASSION FRUIT CRÊPES SOUFFLÉ

Pastry Cream

2 cups milk

1 vanilla bean, split and scraped out

4 egg yolks

¼ cup sugar

2 tablespoons cornstarch

Passion Fruit Sauce

6 tablespoons sugar

¼ cup water

⅔ cup thawed frozen passion fruit puree (see Sources, page 274)

3 tablespoons unsalted butter

3 passion fruits, halved

Crêpes Soufflé

3 cups milk

8 tablespoons (1 stick) unsalted butter plus about 2 tablespoons for greasing the skillet

12 eggs, separated

¾ cup sugar

¾ cup all-purpose flour

3 tablespoons granulated sugar, for caramelizing

Confectioners' sugar, for garnish

MAKE THE PASTRY CREAM In a medium saucepan, combine the milk, vanilla bean, and seeds. Bring the milk to a boil.

Meanwhile in a bowl, mix together the yolks, sugar, and cornstarch. Whisking constantly, pour the hot milk over the egg yolk mixture in a thin stream until smooth and well blended.

Pour the mixture into the saucepan and place it over high heat. Stir constantly with a whisk and bring to a boil. Cook for 4 minutes, or until thickened and smooth.

Pour the pastry cream through a fine-mesh strainer into a bowl. Place a piece of plastic wrap directly on the surface to prevent a skin from forming. Refrigerate until completely cold.

MAKE THE PASSION FRUIT SAUCE In a small pot, cook the sugar and water without stirring, until light amber in color, about 4 minutes. Stir in the passion fruit puree and cook for 2 minutes more. (The sauce can be made up to 3 days in advance. Let cool, then store in a covered container in the refrigerator up to 3 days. Reheat gently before using.)

Just before serving, whisk in the butter. Scoop out the passion fruit seeds and pulp. Stir them into the sauce.

MAKE THE CRÊPES SOUFFLÉ Preheat the oven to 375°F.

In a small saucepan, bring the milk and 8 tablespoons of the butter to a boil over medium-high heat.

In a large electric mixer bowl, beat the egg yolks and 6 tablespoons of the sugar on high speed for 30 seconds. Add the flour and beat on high for 1 to 2 minutes, or until creamy and white. Slowly pour in the boiling milk and stir until blended.

In a large, clean bowl with clean beaters, beat the egg whites until very thick and foamy. Slowly add the remaining 6 tablespoons of the sugar, beating until the egg whites form peaks when the beaters are lifted.

With a rubber spatula, gently fold the beaten whites into the egg yolk mixture, folding the mixture from the top to the bottom.

COOK THE CRÊPES Warm a 10-inch ovenproof sauté pan with ½ teaspoon of the butter over medium heat. Ladle 1 cup of the batter into the sauté pan and cook for 10 seconds, then transfer the pan to the oven for 3 minutes or until puffed and set.

Place a large sheet of waxed paper on a dinner plate. Carefully slide the crêpe onto the waxed paper with the browned side facing down.

While the crêpe is still hot, place a tablespoon of the prepared pastry cream in the center. Fold the crêpe in half.

Repeat with the remaining batter, making 5 more crêpes.

TO SERVE Before serving and caramelizing, warm up the crêpes in the oven for 3 to 4 minutes or in the microwave for 10 seconds, or until heated through.

To caramelize the top, sprinkle 1½ teaspoons granulated sugar on each crêpe and brown lightly with a blowtorch.

Spoon 3 tablespoons of the sauce into the bottom of a shallow bowl. Place a crêpe on top and dust with confectioners' sugar.

WINE SUGGESTION: PINOT GRIS VIN GLACE, KING ESTATE, 2004, WILLAMETTE VALLEY, OREGON. *A late-harvest Pinot Gris with aromas of honeyed peaches, guava, and passion fruit.*

The appearance of rhubarb and strawberries in the market signals the arrival of spring, but this homey cobbler can be made with other fruits that are in season. Good combinations include peaches with blueberries in summer and pears or apples with walnuts in the fall and winter. | Though it is often used in desserts, and is sometimes called the "pie plant," rhubarb is actually a vegetable. Only the stems are edible, so fresh rhubarb is sold without leaves. | SERVES 6

STRAWBERRY-RHUBARB COBBLER

Filling

2½ cups ⅓-inch rhubarb slices

1 cup sugar

2 cups coarsely chopped strawberries

3 tablespoons cornstarch

1 teaspoon vanilla extract

1 orange, zested

Dough

1⅔ cups all-purpose flour

3½ tablespoons sugar

1½ tablespoons baking powder

1 pinch fine sea salt

6 tablespoons (¾ stick) cold unsalted butter, cut into small dice

⅔ cup plus 1 tablespoon heavy cream

Turbinado sugar, for garnish

MACERATE THE RHUBARB Mix the rhubarb and sugar in a large bowl. Let stand 1 hour. Drain the rhubarb and discard the liquid.

MAKE THE FILLING Toss the rhubarb with the strawberries, cornstarch, vanilla, and orange zest. Mix well. Scrape the mixture into a 6-cup oval baking dish.

Preheat the oven to 375°F.

MAKE THE DOUGH In a large mixer bowl or a food processor, combine the flour, sugar, baking powder, and salt. Add the butter and mix briefly, just until the mixture resembles coarse crumbs. Add the ⅔ cup cream and stir just until moistened.

Turn the dough out onto a lightly floured surface and knead 5 or 6 times to mix thoroughly.

ROLL OUT THE DOUGH On a lightly floured surface, roll out the dough to a ½ inch thickness. With a biscuit or cookie cutter, cut out 3-inch circles. Place the circles on top of the fruit touching each other lightly.

BAKE THE COBBLER Brush the top of the dough with the remaining 1 tablespoon of cream. Sprinkle with turbinado sugar. Bake 20 minutes.

Lower the oven temperature to 325°F. Bake 20 minutes more, or until the crust is lightly browned, the rhubarb is soft, and the fruit juice is bubbling.

SERVE Let rest 20 minutes. Serve warm with vanilla ice cream or Crème Anglaise (page 243).

WINE SUGGESTION: CABERNET FRANC ICEWINE, INNISKILLIN, 2003, NIAGARA PENINSULA, CANADA. *An ice wine made from Cabernet Franc grapes, with aromas of cooked strawberries, fresh raspberry, and citrus.*

Key limes are about the size of a ping pong ball—much smaller than the typical Persian limes that are commonly available. They have thin skins and are more aromatic than the larger variety. Their peak season is during July and August, but you can generally get them fresh year-round. Most Key limes come from Mexico and Central America. | This pie is the perfect summer dessert with a glass of good limeade or lemonade. | SERVES 8

KEY LIME PIE

About 18 Key limes

Crust

1¼ cups finely crushed graham crackers (about 8 double crackers)

⅓ cup unsalted butter, at room temperature

3 tablespoons sugar

Filling

8 egg yolks

3 cups sweetened condensed milk

Confectioners' sugar

PREPARE THE LIMES With a hand-held grater, finely grate the zest (just the green part) from the limes until you have 1 tablespoon plus 1 teaspoon zest. Set aside 1 teaspoon of the zest for garnish.

Juice the limes. You should have 1⅔ cups of juice.

Preheat the oven to 350°F.

MAKE THE CRUST In a large bowl, stir together the crumbs, butter, and sugar until well blended. With your hands, pat the mixture firmly into the bottom and sides of a 9-inch pie pan or tart pan.

BAKE THE CRUST 10 minutes or until it is firm. Cool the pie shell on a rack.

MAKE THE FILLING In a large bowl, whisk together the egg yolks and 1 tablespoon of the zest until the yolks are blended. Add the condensed milk and whisk until smooth. Stir in the lime juice. Pour the mixture into the prepared pie shell.

BAKE 30 minutes, or until it rises slightly.

COOL the pie on a rack. Cover with plastic wrap and chill for at least 4 hours or overnight.

TO SERVE Sprinkle with confectioners' sugar and the reserved 1 teaspoon lime zest.

Serve plain or with whipped cream or frozen yogurt.

WINE SUGGESTION: ICE WINE, "SELECT LATE HARVEST," HERMANN J. WIEMER, 2004, FINGER LAKES, NEW YORK. *An American ice wine with aromas of candied peaches, white berries, and hints of honey.*

My business partner Jimmy Haber told me that this was his favorite kind of pie. Once I tasted it, it became a favorite of mine, too. | My version is a little different because I spread a thin layer of chocolate over the crust to keep it from absorbing the moisture from the creamy filling. I like to serve this with Chocolate Sauce (page 246), on the side. | SERVES 6

BANANA CREAM PIE

Crust

1⅓ cups all-purpose flour

½ teaspoon fine sea salt

3 tablespoons chilled unsalted butter, cut into bits

5 tablespoons chilled vegetable shortening

¼ cup ice water

Filling

6 ounces semisweet chocolate, chopped

2 cups milk

¼ cup cornstarch

4 egg yolks

½ cup plus 2 tablespoons sugar

1 vanilla bean, slit lengthwise and the seeds scraped out

2 tablespoons dark rum (optional)

2 tablespoons unsalted butter

Whipped Cream

2 cups cold heavy or whipping cream

3 tablespoons confectioners' sugar

1 tablespoon dark rum

2 to 2½ medium, ripe bananas

MAKE THE CRUST In a medium bowl using a pastry blender or in a food processor with the steel blade, combine the flour and salt. Blend in the butter and shortening until the mixture resembles coarse crumbs.

Drizzle the water over the mixture. Stir or pulse until the dough begins to come together. If the mixture seems dry and crumbly add a little more water a few drops at a time. Gather the dough into a ball, and then flatten it into a disk. Wrap in plastic and chill for at least 30 minutes.

MAKE THE FILLING Grate 1 tablespoon of the chocolate. Set it aside for garnish.

In a small heatproof bowl over a pan of hot water, melt the remaining chocolate. Spread the chocolate evenly on the bottom of the pie shell. Cool completely until the chocolate is firm.

Pour ½ cup of the milk into a medium bowl. Whisk in the cornstarch until smooth. Stir in the egg yolks and ½ cup of the sugar until well blended.

In a medium saucepan, heat the remaining 2 tablespoons of the sugar, the remaining 1½ cups of milk, the vanilla bean and seeds, and the rum until simmering. Remove the vanilla bean.

Whisking constantly, slowly pour in the egg mixture. Cook, stirring, until the mixture comes to a boil and thickens. Remove from the heat. Whisk in the butter.

Scrape the mixture into a bowl. Place a piece of plastic wrap directly on the surface to prevent a skin from forming. Refrigerate until cold.

WHIP THE CREAM In a large chilled bowl with chilled beaters, whip the cream, confectioners' sugar, and rum until soft peaks form.

ASSEMBLE Cut the bananas into ¼-inch slices. Stir the filling briefly and spread half in the prepared pie shell. Add the banana slices. Spread with the remaining filling. Scoop the whipped cream on top.

Sprinkle with the reserved grated chocolate. Store in the refrigerator and serve within 24 hours.

WINE SUGGESTION: VIDAL ICE, STANDING STONE VINEYARDS, 2004, FINGER LAKES, NEW YORK. *A sweet wine made from Vidal grapes, with aromas of pineapple, nuts, and dried apricots.*

Pecan pie seems to have been invented in the test kitchens of a corn syrup manufacturing company in the 1920s. It quickly became popular, especially in the South, where pecan trees are plentiful. You can substitute walnuts for the pecans if you prefer. | Crème Anglaise (page 243) or honey whipped cream go well with this pie. | SERVES 6

PECAN PIE

Crust

1⅓ cups all-purpose flour

½ cup confectioner's sugar

½ teaspoon fine sea salt

3 tablespoons chilled unsalted butter, cut into bits

5 tablespoons chilled vegetable shortening

¼ cup ice water

Filling

8 tablespoons (1 stick) unsalted butter, at room temperature

¾ cup packed light brown sugar

3 eggs

¾ cup dark corn syrup

1 teaspoon vanilla extract

¼ teaspoon fine sea salt

1 cup chopped roasted pecans

16 pecan halves

Confectioners' sugar, for garnish

MAKE THE CRUST In a medium bowl using a pastry blender or in a food processor with the steel blade, combine the flour, sugar, and salt. Blend in the butter and shortening until the mixture resembles coarse crumbs.

Drizzle the water over the mixture. Stir or pulse until the dough begins to come together. If the mixture seems dry and crumbly, add a little more water a few drops at a time. Gather the dough into a ball, and then flatten it into a disk. Wrap in plastic and chill until firm, at least 30 minutes.

Butter a 9- or 10-inch pie pan. On a lightly floured surface with a floured rolling pin, roll the dough out into a ⅛-inch-thick circle. Drape the dough over the rolling pin and place it without stretching it into the center of the prepared pan. Fit the dough into the pan and trim off all but a 1-inch border of dough. Fold the border under to form a high rim. Pinch the dough together all around to form a fluted edge.

Cover with plastic wrap and place the pan in the refrigerator to chill at least 30 minutes.

Preheat oven to 350°F. Line the dough with parchment paper or foil. Fill with pie weights or uncooked beans. Bake for 20 minutes, or until the crust is golden brown. Remove the paper and pie weights. Let cool.

MAKE THE FILLING With an electric mixer, beat the butter and sugar until light and fluffy. Add the eggs and beat until blended. Beat in the corn syrup, vanilla, and salt. With a rubber spatula, stir in the chopped pecans. Scrape the filling into the baked pie shell.

BAKE THE PIE for 20 minutes. Remove it from the oven.

Arrange the pecan halves on top. Bake 30 to 35 minutes more, or until browned and set but still slightly soft in the center.

COOL the pie completely on a wire rack. Store in the refrigerator.

This pie is best when refrigerated for several hours before serving, to allow it to fully set.

SERVE cool or at room temperature, sprinkled with confectioners' sugar.

WINE SUGGESTION: MUSCAT MUSEUM, YALUMBA, NV, VICTORIA, AUSTRALIA. *A tawny-style dessert wine with aromas of dates, prunes, and figs.*

Hazelnut crunch is made of hazelnuts that have been toasted, skinned, chopped into even pieces, and sweetened. You can buy it at bakers' supply stores or see the Sources on page 274. | You can substitute chopped nuts such as almonds, walnuts, or pecans. | If you are looking for a special pie to end Thanksgiving or another holiday dinner, think of this one. I like to serve it with cinnamon whipped cream or bourbon-flavored ice cream. | SERVES 6

HAZELNUT CRUNCH PUMPKIN PIE

Crust

1⅓ cups all-purpose flour

½ teaspoon fine sea salt

3 tablespoons chilled unsalted butter, cut into bits

5 tablespoons chilled vegetable shortening

¼ cup ice water

Filling

3 eggs

1 can (15 ounces) pumpkin puree

1½ cups heavy cream

½ cup granulated sugar

½ cup packed dark brown sugar

½ teaspoon fine sea salt

½ teaspoon vanilla extract

¼ teaspoon ground cinnamon

¼ teaspoon ground cloves

¼ teaspoon ground ginger

¼ teaspoon freshly grated nutmeg

MAKE THE CRUST In a medium bowl using a pastry blender or in a food processor with the steel blade, combine the flour and salt. Blend in the butter and shortening until the mixture resembles coarse crumbs.

Drizzle the water over the mixture. Stir or pulse until the dough begins to come together. If the mixture seems dry and crumbly, add a little more water a few drops at a time. Gather the dough into a ball, and then flatten it into a disk. Wrap in plastic and chill at least 30 minutes.

ROLL OUT THE DOUGH Butter a 9- or 10-inch pie pan. On a lightly floured surface with a floured rolling pin, roll the dough out into a ⅛-inch-thick circle. Drape the dough over the rolling pin and place it without stretching it into the center of the prepared pan. Fit the dough into the pan and trim off all but a 1-inch border of dough. Fold the border under to form a high rim. Pinch the dough together all around to form a fluted edge.

Cover with plastic wrap and place the pan in the refrigerator to chill at least 30 minutes.

Preheat the oven to 325°F.

BAKE THE CRUST Line the dough with parchment paper or foil. Fill with pie weights or uncooked beans. Bake for 20 minutes, or until the crust is golden brown. Remove the paper and pie weights. Let cool.

MAKE THE FILLING In a large bowl, whisk together the eggs. Stir in the remaining filling ingredients. Pour into the prepared crust and bake for 45 minutes, or until the center of the pie jiggles slightly when tapped.

Place on a rack to cool completely.

Hazelnut Topping

2 tablespoons honey

1 cup hazelnut crunch (see Sources, page 274) or 1 cup toasted, skinned hazelnuts, chopped

MAKE THE TOPPING In a small saucepan over medium heat, warm the honey and stir in the hazelnut crunch or chopped hazelnuts. Pour over the pie and spread evenly. Cool completely at room temperature.

TO SERVE This pie is best served at room temperature the day it is made.

WINE SUGGESTION: VIN PAILLE, SHELDRAKE POINT VINEYARD, 2003, FINGER LAKES, NEW YORK. *A Vin Paille–style wine with notes of figs, dates, and luscious raisins.*

The topping on this pie is crumbly when it goes into the oven, but as it bakes a delicious crusty covering forms on the top of the pie. The best pies are made from apples that keep their shape and have a balanced tart-sweet flavor. Other good varieties include Golden Delicious, Winesap, Jonathan, and Jonagold.

SERVES 6

CRUSTY APPLE PIE

Crust

1⅓ cups all-purpose flour

½ teaspoon fine sea salt

3 tablespoons chilled unsalted butter, cut into bits

5 tablespoons chilled vegetable shortening

¼ cup ice water

Filling

8 red or green apples, such as MacIntosh or Granny Smith, peeled, cored, and thinly sliced

½ lemon, juiced

½ cup sugar, or more to taste

3 tablespoons all-purpose flour

1½ teaspoons ground cinnamon

½ teaspoon ground cloves

½ teaspoon ground nutmeg

½ teaspoon salt

Topping

2 tablespoons all-purpose flour

9½ tablespoons (1 stick plus 1½ tablespoons) chilled unsalted butter, cut into bits

⅔ cup packed dark brown sugar

½ cup pecans, coarsely chopped

MAKE THE CRUST In a medium bowl using a pastry blender or in a food processor with the steel blade, combine the flour and salt. Blend in the butter and shortening until the mixture resembles coarse crumbs.

Drizzle the water over the mixture. Stir or pulse until the dough begins to come together. If the mixture seems dry and crumbly add a little more water a few drops at a time. Gather the dough into a ball, and then flatten it into a disk. Wrap in plastic and chill for at least 30 minutes.

ROLL OUT THE DOUGH Butter a 9- or 10-inch pie pan. On a lightly floured surface with a floured rolling pin, roll the dough out into a ⅛-inch-thick circle. Drape the dough over the rolling pin and place it without stretching it in the center of the prepared pan. Fit the dough into the pan and trim off all but a 1-inch border of dough. Fold the border under to form a high rim. Pinch the dough together all around to form a fluted edge. Cover with plastic wrap and place the pan in the refrigerator to chill at least 30 minutes.

MAKE THE FILLING In a large bowl, toss the apples with the lemon juice.

In a small bowl, stir together the sugar, flour, cinnamon, cloves, nutmeg, and salt. Sprinkle the mixture over the apples and toss to coat.

Preheat the oven to 375°F.

MAKE THE TOPPING With your fingers or in a food processor, mix the flour and butter, leaving the butter in pieces about the size of a nickel. Stir in the brown sugar. If using a food processor, transfer the topping to a bowl. Stir in the pecans. Refrigerate the mixture.

FILL THE PIE SHELL Scrape the apple mixture into the crust, mounding it in the center. Place a baking sheet on the lower oven rack to catch any drips. Place the pie on the rack in the center of the oven. Bake for 25 minutes.

Raise the heat to 400°F. Scatter the topping over the apples, covering them completely and pressing gently so that the topping adheres. Bake until the topping is nicely browned and the apples are tender when pierced with a knife, 25 to 30 minutes longer.

COOL THE PIE on a wire rack. Serve warm or at room temperature.

WINE SUGGESTION: LATE HARVEST CHARDONNAY, WOLFFER ESTATE, 2004, HAMPTONS, LONG ISLAND, NEW YORK. *A late-harvest Chardonnay with aromas of baked apple, dried apricots, and preserved lemons.*

A classic dessert is converted into a new and exciting one by flambéing it with rum and serving it with Piña Colada Sauce. | SERVES 6

PINEAPPLE-DATE UPSIDE-DOWN CAKE | PIÑA COLADA SAUCE

Cake

1¾ cups sugar

6 slices fresh pineapple (½ inch thick), cored

6 pitted dates

12 tablespoons (1½ sticks) unsalted butter, at room temperature

3 eggs

6 egg yolks

¾ cup all-purpose flour

⅔ cup cornmeal

¾ teaspoon baking powder

Pinch fine sea salt

Sauce
MAKES 3 1/2 CUPS

1½ cups unsweetened coconut milk

1 cup unsweetened pineapple juice

¾ cup canned sweetened cream of coconut, such as Coco Lopez

½ cup white rum

¼ cup dark rum

MAKE THE CARAMEL Put ¾ cup of the sugar and ¼ cup water in a pot and set over high heat. Cook, swirling the pan occasionally, until the color turns medium amber. Carefully pour the caramel into a 9 x 2-inch round nonstick cake pan.

ARRANGE THE PINEAPPLE Arrange the pineapple slices in a single layer over the caramel. Place a date in the center of each slice.

Preheat the oven to 350°F.

MAKE THE BATTER In a large bowl, beat the butter and remaining 1 cup of the sugar until light and fluffy. In another bowl, whisk together the eggs and yolks. Beat the egg mixture into the butter. Combine the flour, cornmeal, baking powder, and salt in a sieve and sift them over the bowl. Stir until the batter is smooth and well blended. Spread the batter over the fruit in the pan.

BAKE 40 to 45 minutes, or until a toothpick inserted in the center of the cake comes out clean. Invert the cake onto a plate.

MAKE THE SAUCE In a medium saucepan, combine all of the sauce ingredients. Bring to a simmer and stir well.

FLAME THE CAKE In a medium saucepan, heat the dark rum over medium heat. Averting your face, carefully ignite the rum with a long match. Carefully pour the flaming rum over the cake.

SERVE the cake while still warm, drizzled with the warm sauce.

CHEF'S TIP: You can also bake this cake in individual molds. It goes well with ice cream or pineapple sorbet. Make the sauce ahead and store it in the refrigerator, well wrapped. It keeps well for a long time.

WINE SUGGESTION: CHENIN BLANC ICE WINE, TERRA BLANCA, 2003, YAKIMA VALLEY, WASHINGTON. *An ice wine style made from Chenin Blanc grapes, with aromas of honeyed peach, apricots, and pineapples.*

Carrot cake is the perfect dessert for a hearty winter meal. The Butterscotch Sauce makes this cake seem special. It tastes great with ice cream and many other cakes and pies, too. | SERVES 8 TO 10

CARROT CAKE | BUTTERSCOTCH SAUCE

Cake

1⅓ cups all-purpose flour

1 cup packed dark brown sugar

⅓ cup granulated sugar

1½ teaspoons baking soda

1 teaspoon baking powder

1 teaspoon ground cinnamon

½ teaspoon ground cloves

½ teaspoon ground allspice

½ teaspoon grated nutmeg

½ teaspoon fine sea salt

3 eggs

⅔ cup vegetable oil

1½ cups finely grated carrots (about 2 medium)

½ cup canned unsweetened crushed pineapple, lightly drained

Cream Cheese Frosting

8 ounces cream cheese, at room temperature

1 cup (2 sticks) unsalted butter, at room temperature

1 teaspoon vanilla extract

1½ pounds (6 cups) confectioners' sugar

PREHEAT THE OVEN to 325°F. Butter and flour two 9-inch layer cake pans.

MAKE THE BATTER Sift together the dry ingredients into a large bowl. In a medium bowl, whisk together the eggs and oil. Pour the egg mixture over the dry ingredients. Stir in the carrots and pineapple until well blended. Divide the batter between the 2 pans.

BAKE THE CAKE Bake for 35 to 40 minutes, or until a toothpick inserted in the center comes out clean. Place the cake pans on a rack to cool for 10 minutes. Invert the cakes onto racks to cool completely.

MAKE THE FROSTING In a large bowl, beat the cream cheese and butter with an electric mixer until well blended. Add the vanilla. Beat in the confectioners' sugar in batches until light and fluffy. Keep at room temperature for easy spreading.

FROST THE CAKE Place 1 cake layer on a serving plate, bottom-side up. Scoop about one-third of the frosting onto the cake, spreading it evenly over the top. Place the second layer bottom-side up over the first.

Spread the remaining icing over the top and sides of the cake.

MAKE THE SAUCE Place all of the sauce ingredients in a small pot. Cook over medium heat, stirring frequently. Bring to a simmer and stir until smooth. (This sauce will keep for weeks, well covered in the refrigerator. Gently reheat the sauce to thin it out.)

SERVE immediately with the warm Butterscotch Sauce or cover and refrigerate up to 3 days.

Butterscotch Sauce
Makes about 1-1/2 cups

1⅓ cups packed dark brown sugar

½ cup heavy cream

2 tablespoons unsalted butter

1½ tablespoons dark rum, such as Meyer's Dark

¼ teaspoon fine sea salt

WINE SUGGESTION DOLCE, 2002 NAPA VALLEY, CALIFORNIA. *A Sauternes-style wine with aromas of honeysuckle, figs, and baked brioche.*

T he floral design and pastel colors of this cake make me think of my daughter, so I named it for her favorite doll. | SERVES 10

"BARBIE" RASPBERRY LAYER CAKE

Cake

1½ cups self-rising flour

1¼ cups all-purpose flour

1 cup milk

1 teaspoon vanilla extract

1 cup (2 sticks) unsalted butter, softened

2 cups sugar

4 eggs, at room temperature

Cream Cheese Frosting

1½ pounds cream cheese, at room temperature

1 cup (2 sticks) unsalted butter, at room temperature

1½ pounds (6 cups) confectioners' sugar

1 teaspoon vanilla extract

2 to 3 drops red food coloring

4 to 5 drops yellow food coloring

1½ cups Chambord (black raspberry liqueur)

1 cup raspberry jam with seeds, Smucker's brand recommended

PREHEAT THE OVEN to 400°F. Grease two 9-inch round cake pans.

MAKE THE BATTER In a bowl, stir together the 2 flours until blended.

In another bowl, stir together the milk and vanilla extract.

In a large electric mixer bowl, beat the butter until smooth. Gradually add the sugar and beat until fluffy, about 3 minutes. Add the eggs 1 at a time, beating well after each addition.

On low speed, add the flour mixture in 4 additions, alternating with the milk in 3 additions, beginning and ending with the flour. Stir until well blended. Scrape the batter into the prepared cake pans.

BAKE the cakes for 22 to 25 minutes, or until a cake tester inserted in the center comes out clean. Remove the cakes from the oven. Let the cakes cool in the pans on a rack for 10 minutes. Invert the cakes onto the racks. Let cool completely.

MAKE THE FROSTING In a large bowl, beat the cream cheese and butter with an electric mixer until well blended. Add the sugar a little at a time, stirring constantly. Add the vanilla and beat until light and fluffy. Keep at room temperature for easy spreading.

ADD THE COLORING Set aside 1½ cups of the frosting. Divide the remaining frosting between 2 bowls. Add red food coloring to 1 bowl and stir with a rubber spatula until the color is pink. Add yellow food coloring to the second bowl and stir until blended. Leave the remaining frosting uncolored.

Scrape the pink frosting into a piping bag fitted with a ¼-inch flat pastry tip. Scrape the yellow frosting into a second bag fitted with a ¼-inch flat pastry tip.

ASSEMBLE With a long serrated knife, cut each cake crosswise into 3 layers. Using a pastry brush, brush each layer on both sides with the Chambord.

Place 1 cake layer on a serving plate. Spread about 3 tablespoons of the jam over the cake. Place a second layer of cake on top and spread it with 3 tablespoons of the jam. Repeat until you use all 6 layers, ending with a layer of cake, cut-side down.

Ice the entire cake very lightly with the uncolored frosting. With the pink frosting, pipe flower petals over the cake. With the yellow frosting, pipe dots.

SERVE immediately or cover with an inverted bowl and store for several hours in the refrigerator.

CHEF'S TIP: *If you are not comfortable working with a pastry bag, make a simple design of dots and swirls. Practice the design first on a piece of waxed paper.*

WINE SUGGESTION: WHITE RIESLING LATE HARVEST, HOGUE CELLARS, 2005, COLUMBIA VALLEY, WASHINGTON. *A late-harvest wine with aromas of dried apricots, tangerines, and confectioners' sugar.*

One of my favorite indulgences—a classic American sticky bun—inspired this dessert. Eat it fast while it is still warm! This is good with a variety of ice creams. I like it best for breakfast topped with Crème Anglaise. | SERVES 8

CINNAMON-PECAN STICKY LOAF | CRÈME ANGLAISE

¾ cup granulated sugar

1½ cups coarsely chopped pecans

3 tablespoons turbinado sugar (Sugar in the Raw)

2 teaspoons ground cinnamon

⅓ recipe Brioche Dough (page116) prepared through the first rise

Eggwash: 1 egg yolk mixed with 1 tablespoon water

1 tablespoon unsalted butter

2 tablespoons rum

3 tablespoons honey

1 recipe Crème Anglaise (page 243)

MAKE THE CARAMELIZED PECANS Lightly oil a large baking sheet. In a medium saucepan over high heat, combine the granulated sugar and ¼ cup water. Cook, gently swirling the pan occasionally, until the sugar is golden brown. Add the pecans and stir to coat. Spread the pecans on the prepared baking sheet.

Butter and flour a 9 x 4½-inch loaf pan. Mix the turbinado sugar and cinnamon together.

ROLL OUT THE BRIOCHE DOUGH on a lightly floured surface to a 10 x 8 x ¼-inch rectangle. Sprinkle 3 tablespoons of the cinnamon sugar and 1 cup of the candied pecans over the dough. Roll the dough up like a jelly roll, tucking in the ends. Place it seam-side down in the prepared pan. Cover with plastic wrap.

Let rise in a warm, draft-free place 1 to 1½ hours, or until doubled in bulk.

BAKE Preheat the oven to 375°F. Brush the eggwash over the top of the loaf. Bake 25 to 30 minutes, or until nicely browned and a thin knife inserted in the center comes out clean and warm.

MAKE THE SYRUP Place the remaining cinnamon sugar mixture in a medium saucepan with the butter. Add the rum and 1 tablespoon water. Cook, swirling the pan occasionally, until golden brown. Remove from the heat and stir in the honey.

DRIZZLE THE SYRUP Remove the loaf from the pan and invert it onto a rack set over a sheet of aluminum foil. With a thin knife, poke holes in the bottom of the loaf. Drizzle the warm syrup a little at a time over the loaf so that it has a chance to soak into the bread. Scatter the remaining caramelized pecans on top.

TO SERVE Slice the warm loaf and serve immediately with Crème Anglaise.

WINE SUGGESTION: CHAMBERS ROSEWOOD VINEYARDS, TOKAY, NV, RUTHERGLEN, AUSTRALIA. *An Australian "sticky" wine with aromas of molasses, brown sugar, and roasted nuts.*

TECHNIQUES

TO COOK AND SHELL LOBSTERS

For 2 lobsters, bring 6 quarts of water to boiling. Add the lobsters and cook for 10 to 12 minutes, until the lobsters are bright red. With tongs, remove the lobsters from the pot. Cool them over ice.

To remove the meat from the shell, hold the body in one hand and the tail in the other. Twist the lobster in opposite directions until it comes apart in the middle. Remove the meat from the tail in 1 piece and cut it in half lengthwise. Remove the dark intestine. With a shell cracker or the back of a heavy chef's knife, crack the claws and knuckles. Remove the meat. Cut the meat into the desired size dice. The lobster meat can be wrapped and refrigerated up to 8 hours. Remove the gray-green tomalley (liver) and red roe, if any, and set them aside separately. They can be used to finish and flavor sauces.

TO CLEAN SOFT-SHELL CRABS

Locate the front of the crab where the eyes and mouth are. Bring the blade of a long, heavy knife down quickly about ¼ inch behind the eyes. Discard the eye portion.

Locate the gills on either side of the crab by lifting the papery shell at its pointed edges. The gills are feathery and yellowish. Scrape them out gently.

Turn the crab over and locate the bell-shaped flap that lifts up from the center of the body like a kind of lever. Lift it and cut it off close to the back end of the crab.

TO MAKE ROASTED GARLIC BUTTER

Cut off the top ¼ inch of 2 heads of garlic. Place the garlic in an oiled baking pan.

Bake at 400°F until the garlic cloves are soft, about 35 minutes. If they seem dry, add a little bit of water to the bottom of the pan. Test by inserting a sharp, thin knife. When cool, squeeze the garlic from the skins into a bowl. Mash it with the back of a spoon. Measure the garlic and add an equal amount of softened butter. Blend until smooth.

TO MAKE CLARIFIED BUTTER

Put the butter in a pan and melt it over low heat until the fat separates out into a thick layer. Remove the pan from the heat. Spoon off the foam from the top. Pour the liquid into a heatproof container. Cover and refrigerate. When the butter fat becomes firm, pour off and discard the milky liquid from the bottom of the container. Use the clarified butter immediately or cover and refrigerate up to 1 week.

TO CLEAN WILD MUSHROOMS

Many wild mushroom varieties can be very sandy and require careful cleaning. Fill a large basin with cool water.

Add the mushrooms and swirl gently. Lift the mushrooms out with your hands. Using fresh water, repeat at least twice, or until there is no more sand at the bottom of the bowl. Drain the mushrooms and pat them dry.

TO COOK CORN FOR KERNELS

Bring a large pot of salted water to a boil. Add the corn and cook for 3 minutes, or until tender. Drain the corn and place it in a bowl of ice water to cool. Drain and pat dry. With a large chef's knife, cut the kernels off the ears. You should have about ¾ cup kernels per ear of corn.

TO ROAST AND PEEL CHESTNUTS

Line a baking pan with foil. With a small sharp knife, cut an X in the bottom of each chestnut.

Place the chestnuts in the pan. Bake at 400° for 25 to 30 minutes, or until tender when pierced. Remove from the oven. Wrap the chestnuts in a towel for 5 minutes to cool slightly. Crush the shells lightly and remove the chestnuts.

TO TOAST CORIANDER SEEDS

Place the seeds in a dry skillet over medium-high heat. Cook a few minutes, rotating the pan frequently, until the seeds are fragrant. Remove to a plate to cool.

TO MAKE SMOKED SALT

Maldon sea salt from England has a great flavor and the large flakes are perfect for smoking.

1 cup hickory chips

1 cup Maldon sea salt

Mound the chips in the center of a pan and place over high heat. Light the chips and allow them to burn until they turn black. Reduce the heat to low. Line a perforated pan with foil and sprinkle the sea salt evenly in the pan. Place the perforated pan over the chips and put a cover on top. Smoke the salt for 15 minutes over low heat.

TO MAKE SMOKED BLACK PEPPER

1 cup hickory chips

1 cup cracked black pepper

Follow the same method as for the smoked sea salt above, but the smoking time is only 4 to 6 minutes.

TO MAKE SIMPLE SYRUP

¾ cup sugar

¾ cup water

Combine the water and sugar in a small pot and bring to a simmer. Stir until the sugar is fully dissolved. Remove from the heat and allow to cool. Store in a covered container in the refrigerator up to one week. Makes about 1½ cups.

TO MAKE CARAMELIZED WALNUTS

⅔ cup sugar

¼ cup water

1 cup walnut halves (4 ounces)

Butter a small baking sheet with sides. Combine the sugar and water in a medium saucepan. Stir over medium heat until the sugar dissolves. Stop stirring and boil the syrup until it turns a rich golden brown. Remove the pan from the heat and stir in the walnuts. Spread the walnuts in a single layer in the prepared pan. Let cool. Makes about 1½ cups.

MEAT

LOBEL'S OF NEW YORK
877-783-4512
www.lobels.com

Specializes in top-quality meats and poultry

FOIE GRAS, LAMB, DUCK, AND GAME

D'ARTAGNAN
Newark, NJ
800-327-8246
www.dartagnan.com

Named for the fourth musketeer in the famous story, D'Artagnan specializes in foie gras, duck, and related products; also lamb, game, pâté, foie gras terrine, and wild mushrooms.

HUDSON VALLEY FOIE GRAS
Ferndale, NY
845-292-2500
www.hudsonvalleyfoiegras.com

Specializes in American foie gras, duck, and duck products

FISH

BROWNE TRADING COMPANY
Portland, ME
800-944-7848
www.browne-trading.com

Specializes in caviar and smoked and fresh seafood

PISACANE MIDTOWN SEAFOOD
New York, NY
212-752-7560

TRUFFLES AND TRUFFLE OIL

URBANI TRUFFLES USA, LTD.
North Wales, PA
215-699-8780
www.urbanitruffles.com

SPICES, ASIAN SAUCES, AND CONDIMENTS

KALUSTYAN'S
New York, NY
800-352-3451
www.kalustyans.com

Mustard oil, fresh spices, whole grains, dried fruit, nuts, Maldon salt, Middle Eastern and Asian seasonings

CHEESES

MURRAY'S CHEESE
New York, NY
888-692-4339
www.murrayscheese.com

The place to go for both domestic and foreign cheeses

BAKING EQUIPMENT AND INGREDIENTS

NEW YORK CAKE SUPPLIES
New York, NY
800-942-2539
www.nycake.com

A complete line of baking and confectionery equipment and utensils, and decorating supplies

J. B. PRINCE COMPANY
New York, NY
800-473-0577
www.jbprince.com

A large selection of kitchen tools and equipment

PARIS GOURMET
800-727-8791
www.parisgourmet.com

A wide range of products including chocolate; baking ingredients such as feuilletine, hazelnut crunch, etc.

INDEX